D0262045

WITHDRAWN
FROM THE LIBRARY OF
UNIVERSITY OF ULSTER

100317696

JOHN SMITH

John Smith

Playing the Long Game

Andy McSmith

VERSO
London · New York

First published by Verso 1993

Verso
UK: 6 Meard Street, London W1V 3HR
USA: 29 West 35th Street, New York, NY 10001–2291

Verso is the imprint of New Left Books

ISBN 0–86091–475–5

British Library Cataloguing in Publication Data
A catalogue record for this book is available from the British Library

Library of Congress Cataloging-in-Publication Data
A catalogue record for this book is available from the Library of Congress

Typeset by York House Typographic Ltd, London
Printed in Great Britain by Bookcraft (Bath) Ltd

Contents

Acknowledgements

They say that no one is a hero to his valet. For several years, when I was employed as a member of the Labour Party's head office staff, I had to act as a valet, of a sort, to most of its front-rank politicians. My first encounter with John Smith was in 1984 at the Chesterfield by-election, when Tony Benn fought his way back into Parliament. The event was attracting so much interest that the little Derbyshire town quite ran out of overnight accommodation, and the Shadow Secretary of State for Employment and I were obliged to share a hotel room. So I am a biographer who has slept with his subject. I did not know as much then as I do now about the foibles of prominent politicians, and did not know, therefore, how unusual it was that someone who had been a Cabinet minister should accept the inconvenience of this unexpected intrusion with such friendly good nature. There is nothing grand, or self-important, or thin-skinned, about John Smith. He accepts situations as they come, with a matter-of-fact good humour, as I was reminded some years after Chesterfield, when Smith had to appear on a platform with a person, who shall be nameless, of whom I happened to know he had about as low an opinion as anyone could have of a political colleague. I expected him to be in a bad temper about it, and gently suggested to him that he might not be looking forward to the occasion, but he shrugged it off, saying: "Och aye, I've defended some of the worst murderers in Scotland – I can always find something good to say about a Labour politician."

This biography is not authorized. I think if John Smith had had a choice in the matter, no one would have written his biography until after he has taken office as Prime Minister. None of the book's conclusions, or any errors or misjudgements which may have crept in, should be attributed to him. All the same, I have to thank him for being helpful and courteous when he was faced with the fact that it would appear whether he approved of it or not.

Thanks also to the *Daily Mirror* and *Daily Record* for access to their cuttings libraries, to colleagues on the *Mirror* political staff, and to the Labour Party's former librarian, John McTernan; to my wife, Sue Dearie, and my sister, Catherine; and to Will Barclay, Tony Bevans, Janey Buchan, Tom Clarke MP, Tom Condon, Robin Cook MP, Alistair Darling MP, Donald Dewar MP, Andy Grice, Ross Harper, Roy Hattersley MP, Doug Henderson MP, David Hill, Alan Howarth, Jenny Jeger, Neil Kinnock MP, Alan Lawson, Helen Liddell, Bob McLaughlan, Andrew Marr, Martin O'Neill MP, Ann Pettifor, George Robertson MP, Robert Shanks, David Shaw MP, John Smith of Tarbert, Lesley Smith, David Ward, Brian Wilson MP, Colin Robinson of Verso, and many others who have been quoted here, or gave advice and time.

1

The Boy from Argyll

Quiet times breed quiet leaders. Despite the interminable violence in Northern Ireland, civil life in Britain in the second half of the eighties was placid, thanks to the new prosperity generated by North Sea oil and the freeing of money markets. So ended the decade and a half of political turbulence which created the time of "conviction politicians" like Tony Benn and Arthur Scargill on the left, or Margaret Thatcher on the right. Their time had passed, and the era of quiet, bespectacled leaders named John had arrived.

John Smith QC, fifteenth leader of the Labour Party, is famously ordinary. His name is as plain as a name can be. On Sundays, he goes to church. His family life is happy and secure. His political views are moderate, sensible, unideological and unchanging, and he has made a success of two professions. "John is almost irritatingly too good to be true, from a biographer's point of view," says Donald Dewar, an old ally who could claim to be Parliament's longest-serving "Smithite". Or, to quote Parliament's resident wag, Tony Banks, Smith is "sensible two-shoes".[1]

It may be a problem for John Smith's biographer that he has lived such an unblemished and decent life, but it does not cause alarm within the Labour Party. There is no general rule that the best political leaders are the ones who set your pulse racing. Voters may be reassured by the blandness of Smith. The most successful leader the Party ever had was Clement Attlee, who was so personally inconspicuous that he was the butt of a much-repeated joke about an empty taxi drawing up and Attlee getting out. Compared with him, Smith is exciting, self-assured, good company, one who knows how to enjoy himself. His owlish, bank-manager look conceals an exceptional intelligence, sharp wits and a ruthless grasp of reality. A Shadow Cabinet colleague compares him with a crustacean camouflaged in the sea bed: "For a long time, he keeps so still that you almost forget he's there; then when he makes his move, he moves very quickly indeed."

In his youth, John Smith was one of the high-fliers of Scottish politics. No one who knew him then is in the least surprised that he is a prominent figure in national politics now. In his thirties, he was one of the fastest-rising ministers in the Labour government, appearing at every turn to contradict the Peter Principle. No matter what Smith was given to do, he gave the impression that it was well within his competence and he was capable of more. Since he reached the age of forty, politics has not given him nearly enough to do. He and his contemporaries were condemned to spend longer out of office than the average murderer spends in prison, with the same uncertainty about when – or whether – the sentence would ever end. John Smith is not, as some Labour MPs are, a natural oppositionist. He has an image of himself as a member of the political establishment, someone whose proper role is to be making decisions, influencing events, doing things. But most of his prime has been spent marking time. He may have one more chance to govern, and when it comes – if it comes – he will be almost sixty years old.

These long years in opposition have brought out another quality in Smith – his extraordinary patience. To have carried on for so long in a role which did not suit him, hoping it would pay off in the end, remaining a prominent figure in the Labour Party through all its changes and troubles, shows an unshakable dedication, and a will to survive. But then, survival runs in the family.

Almost nothing remains of the ancient settlement of Allt Beithe (pronounced Awlt Bay) on the shore of Loch Fyne, in north Kintyre – just tumbledown outlines of old stone houses, built on a steep hillside about 200 feet above sea level, some other moss-grown stones scattered in the grass, and a track leading to a deep pool which must have served as the village's water supply. These were two-room dwellings, built of stone quarried locally, and with a chimney in one gable. The gables were built towards the sea, to give maximum shelter. These days, bracken grows in the doorways. The Forestry Commission has been busy in the area, planting conifers. The place name means "a burn bordered by beech trees", and an old map, on which it is marked as "Aldbee", provides evidence that there was a community here in Shakespeare's time. The land looks unsuitable for crops, and the shoreline far below seems too boulder-strewn for fishing boats. Yet for at least 250 years its inhabitants eked out a living somehow, possibly by a combination of cultivating what little arable land they could find, rearing stock, and travelling northwards to set out on fishing expeditions.

According to a headstone in Tarbert cemetery, John Leitch, a farmer from "Altbea", was born in 1791, and his wife Catherine, *née* Carmichael, in 1802. The 1841 census confusingly gives his age as forty, hers as twenty-six, and lists him as a "fisherman". Perhaps the Leitches did not feel like giving accurate information to the census-taker about their dates of birth, but presumably what they told him about their children was true. At that stage, there were six who had survived infancy: Mary, Donald, Lizzy, Malcolm, Annie, and Catherine. There was also a "herd" sharing their home, a fifteen-year-old boy named Archie McLean. Another child, Archibald, was born in 1843. His mother was now past forty, and had been bearing children for at least sixteen years, so she must have assumed that the baby boy would be her last. Indeed he was, because a tragedy swept the entire little community away.

According to a story told in the family, it began with a gruesome discovery on the shoreline of Loch Fyne. Death on board ship was as common there as anywhere else on Britain's busy coast. Sometimes, a ship's crew would indulge in the antisocial practice of chucking a corpse overboard in shallow water rather than wait to dispose of it properly in the open sea. It is possible that someone from the little knot of homes in Allt Beithe or neighbouring Baldarroch came upon the bloated, discarded remains of a seafarer washed up on the coast, and buried him in the nearby undergrowth, not knowing that he had died from cholera. Or there may be a simpler explanation for the contagion which destroyed their village: it may just have been caused by living conditions.

For whatever reason, the townsfolk in nearby Tarbert began to wonder why they had not heard from their neighbours down the coast, and two brave men set out to investigate. The sight which greeted them must have been appalling. Everyone in Baldarroch was dead. In Allt Beithe, it was almost as bad. John Leitch was probably already dead. Catherine may still have been alive, and capable of telling them what had happened, but desperately sick. According to the evidence in Tarbert cemetery, he died on 4 December 1845, and she followed him twelve days later. The only survivor in the whole of the little community, according to family legend, was two-year-old Archibald Leitch. The rescue party put the little settlement to the torch, in the hope of destroying the "plague" which had wiped it out. Archibald was taken to live with his mother's parents at Bruach na Suith. Only one memento came with him: the wooden door of his family home. Having survived such a calamity, he doubtless grew up with a reputation as a child blessed with good fortune; but it is unlikely that anyone in the village thought that the great-grandfather of a British Prime Minister could be living among them.

Stories handed down by word of mouth do not always stand up against whatever hard evidence can be unearthed. There is one flaw in the story of Archibald Leitch, sole survivor of the "plague". The headstone on his parents' grave is clearly marked as being commissioned "by their sons and daughters" – implying that they were outlived by at least four of their children. And if the surviving children went to the expense of commemorating their parents, why not their brothers and sisters, who were reputedly carried off by the same contagion? Perhaps there were older children, who had left home to find work before the tragedy, and were able to put together just enough money to have their parents' names carved on a tombstone, but not those of their lost brothers and sisters. Or perhaps the legend of Archibald being found alone in a house of death became exaggerated towards the end of his long life.

Archibald's great-grandson, John, who has studied the family history in detail, believes that two of Archibald's brothers may have been drowned years later when their boat capsized in Loch Fyne. It is a fact that two fishermen named Donald Leitch and James Leitch drowned on 15 October 1881, but, confusingly, they were not brothers. James, who was twenty-nine when he died, had a father named Donald, who was not the same Donald who drowned alongside him. The 1841 census says that Donald Leitch, son of John and Catherine, was born around 1829. The Donald Leitch who drowned in 1881 was born in 1840; Donald Leitch, the father of James, who drowned with him, was born much earlier in the century. The little town of Tarbert was full of Smiths and Leitches.

What is certain is that Archibald was orphaned at the age of two, and achieved an aura of indestructibility as he grew older. He started work as a carpenter in Tarbert, married a much younger woman – as men often did then – and outlived her by more than a quarter of a century. He died in November 1930, at the grand age of eighty-seven. The boatyard he founded and ran as a family business with his sons, Dugald and Callum, became a popular meeting-place for local villagers, and is still standing. It is used by A. McCallum, boatbuilders. His two older boys made at least one journey back to the ruins of Allt Beithe, to collect a large stone handmill which their grandfather had used to grind corn. They rolled it down to the shore, loaded it on to a boat, and transported it safely to Tarbert. It can still be seen there, at a house called Breezycliff.

A third son, Donald, remarkably, went through university to become an MA, but died in 1920 at the age of forty. There was a fourth son, named Archie, after his father; and daughters Catherine, Isabel, and Ann. Ann followed the local custom by marrying a man eight years older than herself: old enough, in other words, to have accumulated sufficient wealth to support a family. He was John Smith, a local herring fisherman, who died in 1952 at the age of eighty-two. Family tradition demanded that the firstborn son was named after his paternal grandfather. John's father was Neil Smith, son of John Smith – who, doubtless, was himself the son of Neil Smith and grandson of John Smith, and so on back through the generations. The first child, born in 1902, was consequently called Neil.

These were not poor people, by local standards. Indeed, old Archibald Leitch might not have allowed his daughter to marry into the family had they not been respected in the village. John and son Neil had their own fishing boat. They practised ring-net fishing, which involved a pair of boats operating together, dragging a long net through the loch to haul in a huge catch. Each boat was operated by four or five men. The other men in the Smith boat were not hired hands working for wages: they had a share of the catch, so they prospered with the Smiths in a good year, and went hungry when the market price of herring fell. Smith father and son were labourers rather than capitalists, but prosperous enough to have been rounded up and deported under a Stalinist regime for being of the "kulak" class. They were also deeply religious Presbyterians and elders of the Church of Scotland, for whom strict honesty in all money matters was a moral imperative.

The older Smith's most prosperous years, ironically, were during the two world wars, when there was never a problem finding buyers for his catch – though in the second war he had to manage without the help of his oldest son, who was in the Royal Navy. At other times the price of herring fell so drastically that they had to give up fishing, and work as hands on merchant ships doing runs along the coast and into European ports. In the end, the herring fishermen of Loch Fyne destroyed their own livelihood. There were too many of them battling to keep up their living standards, the loch was overfished, and the industry died. There was no question of Neil's son John being a fisherman. His first son, born in 1976, is of course Neil Smith. Neil's ambition, at the time of writing, is to be an advocate – the Scottish equivalent of a barrister – and a politician. Not a Labour politician, though. His opinions are well to the right, which is why there was a Conservative sticker alongside the Labour sticker on the Smiths' front door during the 1992 election. (The Labour sticker, for some reason, was taken down first.)

John Smith the younger, meanwhile, decided at some point in his life that he "didn't have the brains" for a flashy profession like politics, although the little that he has written – about his family history – is evidence that he has more brain than many of the nation's legislators. However, the view people form of themselves early on often dictates the course of their lives. John Smith did not study law or run for Parliament, and won't be Prime Minister; he left school at fifteen, and runs his own business as a plumber from his home in Tarbert, where he and his family awake in the mornings to the sound of waves lapping and seagulls quarrelling on the shore of the loch just a few yards from their front door. This must be Tarbert's gain. The world might be a better place if there were no professional lawyers or politicians, but who could imagine civilized society without plumbers?

The Smiths of Tarbert are entitled to have to suffer the intrusive curiosity of outsiders, but it might just be worth recording that John Smith thinks it was lucky for his famous cousin that Labour lost the 1992 election. If he had become Chancellor of the Exchequer, says the other John, he would have had a hard job avoiding the fiasco of Britain's sudden exit from the Exchange Rate Mechanism, and would have been blamed for it. Public opinion would never have believed that such a disaster could happen under the Tories.

John and Ann Smith had five children, born between 1902 and 1915. The last was yet another John Smith, who died in 1987. The brain of the family was their second son, christened Archibald Leitch Smith in honour of his grandfather.[2] Instead of starting work at fourteen or fifteen like the rest of the family, he was allowed to go on to Dunoon for secondary education, and then to Glasgow University. There, he read English and History, and joined the Glasgow Student Labour Club. After university he took up a post as headmaster of a primary school in the village of Portnahaven, on the island of Islay, off the west coast of Scotland. There he met Sarah Cameron Scott, who was working as a commercial artist. Her father, Robert Scott, came originally from south-west Scotland, close to the Cumbrian border. He had worked as a quarryman at Bonawe, near Taynuilt, close to where the River Awe runs into Loch Etive, north-east of Oban. He died young before the war. Sarah's mother, who was a Cameron from northern Scotland, then moved further inland to Dalmally, near the northern tip of Loch Awe, to run a boarding house called Baddarroach. At the time of writing, Mrs Sarah Smith is alive and still vigorous, at the age of about eighty, and living in Aberdour, Fyfe, where Gordon Brown is her constituency MP. She moved there to be near one of her daughters, Mrs Anne Kelly, who is married to a local headmaster.

When Sarah Smith was pregnant for the first time, she evidently preferred not to give birth on Islay, and made what must have been a formidable forty-mile journey across sea and land to her mother's boarding house, which is where her son was born on 13 September 1938. Like his grandfather, he was called John. When the boy was two years old, Archibald Smith was appointed headmaster of Ardrishaig primary school. This brought the family back to the Scottish mainland, and into the little house attached to the "wee" school on the slope above the Tarbert Road in Ardrishaig. This was another little fishing port, hit, like Tarbert, by the collapse of the herring industry. It is about eleven miles north of Tarbert, in the Knapdale area north of Kintyre, on the shore of Loch Gilp, which adjoins Loch Fyne. Nowadays, the car journey to Tarbert takes only a quarter of an hour, but in the 1950s the distance was great enough to make a family reunion a rare event.

Archibald Smith's employer was Argyll County Council, now the Argyll and Bute district of Scotland's massive Strathclyde region. It may soon be a county again, but it is to be hoped that this time the local lairds will be able to agree on where the seat of local government should be. In the old days several communities fought jealously over this right, and the local bureaucracy became dispersed. The county clerk and chief constable were based in Lochgilphead, just up the road from Ardrishaig. The county treasurer was in Campbeltown, many miles to the south, in Kintyre. The county architect was far over to the east in Dunoon, on Clydeside. The chief medical officer was way up north in Oban, on Scotland's west coast. The motor taxation department was in Ardrishaig. Where the county council met depended on the time of year. As a young MP, John Smith watched disapprovingly as this fine old mess was tidied up and centralized, and local decision-making was divided between a district headquarters in Lochgilphead, and the headquarters of the massive Strathclyde region. "I doubt whether we are wise to create such a monster in such a small country as Scotland," he warned.[3]

The older residents of Ardrishaig all remember their school headmaster and his clever young son very well. His pupils instantly nicknamed him "Hairy", which suggests that he did not look quite as his son does in middle age. By reputation he was a strict master, but popular for all that. George Bruce, a son of Ardrishaig who emigrated to Australia, claims: "I had the honour of being the first pupil in the class that he gave a clip over the ear to. I was walking out of the class, talking to another boy, when I got a lift under the ear from Hairy Smith for talking in class. Two strides further on, I would have been out of the door." One of his former female pupils remembers him as being stricter with the boys than with the girls. He was sternest of all with his own son, who entered the "wee" school adjoining the family home at the age of five, and by eleven was in his father's class in the larger building across the road. John Smith's own recollection, supported by other former pupils, was that old Hairy expected young Hairy to get it right even when other children were out of their depth. "It was always 'Why weren't you top of the class?' In the end, it was easier just to be top of the class," he has been quoted as saying.[4]

The rest of the family were just as well-known in the village. There were the two little girls, Mary and Anne, who would come out of their house to watch the older children in the playground, and their mother, Sarah Smith – "a lovely, gentle woman", according to Mrs Jennifer Phillimore, one of John Smith's contemporaries. It was too small and too close a community for the social gap between the Smiths and the other families to matter.

There was no temptation for Archibald Smith to seal himself socially in a little crowd of university-educated professionals: he was almost the only man in town who had been to university. Besides, he was aware that he owed his position to the solidarity of the local community. Early in the war, the county council had decided to close the school and move the pupils to neighbouring Lochgilphead, whereupon the parents organized a "strike", keeping their children out of school for several weeks until the authorities caved in.

The only real experience Ardrishaig people had of being cold-shouldered by people with money was when yachts belonging to well-off families from Glasgow sailed into Loch Gilp. The local boys quickly found a way to take revenge. Fishing for live eels was a simple skill, which anyone could master. The game was to toss them on to the deck of a visiting yacht, preferably one with women or girls on board. It cannot be proved, but it is suspected that the young John Smith was guilty of this prank.

The easy manners and friendly sociability of the future Labour leader are undoubtedly the result of being raised in a small community where everyone knew everyone else. All those who remember him seem moved to say how little he has changed over the years. "He wasn't at all stand-offish," says Mrs Grace Clifford, another contemporary. "When I see him on the television, I think he is just the boy I knew at school. I feel I could carry on a conversation where we left off." Peter Clarke, who left Ardrishaig to become a writer and economist – and a Tory – was a few years younger than the headmaster's son, and consequently a little intimidated by him, and more taken with his sisters. He was very impressed, though, by John Smith's toy bow and arrow, and the sling improvised from an old Ajax carton, with its top ripped off, in which the arrows were neatly stored. "The most striking thing is that he has simply not changed," he says. "He was a wee bit lighter, but jowly even then, and slightly sanctimonious. Not one of the lads. Bookish, but he wasn't thought to be a scholar. He was owlish – that was his most memorable quality. That owl-like little boy that I remember in short trousers is the leader of Her Majesty's Opposition."

One thing that marked out the Smiths as different, though, was their interest in politics, and Labour politics at that. This was a deeply Conservative area. To this day, Argyll has never had a Labour MP – though, in a surprise result, it was captured from the Tories by a Liberal, Mrs Ray Michie, in 1987. Alex Bruce, now one of the stalwarts of the local church, was just old enough to vote in the 1945 election. He was away with the forces, and scandalized his parents by writing to ask them to cast his proxy vote for Labour. "It just wasn't done round here. Too many lairds living nearby," he says. Archibald Smith may have thought it prudent not to retain his formal link with the Labour Party, to avoid incurring the disapproval of Argyll County Council's education department; but he must have been Ardrishaig's only subscriber to the *New Statesman*, and after he had retired to Dunoon, he had no hesitation in rejoining the Party. He was a steward at a Scottish Labour Party conference in the 1970s, and was out campaigning for a "yes" vote in the 1979 referendum on Scottish devolution, which took place under legislation which his son had piloted through the House of Commons. (He died in 1981, at the age of seventy-three.)

In or out of the Party, there was not much doubt about Archibald Smith's sympathies. "I remember him enthusing about the council houses in Ardrishaig," says Peter Clarke. "I thought my relatives who lived in them were folk you should feel sorry for, but he thought they were terribly advanced."

Anyone who doubted the father's allegiance had only to listen to his young son. There was a shop in the town centre called Tibby's, run by a Mrs MacVicar, where lively arguments were to be heard on a Saturday. Mrs MacVicar's son Angus, now in his eighties, remembers John Smith as "quite brilliant – in a class of his own". Ian "Eeny" McGregor, who runs an old people's home close to the former primary school, which is now a toy library, says: "I remember him talking about Nye Bevan and telling us that the introduction of the National Health Service would mean the end of people having to have their tonsils or appendix out on the kitchen table. We were more interested in Dan Dare and the McFlannels. But John would talk politics. Even then it was his great passion."[5]

At the age of eleven John moved on to junior secondary school in the neighbouring village of Lochgilphead, a couple of miles up the road. There, he devoted part of his spare time to membership of the Scripture Union, which earned him a place on a day trip to Glasgow. This entailed a four- or five-hour journey by bus along windy, bumpy roads, an overnight stay, and a return journey the following day. Jennifer Phillimore's enduring memory of the outing is of being violently sick during the journey. Glasgow is usually thought of as west Scotland, but for these children from Argyll it was the furthest east they had ever been in their lives.

An interesting question is: how religious was the young John Smith? He volunteered for activities connected with the church, yet he was probably not as profoundly devout as his uncle and grandfather. He made an early discovery that he had an exceptionally fine singing voice. As a boy soprano he had a repertoire of Gaelic songs, and even won a silver medal at the Mod, the Scottish equivalent of the Eisteddfod. He wore a kilt for the performance, of course. He also used to sing in his local choir. Bob

McLaughlan, who knew him as a teenager, suspects that it was music, more than religious devotion, which drew him to the church. On a visit to the Smith household in Ardrishaig, he was surprised to learn that the family cat was called Billy Graham, "because he's so pure" – which implies that John's parents' attitude to religion was a little less reverential than that of other members of the extended family. Even so, religion was as much part of his mental make-up as Labour politics, then and during his adult life.

The simplicity and consistency of the whole Smith philosophy is rooted in Argyll. The co-operative good neighbourliness, the absence of snobbery, class division and crime, the cheerful sense of belonging which he experienced as a small boy, is how John Smith thinks people should live. If he had his way, all of Great Britain would be like an untroubled hamlet in western Scotland. Peter Clarke says: "I was taught that of all the Scots, we were the nicest and happiest and the best, because we lived in the beauty of Knapdale. It was the general view that we were the tops. I guess Smith would have shared that assumption."

2
Student Days on Clydeside 1952–62

Until he was fourteen, John Smith had no experience of life outside the picture-postcard communities of western Scotland. That had to change if his education was to go any further. There were only three schools in the two-million-acre county of Argyll which took pupils over fourteen, all in towns a formidable distance away – Campbeltown, Dunoon, or Oban. John Smith followed in his father's footsteps to Dunoon. As the crow flies this is only about twenty miles from Ardishraig, assuming that the crow overflew Loch Gilp, Loch Fyne, Loch Striven and Glendaruel Forest before landing on the west bank of the Clyde. For a human, it was as long as the journey to Glasgow. Little John Smith, like other children from all over Argyll, said goodbye to his parents when term began, and saw them again when term was over. And he was, in effect, saying goodbye to Ardrishaig. Although he would return even as a university student, to take summer jobs with MacBreyne's bus and steamer company or the motor tax department, he was no longer part of the village where he had grown up. The link became even weaker when his father was moved to another teaching job in Dunoon. But Ardrishaig people remember him coming back in December 1973 for the funeral of his aunt, Mary MacPherson, whose son is currently Strathclyde's Director of Education. By then, wee "Hairy" Smith was a Member of Parliament, something no one from Ardrishaig had achieved before.

Meanwhile, he was at the mercy of a Dunoon landlady. Fortunately for him, he was taken in by a kindly soul named Mrs Irene McGilp. Peter Clarke, who followed the trail to Dunoon some years later, recalls her as having "ample bosoms" and as being "one of the great scone-makers of Argyll". The boys usually lodged in pairs, but John Smith was her only lodger – either because his father was slightly better off than others, or because he was lucky. Some of Dunoon's little lodgers came from as far afield as the Isle of Islay – for instance William Stewart, who went on to be appointed Chief Adviser at the Cabinet Office in 1990.

For the first time in his life, John Smith was living in a place where he could walk down the street without meeting anyone he knew; where there was even crime, and residents might think it prudent to lock their doors when they left the house. "To us, it was the big metropolis," Peter Clarke recalls, with some contempt for Dunoon's pretensions. "It was where the working class who have made it went to retire. It thinks it's rather grand, but to anyone else it seems rather naff – the Essex of Argyll, with more rain." None of this bothered the bright little boy from Ardrishaig, who continued to shine in class. His essay on Ernest Hemingway was published in the school magazine – and his political interests continued unabated. He joined the Dunoon branch of the Argyll Constituency Labour Party at sixteen. Bob McLaughlan, who has long since left the Labour Party and is now a leader writer for the *Herald* in Glasgow, claims to have signed him up.

It would be impossible to overstate the influence of his west Scotland upbringing and his schooling on the way the adult John Smith sees the world. The Smith vision of a classless society begins with young children of different natural abilities, from all walks of life, rubbing shoulders in the same playground, with none of the unfair social privilege or exclusiveness which money can buy. It was a vision he acquired in Argyll; in one of his first parliamentary speeches, he boasted: "I received the whole of my secondary education in the county of Argyll, where fee-paying schools were never heard of, never demanded and never likely to be asked for by people who live there."[1] It was an attitude he had learnt at home: "My father, who was rather a wry old gent, said that the great thing about Argyll, in educational terms, is that it was so far behind that it was always ahead – ahead of the next change in fashion."[2] And the lesson stuck: "I still believe education is the great liberator," he told an interviewer a few days before he became leader of the Labour Party. "Apart from anything else, it opens the doors of the imagination, breaks down class barriers and frees people. In our family, the person who was educated was the person you should admire. Money was looked down on and education was revered. I am still slightly contemptuous of money."[3]

To this day, Smith is keen for it to be known that the name Dunoon Grammar School had nothing to do with selection or the eleven-plus. It dated back, in fact, to Tudor times. When the school celebrated its 350th anniversary in 1991, John Smith, the Shadow Chancellor, was there to propose the toast. Two more Labour MPs, George Robertson and Brian Wilson, were also among the old boys present on that occasion. There was no secondary modern school to take the exam failures. Argyll children either left school at fourteen, or they went to "grammar school". Other old boys of Dunoon Grammar School, like Bob McLaughlan and Peter Clarke, accuse Smith of seeing his school days through rose-tinted spectacles. There were private schools in Dumbarton and Edinburgh, where the children of Argyll's wealthy families could avoid contact with the rest of the population. There was also a loose system of selection. Even at Lochgilphead, the children were divided into three or four streams, according to ability. "A" stream pupils, like John Smith, were exempted from technical subjects like woodwork and metalwork, while "C" streamers were spared Latin. The expectation was that the "A" stream would stay on, and perhaps go to university; those in the lowest stream would start work at fourteen or fifteen. So, in a sense, those who went to Dunoon Grammar School had already been selected. None the less, it was a far less rigid form of streaming than the one adopted in English state schools at the time; while the number of privately educated children was very small. It was also a system which encouraged. Children from humble backgrounds had a better chance of reaching university here than they did in southern England.

In John Smith's case, of course, there was never any doubt that he was bound for university. He had decided to read Law, which meant that he had to spend four years completing an arts course before he even opened his law books. He obtained an MA in History and an LLB in Law, arriving at Glasgow University in the year of Suez, 1956, and leaving in 1963, a few months after the death of Hugh Gaitskell. It was here that he learnt the art of public speaking. It is often assumed that he can speak so well because of his legal training, but old friends say it was the other way round: he was an accomplished political orator long before he was called to the Scottish Bar, having developed his speaking style during arduous student debates. There was a debating tradition at Glasgow which was taken very seriously by both the students and the authorities. Debates began at lunch time on a Friday, and would continue until midnight. The liveliest session would be towards the end, before the student bar closed at 10.30 p.m., when the students would put on review sketches, known as "stunts", for the amusement of a none-too-sober audience. Earlier in the day, they would mimic the proceedings of Parliament. One of the various political clubs would take it in turns to act as the "government", and produce a piece of legislation which the others would then oppose.

There were six clubs in John Smith's day, all training grounds for young men who went on to achieve prominence in Scottish public life. The Conservatives included Teddy Taylor, now Sir Edward Taylor, the right-wing MP for Southend, who was a maverick even then. The Liberals had Menzies "Ming" Campbell, a future Olympic athlete and Liberal Democrat MP for North-East Fife, and John McKay, now Lord McKay, a former Dunoon Grammar School boy who switched to the Tories and became MP for Argyll. The Scottish Nationalists included Iain and Neil MacCormick, sons of the celebrated "King John" MacCormick, who had founded the SNP when he was a student at Glasgow at the same time as John Smith's father. There were "The Distributors", a Catholic club based on the ideas of G.K. Chesterton and Hilaire Belloc, chaired for a year by Jimmy Gordon, later the founder and head of Radio Clyde; the Independent Socialists, an amalgam of Bevanites and Communists, including John Ryan, later Labour MP for Uxbridge; and there was the University Labour Club.

The Labour Club's reputation spread beyond the university perimeter. Its stars were thought to be very bright, very ambitious, and very Gaitskellite. When Gaitskell died, the club members were all on the side of George Brown rather than Harold Wilson. Successive presidents included Arthur Houston in 1956–57, Bob McLaughlan the following year, John Smith in 1959–60, Donald MacCormick in 1960–61, and Donald Dewar in 1961–62. One of the most academically gifted members was Alexander Irvine, who was not then as active in politics as Smith or Dewar, but is now one of England's foremost QCs, a Labour peer, and a potential Labour Lord Chancellor. "If there were any Bevanites in the club," says Dewar, "I can't remember them." There were a few, however, including Hugh MacPherson, a columnist for *Tribune* since the early 1970s, who became the club's president in 1962, when the influence of the left in Glasgow generally was at a peak.

At that time, Gaitskell was under continual challenge from the left over a range of issues, but particularly nuclear disarmament, and was grateful for any support he could get. The right wing of the Scottish Labour Party was not over-endowed with intellectual talent. A club which turned out bright, energetic, hard-line Gaitskellites, ready and willing to go out of the university perimeter to be involved in real politics, was a jewel worth polishing. Willy Marshall, General Secretary of the Scottish Labour Party, kept a close eye on them for years. Smith had come to his notice even before he was a university student. Marshall used to hire university students to spend a week or a fortnight in specially selected constituencies, going from door to door, recruiting new members to the Party. The pay, which came from Co-operative Party funds, was very poor. In fact, just before Smith's arrival, the student canvassers went on strike. Even after they had extracted a pay rise out of Willy Marshall, they were working for love rather than money. Smith joined a canvassing team in summer 1956, just after leaving Dunoon Grammar School – having no doubt been recruited by Bob McLaughlan. The four youngsters went knocking on doors in Glasgow, and then in parts of Argyll. Jimmy Gordon was one of them. He recalls: "It was all too easy. The subscription wasn't much. If you were at all persuasive, people signed up like mad; but they fell away equally quickly, because the party organization was bloody awful even then."

Marshall also encouraged his young charges to think of themselves as future MPs. He tried to persuade at least three of them to stand in the 1959 general election, in safe Tory seats where they would have no chance of winning but would gain experience which might be useful later. Arthur Houston, in fact, contested East Renfrewshire. Jimmy Gordon, who was not even a party member, declined the offer. As for John Smith, he had to point out that he was not yet twenty-one, and would have been disqualified on grounds of age. However, he had an unexpected break two years later, when the MP for East Fife suddenly died. Douglas Young, a classics lecturer at St Andrews University and a member of East Fife Labour Party, knew him by reputation, and wrote to him suggesting he stand in the forthcoming by-election. He leapt at the idea. At the age of just twenty-two he descended upon the voters of East Fife bubbling with enthusiasm, and backed up by coachloads of student helpers. Every member of the Glasgow University Labour Club was expected to make the journey at least once, if not every weekend, to help out. Donald Dewar recalls leading raiding parties of forty or fifty into the fray. Jimmy Gordon enjoyed himself so much – especially when he met the Labour MP for the neighbouring seat, Willie Hamilton – that he finally joined the Party, and stayed for four or five years.

This was also one of the first by-elections to feature a televised debate between the candidates, which proved decisive in the fight for second place. There was no prospect whatsoever that John Smith would win, but he did have a chance of coming second. The dead MP, Sir James Henderson-Stewart, had been one of the last candidates to stand on a joint Conservative/Liberal ticket. His Tory successor, Sir John Gilmour, had a Liberal opponent. Despite pockets of solid Labour support, it was an area rather like Argyll, where deference was the norm, so it was plain that most of the vote would now go to the Tory. Smith was told by one working-class voter whose support he had asked for: "No thank you, young man. I think Sir John is just the right man to succeed Sir James." The Liberal turned out to be a poor television performer, while Smith was confident and quick-witted, as always. When the votes were counted, Labour's share had dropped a little from the 1959 result, but that did not bother Smith at all. What delighted him was that he had come second, with 8,882 votes, 96 ahead of the Liberal. His reputation as a rising star of the Scottish Labour Party was made. In all, he says, it was a "hilarious event".

By now, John Smith was a veteran of the student circuit. He and Donald Dewar were well established as two of the best debaters in a competitive field. They were not necessarily the wittiest, nor the most theatrical performers. They did not play for laughs, but came to present a well-argued case, usually about the pragmatic advantages of electing a Labour government. Ming Campbell recalls: "Even as a student there was a political hardness about John, which stamped him out among others. It was evident then that if he continued in politics, he was going to be extremely successful." Hugh MacPherson says: "He was very adult and very political, very quickly."

As a pair, Smith and Dewar won a trophy in a competition sponsored by *The Scotsman*. This brought them an invitation to speak at a Fabian weekend school in Guildford. Their plan was to hitch-hike all the way. After hours of misery standing on the roadside, smartly attired in blue suits and carrying heavy bags, being ignored by passing motorists, they were at last picked up by a fish lorry, which took them to Darlington. Its driver came from Ardrishaig and had recognized Hairy Smith's son, despite the smart suit. Smith and another student did even better in 1962, winning the coveted *Observer* Mace award. However, not everyone liked this elite young group of hard Gaitskellites. Even Hugh MacPherson, who had a soft spot for Smith, was taken aback by the pragmatism of the political circle in which he mixed. "I liked to think politics was about having ideals, not winning elections," he says. On the Labour left – especially in Glasgow's Woodside and Hillhead constituencies, in which the student lodgings were located – they were known as the "seat-seekers": ambitious, pro-establishment, and careerist. Tension in the Glasgow Labour Party exploded into open conflict in 1962.

First there was the May Day parade, an annual event jointly organized by the Labour Party, the Co-op Party and Glasgow Trades Council. It was the Party's turn to select the main speaker, and they loyally plumped for Hugh Gaitskell. But choosing a political theme was a joint decision, and the organizers resolved to make the occasion a demonstration against Polaris missiles. Hugh and Dora Gaitskell turned up none the less, to be at the head of a march from George Square to Queen's Park. Snaking along behind was a large and noisy assortment of CND members, Young Socialists, Communists and others for whom Gaitskell was the living embodiment of rotten compromise. Fearful of trouble, Willy Marshall had sent for his protégés from the university to form a Swiss guard around the leader. As the march made its way through Glasgow, they passed a long wall where someone had been busy with whitewash the night before, writing "(H)UGH" in large letters several times over. Worse was to follow in Queen's Park. On an old bandstand decorated with a large anti-Polaris banner, Gaitskell had to struggle through his speech as his audience became ever noisier and more rebellious. It got out of hand when he claimed to have been speaking to a "socialist shipyard manager". Gaitskell turned on a section of the crowd which seemed to be making the most noise, apparently believing they were Communists. He exhorted everyone to ignore them because they were "peanuts". That only made matters worse, and eventually the police were called to quieten down the crowd. To Willy Marshall's horror, a banner was raised aloft right in the thick of the trouble. It was the contingent from the Glasgow Woodside Labour Party, the very one to which John Smith and other students who were watching over Gaitskell belonged.

The day was not over when the May Day march dispersed, and there was one more embarrassment in store for the unfortunate Gaitskell. He was to be guest speaker at a university dinner, which was celebrating the success of a combined campaign by the university's left-wing clubs to have Chief Albert Luthuli of the ANC elected Rector of Glasgow University. It was, incidentally, common to choose a political figure; R.A. Butler and Lord Hailsham were previous rectors; but the left managed to have the distant Luthuli elected in preference to the Lord Privy Seal, Edward Heath. This time, having seemingly underestimated earlier in the day how much the Glasgow Labour Party had shifted to the left, Gaitskell seemed to misread the conservatism of the students: he turned up in a red tie and lounge suit, while his young hosts were all in dark suits and gowns. But his miseries were dispelled as he heard the two students' speeches which preceded his. The first was from a Liberal, who confessed that he felt like "the curate before the archbishop". Next came John Smith, whose speaking style must already have been very similar to the one which has served him so well in the Commons: reasonable, lucid, with fact piled upon fact, and wit injected only where it helped to emphasize his point. Gaitskell not only loved the style; he was even more impressed by the message. Smith's theme was that Labour's main function was to win power, and if it was to do that, its members must learn self-discipline and not pursue their political quarrels to a point where they might harm the Party's electoral prospects. A delighted Gaitskell opened with a quip: at first, he said, "I was conceited enough to think I was the archbishop . . ."[4] Later, he confided to Bob McLaughlan, who was then at Oxford University with his daughters, that Smith was "the most impressive student speaker he had ever encountered".

That was Sunday. Monday's newspapers speculated that the Woodside Labour Party would be disbanded. Its members would automatically lose their party membership and would have to reapply individually – a well-known method for purging the Bevanite left. That might very well have happened if the Party's formidable national organizer, Sarah Barker, had taken charge. However, the decision was, in effect, delegated to officials of the Glasgow City Labour Party. They went into Woodside to cross-examine party members suspected of being involved, including Paul Foot, a young socialist whose uncle, Michael, had recently been expelled from the Parliamentary Labour Party over his support for unilateralism. Asked if he had shouted, the younger Foot confessed to being a "pretty childish" sort who, if shouted at, shouted back. The district Party decided to be lenient, and let Woodside off with a reprimand. They needed to defuse the conflict and allow things to settle down quickly, because Woodside's Tory MP had resigned on becoming a law lord, and a by-election was suddenly in prospect, which Labour had a good chance of winning. The Tory majority in 1959 had been a little over 2,000. Everyone, from Gaitskell down, now became interested in the question of whom the local Party would select as its candidate.

This was long before the days when ordinary party members took part in choosing candidates. It was for delegates of the General Management Committee to decide, at a special meeting at which all the shortlisted candidates were allowed to speak. This gave local trade-union bosses an immense advantage. A large union might have twenty or more branches in a city the size of Glasgow. Each would be allowed to send its coterie of delegates, who would have been tipped off beforehand by the union's regional office on the merits of the competing candidates. In that way, one determined trade-union organizer might wield fifty or more votes.

In general, where there is a power struggle between right-wing union fixers and left constituency activists, as there was in Woodside, the union bosses could be expected to win every time. On this occasion, however, the left managed to be well organized and united behind a left-wing Glasgow councillor named Neil Carmichael, who won the nomination and the by-election and served as an MP for over twenty years, becoming Lord Carmichael of Kelvinside after losing his seat in 1983. But before the matter was settled, there were all manner of shenanigans, some involving John Smith. Many years later, when Smith became a Cabinet minister, Paul Foot wrote a piece in the *New Statesman* claiming that Smith had voted at the selection conference, as the delegate from a moribund branch of the National Union of General and Municipal Workers – forerunner of the present-day GMB – which had once represented the cleaners at a bus station. Given that Carmichael was by now a respected parliamentary colleague, it was an embarrassing story which has hung around Smith for decades.

One reason why the unions lost is that they were fielding competing candidates. The favourite was a right-wing Glaswegian, Jimmy White, who had the Transport and General Workers' Union behind him. But the NUGMW had a new Scottish Regional Secretary, Alex Donnet, who rose to be one of the biggest names in the Scottish trade-union movement. There are still a number of Scottish Labour MPs who began their careers as his protégés, including George Robertson, who remembers him as "an old-style Tammany Hall fixer – a quite brilliant, self-educated trade-union leader". Doug Henderson, another former union official, says: "He used to give us younger members of staff hell." Donnet was impressed by the Glasgow University Labour Club, and had signed up its stars, including John Smith, as union members. He decided that Arthur Houston, who had already fought a general election, was the right man for Woodside.

Houston never achieved anything like the prominence of John Smith or Donald Dewar, but he had an interesting early history. He was the self-made working man in a circle of much younger middle-class intellectuals, acting sometimes like an older brother to the newer members of the Labour Club. He was close enough to John Smith to join him on a trip home to Ardrishaig. According to his widow, Christine Houston, the elder Smiths seemed pleased that this naval veteran should have taken their son under his wing. Houston had joined the Royal Navy at the age of fourteen, and spent the whole of the war at sea. The story goes that when he was a leading signalman, in 1952, the Admiral of the Mediterranean Fleet advised him that there was nothing else he could achieve in the navy, and that he should go back to civilian life to complete his education. He graduated from Glasgow University in 1959, at the age of thirty-five, then worked for the Education Institute of Scotland, the main teachers' union. In 1961 he organized one of Glasgow's first teachers' strikes.

Meanwhile, the left was operating out of makeshift headquarters at the home of Norman and Janey Buchan, who had learnt a thing or two about political organization in the Communist Party before they left it in 1956. They were in regular touch with Ian Mikardo – arguably the best political fixer the Labour left had – and with his secretary, Jo Richardson. The Buchans' home was like a sprawling political office, with beds in the corners of upstairs rooms. At the time when the battle over the Woodside selection was being fought, it was also cluttered with 300 fruit pies, 500 Marmite rolls, 150 toilet rolls, and 100 lumps of cheese left over from a CND demonstration which had not attracted the expected numbers. The singer Ewan MacColl was staying as a guest. The Buchans combined a bohemian lifestyle with a puritanical dedication to the traditions of the socialist pioneers: populism with only a touch of Karl Marx. They were the antithesis of John Smith. At about this time, Norman Buchan succeeded in getting himself adopted for a nearby parliamentary seat, which he won in 1964; he was an MP until his death in 1990. Janey Buchan, now in her late sixties, is due to retire as Glasgow's Member of the European Parliament in 1994.

With the candidates lined up, the next step in the tortuous political game is to get the maximum number of delegates affiliated in time for the selection conference. Only people who turned out on the night, with valid credentials, could vote. The rules were pretty loose. Delegates did not even have to be party members; they had to be "available to join" – a form of words devised to bar Communists and members of other parties. Union delegates had to be on the list of names supplied by their union's regional office, but they did not have to prove that they had actually been selected by the body of union members on whose behalf they were voting. In the event of disputes, it was Willy Marshall's job to adjudicate, and Marshall, obviously, was not keen that a CND member and former conscientious objector like Neil Carmichael should win. The Bevanites were convinced, therefore, that the whole apparatus was unfairly stacked against them. Janey Buchan insists that they never expected to win, but decided to make a fight of it anyway.

The first battle was to get Willy Marshall to surrender the list of delegates, so that it could be checked. Their suspicions had been aroused, she says, because they discovered by chance that some of the NUGMW delegates were students who had given an address in the constituency – lodgings in Lillybank Gardens, where the landlord denied knowing them. When Marshall reluctantly handed the list over, Janey Buchan assembled a troop of Young Socialists including Paul Foot, Maria Fyfe, now Labour MP for Glasgow Maryhill, and Jean McCrindle, who rose to prominence in the 1984–85 coalfield campaign – and sent them out to check who the union delegates were, and whether they knew what they were involved in. There appear to have been a series of minor pitched battles over individual names. Janey Buchan claims: "There was one elderly man who said, 'Sir, I am not a member of your union. I think I may have been a member of your union once.' He was a poor wee soul living in a tenement. They told him not to come. They said, 'You'll not be allowed to stay.' It was just awful. Willy Marshall said that's a mistake, they'll be entitled to send another." None the less, on the night some 300 accredited delegates turned out to conduct the selection under the watchful eye of Sarah Barker. Some were delivered to the door in transport laid on by the students, with John Smith in charge. There was one, in particular, who became the unwitting subject of an argument on the dance hall floor, with party members angrily demanding that Willy Marshall should rule his credentials were invalid. Janey Buchan says:

> "Willy Marshall asked Mr X to stand up and identify himself, and in front of 300 people, including his friends and neighbours, told him he had to leave. He was one that John Smith's team had brought in a car. I was standing there

> choking. I wondered: do these people understand how humiliating it was for him, what contempt they had shown for working people, and they would do a thing like that to them, in pursuit of one vote. I've heard people say they were young, and didn't know what they were doing, but they were all law students. They knew. When we went out of that hall, I saw John Smith and I shoved my umbrella across his path so he could not get past, and I asked him if he was ashamed to humiliate a working person like that. He was very shamefaced. Then we went to Neil Carmichael's house, and I said, here's to 1963, and let's hope to Christ it's not like 1962."[5]

Janey Buchan says that she remembers it all as if it happened yesterday. She is adamant that Smith was not only ferrying delegates to the door but stayed, as a delegate, to cast his vote for Arthur Houston. She remembers it so clearly, she says, that she would swear in a court of law that this is true: "He was a delegate, and he was at the meeting. Smith came as the delegate from a branch of the G&M that did not exist. It catered for women cleaners at the bus garage. I am in absolutely no doubt about that. Why else would I have met him coming out at the end?"

It was beyond doubt that the NUGMW was doing everything it could, within a generous interpretation of party rules, to pack the meeting with delegates who would vote for Arthur Houston. One participant, who asked not to be named, says: "The G&M were doing everything to maximize Houston's vote. You would expect them to. The Bevanites were doing the same." And in so far as the story can be accurately pieced together after thirty years, it appears that John Smith really did turn up with a credential, as the delegate from a branch of the NUGMW. He himself is reluctant to talk about it. There are times when he has a lawyer's habit of not remembering what he prefers not to have on record. His powers of non-recollection can be quite formidable at times, and they include any political infighting between right and left which may have taken place in the Glasgow Labour Party in the early 1960s. He does not recollect being involved on Gaitskell's side of the struggle with the Bevanite left. His recollection of the meeting which selected Carmichael as the Woodside candidate is also hazy. "I think I was knocked out from being a delegate. . . . I wasn't confirmed as a delegate," he says.[6]

Bob McLaughlan, who was by now employed as research officer at the NUGMW's Scottish office, is much clearer. He says that when one of the union's delegates dropped out – probably because he was unable to spend a long evening listening to candidates' speeches – John Smith, as a NUGMW member, was persuaded to try to take his place. It would appear that someone then complained to Willy Marshall, who advised Houston's partisans not to push their luck. "John thought he was a delegate. John was not entitled to use somebody else's credentials, but he did not know that. He was a victim of Arthur Houston's enthusiasm. Arthur had enormous energy, but poor political judgement," McLaughlan says. Whatever the truth of it, Smith had now been taught that there is more to politics than brilliant speeches to crowded halls. It was his introduction to internal party warfare, in which lifelong enmities are forged in a day, and no doubt it contributed to his abiding aversion to internal party disputes. Alex Donnet, the union fixer behind it all, had no regrets – except, perhaps, that he had not been able to fix a few more votes for his man. Years afterwards, he liked to regale younger members of his staff with the story of how he had made the young John Smith learn to keep his head above water.

Smith, however, has a ready answer to those who attacked him for being too right-wing and devoid of ideals when he was young. Shortly before he became leader of the Labour Party, he said: "I was a socialist then as now, and I have no reservations about using the word. I remember all sorts of people then attacking me for not being left-wing enough. . . . They are all now stockbrokers and Thatcherites, so I think I got the better of them."[7]

3
The Lawyer 1963–70

However embarrassing it may have been, the Woodside incident did no damage to Smith's political prospects. In Labour Party circles his name was known right across Scotland, and there were numerous people – some of whom he had never met – who were willing to help propel him onwards. He was shortlisted for Rutherglen, where the frontrunner was a Glasgow councillor, Gregor MacKenzie. "That wasn't really serious," he says, "because I was a lifelong friend of Gregor MacKenzie. It was really, in a sense, to make up the shortlist: they needed four or five. I didn't want him not to get it." MacKenzie, in fact, held the seat from 1964 to 1987. The next approach came from South Aberdeen, a Tory seat which Labour had a good chance of winning, but Smith turned them down, recommending Donald Dewar instead. Dewar fought the seat in 1964 and won it in 1966. All in all, there is no doubt that Smith could have become a Labour MP in his mid twenties, if he had seriously wanted to. Instead, he decided to put loyalty first. The East Fife Labour Party had given him a unique chance to perform before TV cameras in a by-election, and he felt he owed it to them to stay to fight the October 1964 general election. This time his vote went up to 9,765, but his share of the total fell a fraction further: to just over 25 per cent, primarily because the Scottish Nationalists had also put up a candidate. His one satisfaction was that he came back even further ahead of the Liberal. As it turned out, this whimsical loyalty to a little Labour Party in a hopelessly Tory seat cost him his chance of being a government minister before he was thirty-five and might have delayed his entry into the Cabinet by a year or so, but in the long run it has done him no harm. Not every young career politician would have seen that there are times when it is better to be patient. The fact that Smith did the honourable thing bears out a claim he has frequently made about himself: that he is not one of those people for whom the whole meaning and purpose of life is to get to the top quickly.

In John Smith's day, university students were well-dressed and well-behaved. That changed later in the 1960s, of course: hence the celebrated photograph of Gordon Brown as a student leader, with an abundance of dark hair curling over his shoulders. Nothing like that exists from Smith's student days. His generation turned up to lectures in tweed jackets, flannels, collars and ties. Anyone daring enough to wear a polo-neck sweater would cause eyebrows to be raised. Drugs were unheard-of, and relations between the sexes were respectful and distant. Sexual intercourse, according to the Philip Larkin poem, began in 1963, after Smith had left university. Anyway, he was not the type to have gone womanizing even in a more liberated era. He preferred to unwind with male companions in the student bar, where he indulged in earnest arguments on matters of consequence.

In his photographs he may look like a neatly dressed man with a sharp haircut, but, surprisingly, all his contemporaries remember how wild and gregarious he was, how much he enjoyed life, and his remarkable ability to drink until well into the night and be up on time for his morning lecture looking alert. And he could be careless with clothes. Like other student politicians, he would hire a dinner jacket for the Friday debates; but on one occasion, at the end of the evening, in an outburst of adolescent exuberance, he ran towards a nearby lamppost, put out his arm to swing around it, and severely ripped his hired trousers.

Arthur Houston's widow, Christine, says: "I always think of him with his shirt-tail hanging out. I was always having to say, 'John for goodness' sake tuck yourself in.' It's the thing which comes into my mind now when I see him in public, looking so sober. He was great fun, and quite wild." He was, says Bob McLaughlan, "the untidiest boy I ever met – but he could get away with things which others couldn't. He was full of energy, full of mischief, and full of fun. He had a great bubbling quality. He was always throwing himself into politics with a serious intensity which was quite remarkable." Donald MacCormick, now a familiar face to viewers of "Newsnight", says: "He was always very determined, very much the life and soul of the party, always a bit 'I'm in charge'. John always made the weather, as they say – socially as much as politically."

There was an occasion when Smith and MacCormick's Scottish Nationalist cousin Neil, now Professor of Law at Edinburgh University, were stopped by a policeman on their way home after a Friday debate. *The Times* went so far as to allege, many years later, that they were caught urinating against a wall – making this "the raciest story anyone has been able to dredge up on the sombre and serious new Labour leader".[1] However, Professor MacCormick says that Smith, far from polluting Glasgow's environment, was trying to improve it: he had found a brush carelessly left lying about by a street cleaner, and was waltzing down the street with it. When he gave his name to the policeman as "John Smith", the officer retorted: "Aye, and I wrote the collected works of Shakespeare."

In one of his summer vacations he took a job as cook and general dogsbody on a "puffer", a small boat which delivered freight along the west coast of Scotland, and to nearby islands. It was an adventurous job for a university student, certainly much more exciting than another of his holiday earners, at the motor taxation department in Ardrishaig; but life aboard a small boat is more rough and ready than life at home. To protect the lad's sensibilities, the skipper thoughtfully put up a notice: "Don't call the cook a —." After one choppy passage, however, when our intrepid student seafarer had thrown up whilst peeling the potatoes, the notice was amended to "Don't call the — a cook." Then on another day while the boat was moored at a loch, Smith used the toilet and flushed it, forgetting that the skipper was standing by the effluent pipe adding a touch of paint. Such, anyway, are the stories his contemporaries tell about him.

But once his law studies began, he had to settle down. The sheer demands of the course might have put a less energetic youngster right off politics or any other tiring pastime. In his final year he was required to combine his university studies with an apprenticeship in a firm of Glasgow solicitors called Joseph Mellick. A typical day would involve early classes at 8.30 a.m. and 9.30 a.m., a bus journey to the office, where he would put in four and a half hours, then back to the university for classes at 4 p.m. and 5 p.m. He could not go on being scruffy either. Three-piece suits and stiff collars were required wear. Even Christine Houston was impressed. He stuck to it to insure himself against the possibility that he might never make a living out of politics. "I decided I wanted a legal qualification because I thought politics was a very risky business," he says.

He stayed on with Joseph Mellick for a year after he had qualified as a solicitor before moving to another firm, Donaldson and Alexander, in 1964. After two years, they offered him a partnership. He was conscious now that his life was at a crossroads. He wanted to return to politics, but he also wanted to marry, so he needed a secure profession. Accepting Donaldson and Alexander's offer would be the safest course. He would then be secure in the knowledge that while he was away pursuing his political interests, other partners would be back at base making sure the money came in; but it would deny him the chance to show off his gift for public speaking. On the other hand, if he was called to the Bar, he would have the fun of performing before an audience, and the freedom of self-employment, but with it would come the risk that there would be no work and no money. He weighed it up in his mind, but really it was no contest: he desperately wanted to go to the Bar.

Incidentally, there was a comical exchange in Parliament years later, when the Tory MP Ian Gow made a passing reference to Smith's legal training:

Gow He is a solicitor.
Smith No, I am not.
Gow A barrister?
Smith No, I am not.
Nicholas Fairbairn Perhaps I can help. The Minister of State is not a solicitor and he is not a barrister. He is an advocate, although few people realize it.[2]

There are no barristers practising in Scottish courts, and an advocate, like Smith, is not allowed to handle a case in an English or Welsh court. The world he entered is a small one. Scotland had fewer than a hundred advocates when he first qualified, less than half the number there are now. The profession had more than its share of politicians. Nicholas Fairbairn, Malcolm Rifkind, Lord Mackay of Clashfern and others became Tories. Ming Campbell became a Liberal. Much of Smith's court work has come through the Glasgow solicitors Ross Harper and Murphy, whose head, Ross Harper, is a former President of the Scottish Conservative Association. Unlike Neil Kinnock, Smith is well used to professional dealings with political opponents. His legal qualifications and the contacts they have given him make him – rightly or wrongly – less vulnerable to the destructive ridicule his predecessor had to endure.

His immediate problem was that tradition required him to go "devilling" before he could make the switch from solicitor to advocate. "You have to be out of the practice of the law, so I couldn't earn any money being a lawyer," he says. He was attached as a trainee to an advocate named Ian Kirkwood, now the Honourable Lord Kirkwood QC, a senator of the College of Justice in Scotland. His law degree enabled him to work as a part-time lecturer, teaching law for surveyors at the College of Building in Glasgow. He also took up a much more interesting sideline as a night lawyer for Scotland's biggest-selling newspaper, the *Daily Record*, and its sister paper, the *Sunday Mail*. This involved turning up to work at about 6 p.m. and checking copy for libel or contempt of court before it went into the newspaper. The papers were, of course, printed in the old-fashioned way, with blocks of soft metal laid out "on stone". Since money was tight, Smith did as many shifts as he could get, but was never once responsible for allowing something through which landed the newspaper in court. He carried on doing shifts for the *Sunday Mail* every Saturday night for two or three years after he began practising as an advocate, although by now he was a married man with a new home in

Edinburgh. A Saturday shift was worth eight guineas, compared with six guineas for a weekday. When it was done, he would join the journalists in the pub before taking the last train to Edinburgh. One of the journalists who knew him from those days, Endell Laird, rose to be editor-in-chief of both papers in 1988. He says, as others have, that the most striking thing about Smith is how little he has changed over the years.

Smith also supplemented his income – so he says – with an astute piece of gambling, using his specialist knowledge of politics. "It was a double bet. We discovered what I thought was an error by the bookmakers. They were giving evens in Conservative seats with a majority of under 5,000, but we thought there was no way Sir Fitzroy Maclean was ever going to lose Bute and North Ayrshire. So we put money on that. Then I didn't like the notion of betting on Conservatives winning, so we got 2:1 against John Mackintosh winning Berwick and East Lothian. And we put the two together and did very well."[3]

The temporary loss of a secure income was inconvenient – not least because of his marriage plans. It had been a long courtship. He had met Elizabeth Bennett, a student reading Russian and French, at a university dance in 1961, when he was twenty-three and she was twenty-one. Says Donald Dewar: "I remember John very well in those days, but I don't remember him ever going out with anybody else." Jimmy Gordon says the same: "In the sense of going out with anybody more than two weeks running, I don't think there was anybody but Elizabeth."

Inevitably, given the position her husband has taken over, Elizabeth Smith has to endure being compared and contrasted with Glenys Kinnock. This must be irritating for both women; but it is perhaps made a little easier by the fact that the contrast is so stark. There is no record that Elizabeth's father, Frederick Bennett, manager of the Glasgow office of the Eagle Star Insurance Company, or any other member of the Bennett family, was ever interested in politics. Elizabeth was born in Ayr, raised in Glasgow in reasonably comfortable middle-class surroundings, and educated at Hutchesons' Girls' Grammar School. Her father died at the age of fifty, when she was still at school. Her mother, born Elizabeth Shanks in 1906, also kept out of active politics, though she came from a political family. Her uncle, Robert Shanks, had been prominent as a Liberal town councillor in Glasgow before the 1914–18 War. As a pacifist and conscientious objector, he lost his council seat after 1914, but founded a Study Circle dedicated to "the discussion of the principles and problems of national and international life in the light of the teachings of Jesus". The Study Circle continued years after Robert Shanks's early death in 1921.

Elizabeth Smith's grandfather, William Shanks, who worked as an engineer for the Post Office, was a similar combination of devout Christian and political radical. As a youth he joined the League of Young Scots, who petitioned for a Scottish Parliament. He was in his early twenties when Queen Victoria died, and he took exception to her successor's designation as King Edward VII, since he was the first Edward to be crowned King of Scotland as well as England. When new pillar boxes were installed in Glasgow with the legend "ER VII", Shanks and other Young Scots went round in the night with chisels to remove the "VI". When the Scottish home rule movement collapsed, after the outbreak of war, Shanks became a Liberal like his younger brother. He joined the Scottish National Party soon after its launch in 1928. His son Robert Shanks, Elizabeth Smith's uncle, who was seventy-five in 1992, still has a vivid childhood memory of marching behind "King John" MacCormick from Stirling station to the field of Bannockburn. He is another political activist, a paid-up Liberal Democrat in Sir David Steel's Peebles constituency.

The first job Elizabeth took on leaving university showed that she had mental horizons which stretched a long way beyond Glasgow. For two years, while her future husband was establishing himself in a solicitor's office, she worked in London as administrative assistant with the Great Britain–USSR Association. This was the officially recognized conduit for informal contacts between London and Moscow, with no links whatsoever to the British Communist Party. It was not a place for people with illusions about the Soviet version of socialism. Sir Fitzroy Maclean, who had personally witnessed the Moscow show trials, was one of the people with whom the young Elizabeth came into regular contact. However, relations between Britain and the Soviet Union were going through a relatively good phase, before Khrushchev's removal, and in her early twenties, therefore, she became experienced in dealing with high-level official exchanges between London and Moscow, and met several groups of eminent Soviet visitors. After two years in London she returned to Scotland, obtained a teacher training diploma, and taught French for three years in schools in Glasgow and Edinburgh.

When the couple first decided to marry, there was the problem of how to pay for an engagement ring. As a solicitor, John Smith had been able to afford a Triumph Herald car, but he knew that it would be beyond his means during his year of "devilling". The pain of parting with it has lingered for a quarter of a century. "It was my pride and joy," he says. However, it paid for the ring. They were married in July 1967. Jimmy Gordon was best man. Smith's *Daily Record* contacts stood him in good stead: the paper carried a picture of him, with his bride, on page 16. Interestingly, they described him as a lawyer, without any reference to his political ambitions, although he had been a candidate in a highly publicized by-election. Four months later he qualified as an advocate; around the same time the couple moved from Glasgow to Edinburgh, where they have lived ever since. At first they shared a small flat in the Royal Mile, the old part of the city, near the law courts. They moved into their present home, in Edinburgh's Morningside district – the setting for Muriel Spark's novel *The Prime of Miss Jean Brodie* – in 1977.

By the time her husband entered politics, Elizabeth Smith was the mother of an eighteen-month-old baby. For the next decade and a half, she remained resolutely private. There is only one recorded occasion on which she was interviewed by a local newspaper reporter, to whom she confided: "I see my role as wholly supportive. I am not one of those women who wants to be independent." Friends say that Mrs Smith, who was well into her thirties before feminism began to impinge on British society, can be quite irritated to hear it suggested that keeping house and bringing up young children is not a valid way for a woman to spend her time.

The Smiths had three daughters, who burst into the public eye when their father was elected leader of the Labour Party. Until then, their parents had taken care to shield them from the sort of publicity which can be ruinous to family life. Smith was never the sort who would parade his small children before the TV cameras for the sake of a few votes. Sarah, born in 1969, Jane, born in 1971, and Catherine, born in 1973, were brought up and educated in Edinburgh, in preference to Westminster, like the children of any other private, Presbyterian middle-class Scottish family. To quote Donald Dewar again: "He has always, throughout his life, made time for the family – family gatherings, family holidays, family Sundays. And he is unusual among MPs because he is a regular churchgoer." This secure home background was almost invaded by tragedy very early on. As a newborn baby, Catherine, the youngest, was found to have cancer of the thigh bone. Her horrified parents were warned to brace themselves against the possibility that she might not survive. Mercifully, an operation was successful.

Elizabeth gave up teaching in 1968, when her first child was on the way, and resumed her former interest in Soviet politics fourteen years later, when she became Scottish Secretary of the Great Britain–USSR Association. This was the year when Brezhnev died, and Moscow politics came back to life. She had missed the entire stultifying Brezhnev era. She kept up the secretaryship for six years – until 1988 – then stayed on as vice-chairman. Once again she was kept busy organizing trips to and from Moscow, and receiving Soviet luminaries in Scotland. They included Gennadi Yanayev, who later achieved notoriety as the Soviet Union's last vice-president and a leader of the August 1991 Kremlin coup. Just before the coup, Elizabeth Smith organized an extraordinary three-day event in which the cream of Scotland's business community travelled to the USSR to celebrate Burns Night in the Kremlin. In a massive hall, where tsars and commissars had been entertained, the gathering listened to the actor Tom Fleming reciting "The Immortal Memory". On another evening in another building, which smelt of urine, Lord McFadzean of Kelvinside, a former director of Shell and one of Scotland's foremost businessmen, was to be seen with tears in his eyes as he listened to Elizabeth Buchanan singing Burns songs. "If the plane which took them to Moscow had gone down, Scottish industry would have taken a severe setback," claims Helen Liddell, who was on the trip as a director of the *Daily Record*. "The *crème de la crème* were there. And Elizabeth organized it all in a voluntary capacity. She'll always have a special place in the minds of everyone who went on that extraordinary trip." Incidentally, one entrepreneur who should have been there but cancelled at the last moment was Liddell's employer, Robert Maxwell.

Like any other young advocate, John Smith had to spend several years acting as junior counsel in court cases where the defendant's costs were being paid through legal aid. His best-known case from these early days was not the sort that a lawyer likes to remember: his client was wrongly convicted of murder and, as a result, spent seven years in prison for a crime he did not commit. He was Paddy Meehan, a well-known Glaswegian villain whose earlier exploits had included escaping from Nottingham prison, only to turn up in East Germany. Meehan was accused of a brutal robbery, in which two men had broken into the home of an elderly bingo hall owner named Abraham Ross, in Ayr. Mr Ross and his wife were dragged from their bed, manhandled, tied up and left helpless, while the raiders made off with £2,000. As a result, Rachel Ross, who was seventy-two, died. Meehan's problem was that he had been out stealing on the night of the burglary, so that when he was arrested, he was at first more interested in covering his own traces than in helping the police with their inquiries. To make matters worse, his accomplice chose to shoot it out when the police caught up with him. Since he was dead, with a bullet in him, his criminal record was admitted as evidence at Meehan's trial. After Meehan had been convicted and sentenced to life imprisonment – which he insisted on serving in solitary confinement – his senior counsel, the Tory MP Nicholas Fairbairn, aided by the broadcaster Ludovic Kennedy and many others, ran a long public campaign to have his conviction overturned, even raising the case in the House of Commons. He was finally pardoned in 1976.

Smith has been accused of doing less than he might have done to help. Fairbairn was quoted as saying: "He preferred not to get involved in the Paddy Meehan case because it was extremely controversial. He chose to stand well back and keep clean."[4] It would not be true to say that he abandoned Meehan altogether. In the early 1970s he wrote privately to the Secretary of State for Scotland, warning that there had been a serious miscarriage of justice. However, to get publicly involved in a single-issue campaign, away from the mainstream of politics, was not John Smith's style. Meehan did not appeal to him very much. Smith remembers him as a "strange character" and "not a perfect client". (Jimmy Boyle, a fellow prisoner in Peterhead, says that Meehan was not very popular there either, although the underworld was unanimously convinced of his innocence.) Perhaps Smith was too protective of his political reputation to want to link it in any way with a hardened criminal.

His political career, though, was something else which had to go temporarily into abeyance because of his ambition to be an advocate. The surprising thing about the young John Smith is not that he reached the House of Commons at the age of thirty-one, but that it took him so long. In 1966 for the first and only time since he became old enough to vote, he allowed a general election to go by without contesting it. Once he had qualified, however, he was back in the market for a Commons seat. He was shortlisted for Hamilton in 1967, when the sitting Labour MP resigned, but failed to get the nomination. He was lucky. The Hamilton by-election turned into a seismic political event, whose effects were still being felt when Smith was a senior minister a decade later. The tiny Scottish National Party picked a young Glasgow solicitor, Winnie Ewing, as their candidate, and ran an inspired campaign which won them a seat in the Commons for the first time in their history. Smith does not like to admit how lucky he was not to have been Labour's fall guy. "Maybe I would have won it," he claims. That is a possibility, or he might, of course, have been allowed a second try at the seat in 1970, in which case he, rather than George Robertson, would now be MP for Hamilton. On the other hand, he might have had a disastrous start to a parliamentary career by being trounced in a traditionally safe Labour seat.

Soon afterwards he was shortlisted again – this time for East Stirlingshire and Clackmannan. He arrived at the selection conference with a reputation as the preferred choice of the Scottish Labour Party establishment generally, and Willy Marshall in particular. None the less, the local Party selected Dick Douglas, a former Clyde shipyard worker with more experience than Smith, since he had fought two general elections as well as a recent by-election. Once again, Smith was lucky: in February 1974 the seat was taken by George Reid of the SNP. If he had beaten Douglas at the selection conference, he might never have been a government minister.

The next approach was the one which mattered. When John Smith was being paid to go canvassing in his student days, he had made several forays into North Lanarkshire, where he had been spotted by the local party agent, Dick Stewart. An ex-miner, forced to leave the industry after a serious injury underground, Stewart later became a substantial figure in Scottish politics as leader of Strathclyde Regional Council for the first twelve years of its existence. In October 1992, John Smith began the first ever "Richard Stewart Memorial Lecture", at Strathclyde University, with a tribute to his former mentor's "sharp analytical brain and rock-like integrity". He said: "Dick was the most remarkable man I have ever known. He was my agent in six general elections, and I think that everything I know about electoral politics I learned from Dick."

The first important piece of political intelligence he learnt from Dick Stewart was that North Lanarkshire's MP planned to retire at the next general election. Peggy Herbison had long been a reliable pillar of the right on Labour's national executive, and was Minister for Pensions in Harold Wilson's first government. After she had left the Commons, she went straight on to become the first woman Lord High Commissioner to the General Assembly of the Church of Scotland. At the time of writing, she is a vigorous eighty-five-year-old. According to Roy Hattersley, who was her Parliamentary Private Secretary from 1964 to 1967, "she was an austere, non-drinking, non-swearing, non-plotting Scottish lady. We got on, even though that is not exactly my line of business. And I remember after I had been her PPS, she introduced me in the House of Commons to John Smith, whom she described as a Scottish advocate, and that was my first sighting of him. I can't remember anything more about him, except her saying he was going to be her successor."[5] This high opinion of her was not shared by everyone: Richard Crossman thought she was a "silly woman" and a "weakling".[6] Be that as it may, she had set a tradition that North Lanarkshire should be represented by someone austere, religious and right-wing. Having held the seat since 1945, she was in a strong position to influence the choice of her successor, and trusted the advice she got from Dick Stewart, who highly commended the young advocate from Glasgow University. Even with the backing of the outgoing MP, Smith had to talk his way through an uncomfortably close selection contest. His main rival was Tom Clarke, who was better known locally, having been brought up just outside the constituency, in Coatbridge. Clarke, in fact, led on the first two ballots, and was expecting to win. He was beaten on the third by nine votes – a statistic both men can still quote from memory almost twenty-five years on.

North Lanarkshire was a rural mining seat which curled around the northern edge of Glasgow and the neighbouring towns of Coatbridge and Airdrie, taking in most of the countryside west of Edinburgh, with a tradition of deference as deep-rooted as Argyll's – with the difference that it was directed towards a Labour establishment. Jenny Lee had first taken the seat for Labour at a by-election in 1929, though she lost it two years later. By 1970 every seat in rural Lanarkshire, and seven out of nine Glasgow seats, had Labour MPs. When Dick Marshall visited the area, as a party official all the way from Glasgow, local party members called him "sir". Smith would soon have become accustomed to being treated with great respect by his prospective constituents. Helen Liddell, who also came from Coatbridge and went on to be General Secretary of the Scottish Labour Party for twelve years, says: "Peggy Herbison was regarded almost as a saint, and John was pretty much her protégé, which was greatly to his benefit. In the Labour mining villages, to have an advocate arrive was like a Martian arriving. They would not have known what an advocate was. They would have known him as a lawyer, and a lawyer was something quite special. They would be very deferential to that kind of person, and the fact that he could speak their language would be a marvellous thing."

One of the immediate benefits John Smith could bring his constituency Party was trade-union sponsorship. With the whole Party–unions relationship up for review, it may be that union sponsorship will begin to wither away under Smith's leadership, but for decades it has been seen as a highly desirable way of attracting cash into impecunious constituency party organizations. The trade union will pay an annual sum towards maintaining an office in the constituency, or towards general election expenses, in return for very little. The money certainly does not guarantee that the MP will vote in line with union policy, and there is no such direct obligation. On the other hand, unions do not sponsor MPs unless they judge them to be politically reliable. In the light of Smith's past connections, the logical place for him to go for sponsorship was to the GMWU. Within that organization, however, Alex Donnet was thought to have quite enough influence already, and he was not allowed to add another Scots MP to its list. Smith was then spotted by another powerful union boss from Clydeside: John Chalmers, who had risen to be General Secretary of the Boilermakers' Union, based in Newcastle upon Tyne. The Boilermakers were an elite craft union, notorious within the union movement for the jealous way they protected their pay differentials. In Parliament they liked to sponsor very able, ambitious MPs like John Smith and Gerald Kaufman – clever men who knew a lot about many things, but not much about making boilers. Later, the Boilermakers amalgamated with the GMWU to become GMBATU – now the GMB; so the union which had originally declined to sponsor Smith inherited him anyway.

It was not long before the lawyer was a Member of Parliament. Harold Wilson called a general election in June 1970, when opinion polls told him he would win. The country unexpectedly chose Edward Heath. Even in North Lanarkshire the Labour vote dropped a little; but nothing like enough to give John Smith a bad night. With a majority of more than 5,000 and nearly 52 per cent of the vote, he was safe.

4
The Backbench MP 1970–74

The MP for North Lanarkshire arrived to find a Parliamentary Labour Party numbed by defeat. Harold Wilson even summoned the Cabinet to Downing Street on the afternoon after the poll, as if he was refusing to accept what had happened. "They were stunned because they thought they were going to win," Smith recalls. "It was the election where everybody said that Labour was going to cruise it, that Harold Wilson was brilliant, and all that. But there is a curious thing: if you've just been elected for the first time yourself, your view is different."[1] Anyway, those were more optimistic days for Labour, when politics was more like a revolving door, and if one election was a defeat, everyone could assume the next would end in victory. Later, Smith would have to get used to returning from the campaign trail to the dreary disappointment of four or five years out of office, without much realistic hope of victory next time.

It was a much younger Parliamentary Labour Party which reassembled after the 1970 election. No fewer than fifty sitting Labour MPs had chosen to retire: more than at any other election in the Party's history. Another sixty-one had lost their seats, including famous Members like George Brown, Dingle Foot, Robert Maxwell and Woodrow Wyatt. The generation of Labour MPs who had entered Parliament in the landslide of 1945 had, with some notable exceptions, dispersed. A generation which had been too young even to vote in 1945 was pushing its way up.

John Smith was accustomed to the smaller world of Scottish Labour politics, where he could move confidently around as an established and promising figure. Now he was thrown into a wholly strange milieu, as one of fifty-four MPs – more than twenty of whom were under thirty-five – all trying to make a mark. Of the new intake, Gerald Kaufman was the one who understood the most about how Westminster worked; but he was too wise to assume that having worked in 10 Downing Street at Harold Wilson's side would give him automatic access to the front bench now. Denzil Davies, from Wales, was soon recognized as outstandingly bright. Dennis Skinner was the first to establish himself as a left-wing rebel, playing a role which has not altered in twenty-two years. Neil Kinnock and Gavin Strang, the youngest of the new Labour MPs, Stanley Clinton Davis, who lost his seat in 1983, and Eric Deakins, defeated in 1987, became "blue-eyed boys", whom Wilson sent off together in 1973 on a courtesy trip to the USSR.

As for John Smith, the first time he was really noticed down south was when he was mistaken for someone else. Some of the mail delivered to him turned out to be intended for a former Tory MP named John Smith of the famous family of newsagents, who had stood down at the 1970 election after representing Westminster and the City of London. When the 1922 Committee – the conduit through which Tory Prime Ministers and ministers are kept in touch with backbench opinion – was due to celebrate its fiftieth anniversary at the Carlton Club, an invitation was mistakenly sent to John Smith MP, and his wife. He seized his chance. Journalists were told at once, and the unwelcome guest announced that he was accepting his invitation. He did not go, in fact, but an embarrassed chairman of the 1922 Committee offered him a free drink at the Carlton any day but the day of their anniversary – and for the first time the new MP from Lanarkshire was mentioned in the national newspapers printed in England. He had been in Parliament for three years. Otherwise, he was so quiet that Neil Kinnock, for one, scarcely noticed his existence. "I knew he was there," he says. "We probably made ourselves known to each other, shook hands, because there is a certain camaraderie among newcomers, especially since there was quite a generation shift in 1970." Their relations were "a sort of fraternal acquaintance rather than friendship" – but then, in Parliament, "Some people hit their stride immediately, are precocious, and never look back. Other people run like a thunderclap and disappear like a shower of rain. The first few years are absolutely no guide as to how someone is going to fare after that."[2]

The large number of new MPs, both Labour and Tory, meant a crush of hopefuls wanting to make their maiden speeches. This is a useful hurdle to cross: an MP who has not made a "maiden" is expected not to ask questions or interrupt others' speeches in the chamber. Kinnock, Kaufman, Skinner, John Cunningham, Michael Meacher, John Prescott and many others managed to fight their way past all the difficulties and have their opening speeches over and done with in the fortnight between the election and Parliament's summer recess. Smith let it wait until the autumn. One thing he could do in the meantime was submit written questions to ministers. His first, dated 13 July, is somewhat shocking to read in these post-feminist days. Noting that a new factory was about to be opened in his constituency as a result of regional aid dispersed by the outgoing Labour government, Smith pleaded with the new Minister for Technology that the firm granted occupancy of the site would be "one which predominantly employs male labour". The Minister, one Nicholas Ridley, reassured him that the government understood the importance of jobs for men. At the time, this question showed that Smith's mind was on the basic bread-and-butter issues which directly affected his own constituents. Unemployment was the biggest social blight in North Lanarkshire, and in those days it was normal to measure the seriousness of the problem by the number of men who were out of work. For a woman to be the breadwinner in a working-class family generally meant hardship and conflict in the home; women were less well paid than men, and cultural taboos made it impossible for an unemployed man to take over domestic chores from his working wife.

The debating chamber heard John Smith's Scottish lilt for the first time on 10 November 1970. New members are advised to be worthy rather than witty in their maiden speech, to praise the achievement of their predecessor, make no jokes, and keep their remarks parochial and uncontroversial. Smith followed most of the ground rules; but, having chosen to take part in a debate on family income, he chided the Conservatives for the meanness of state assistance for the low-paid, and for their wilful ignorance of where there was real hardship in the community. He accused them of being committed to redistributing wealth upwards, through cuts in income tax, but opposed to redistribution downwards. It was a workmanlike performance, without a word in it which John Smith might now wish to withdraw.

Having made his maiden speech, he could return to the green benches the next day to oppose a government Bill which would allow local education authorities in Scotland to send the bright children of poor families to public schools, with their fees paid from the rates. The headmaster's son was there to attack the very idea of fee-paying schools as a "class symbol". It was a theme to which he returned every time the Commons concerned itself with Scotland's education system. The ambitions of middle-class parents ready to pay huge school fees to ensure that their children were given an educational advantage, and taught manners and a way of speaking which would mark them out as the products of comfortable families, left John Smith cold. "The reason people send their children to fee-paying schools", he told the Commons when the Scottish Education Bill came back for a third reading, "is that they think it will cut them off from other children and feel their children will receive a better education if they are fenced round with fees. I do not know what justification there is for it. Of course we should have freedom of choice. Parents should be free to decide where they send their children. But we do not need fees for that."[3] Some months later, he was to be heard objecting that the social stratification which grant-aided schools had introduced to the education system in Edinburgh created, "great dismay throughout the city. . . . One doesn't object to the schools themselves, but to the fact that a fee has to be paid for entry to them."[4]

His second performance was more relaxed than his first, and included a happy little dig at Teddy Taylor, who had been his fellow student at Glasgow University and was now a very young Undersecretary for Scotland, whose Glaswegian brogue helped to disguise how upper-class the Scottish Tories were. "He is a gillie among the lairds." Smith claimed. "He is the one whom they can use as a popular exhibit whenever they are accused of popular prejudice."

John Smith's speaking style was quiet, insistent, clever, and full of hard information. He never attempted flights of rhetoric: Neil Kinnock and Dennis Skinner were infinitely more skilled as crowd-pleasers and rabble-rousers, at home in a hall packed with excited supporters. They consciously chose the party route to prominence, making themselves known around constituency Labour parties and at fringe meetings at annual party conferences, making themselves out as left-wing rebels with no intention of being bought off by the offer of a job in government. It won them quick recognition. In 1978 they were both elected to Labour's national executive, something John Smith would never achieve. He took the slow, grey route as an unobtrusively conscientious backbench MP. He never attempted to discover how to whip up passions among the faithful. He never denounced the Tories; his technique was to demolish his opponent with a mixture of solid fact and clever ridicule. He would exhort his adversary to think again and change his ways, but he would never appear to want him out of public life. He could be ruthless in pointing out that others were being stupid, but he would never accuse them of being bad. It was a style which worked in the Commons, earning him the respect of his fellow professionals without making him famous.

And the issues in which he chose to involve himself matched his style: solid, worthy and important in North Lanarkshire. Jobs came first. "One thing which has impressed me most during the short time in which I have been an MP is meeting a number of people who had been made redundant in a small village in my constituency," he said during the annual debate on the Queen's Speech. "The experience of meeting these people face to face, seeing the anxiety in their eyes and understanding the genuine fears they felt for the future made me realize how direct the effects of unemployment are upon the lives and aspirations of ordinary people."[5] Time and again, he was on his feet protesting that the regional employment premium introduced by the Labour government, which was worth £40 million to Scotland, must be saved.

Education was another specialist subject. Hector Munro, the Scottish Education Minister, complained one day of being awoken at 7.30 a.m. to hear BBC radio broadcasting an allegation that teacher shortages on Smith's patch had reached a point where a headmaster was having to teach an entire primary school of a hundred pupils all on his own. A cross Mr Munro claimed that this was not true: there were actually two teachers at the school in question, with a third about to join them. Perhaps, for once, Mr Smith had exaggerated. However, he was able to get the Commons arguing for an hour and five minutes over whether the educational needs of Lanarkshire schoolchildren were being satisfied.[6]

For several hours a week in the latter part of 1970 he was shut away in a committee room, where a Bill to loosen Scotland's rigid divorce laws was being examined line by line. It proposed that couples who had been living apart for five years should be permitted a divorce without the gruelling obligation to prove infidelity, cruelty or any other misdemeanour. Unsurprisingly, John Smith was in favour of what he saw as a humane and pragmatic piece of social reform which, he anticipated, would reduce the number of Scottish children born to parents unable to marry because one or both was legally tied to a relationship which had long been over. "It is absurd that people should continue to be regarded by the law as married when, in reality, the marriage has long been dead and buried," he claimed. "When people find that the law is not responding to social needs and social change, it brings the law into disrepute." There were those, however, who saw this as another case of the permissive sixties sneaking into the Statute Book to corrode the foundation of family life. "Bigots" is what Smith might have called them but, as usual, he did not: however, he made them check their facts. Here he is, reacting off the cuff, without notes, to something said on the floor of the House of Commons by a Tory MP:

> "I think the honourable Gentleman misunderstands the purpose of having Clause 2 (1) (c) and (d) in the same bill. Clause 3(3) provides that where a pursuer takes an action under Clause 2 (1) (d), that action can be defeated by the defender appearing in the process, so that that can be an end of it. That is why there is this difference between paragraphs (c) and (d). They are not a repetition of the same thing. There is a substantial difference here which the honourable Gentleman does not understand."

It is not easy to argue with a lawyer who can retrieve that sort of detail from his memory, at will. The Tory on the receiving end of this wisdom, Robin Maxwell-Hyslop, could only reply: "That may well be so. . . . " Before he had finished his speech, he had to endure yet another of Mr Smith's constructive interruptions – this time to inform him that he was being "unnecessarily concerned" about provisions in Clause 10 (1) (c), which, he might like to know, were no different from what was already enshrined in law, as Section 26 (1) (b) of the Succession (Scotland) Act 1964. This time Mr Maxwell-Hyslop managed to come back with a retort that it was typical of a lawyer to think that having something foolish appear in one statute was a good enough reason to include it in another.[7]

At last a breakthrough: two years into his parliamentary career, the backbencher's dedicated attention to arduous, detailed committee work enabled him to alter the law of the land north of the border. Not a lot of people know it, but Amendment 11 to page 8, line 17 of the 1972 NHS (Scotland) Bill, which required local health councils to submit annual reports on their activities to their Health Boards, and required Health Boards to transmit a copy of any such report to the Secretary of State, was all John Smith's work. He proposed it while the Bill was being examined in committee, as the minister in charge, Hector Monro, graciously acknowledged when it went back to the Commons for approval.[8]

All this hard work brought him respect within the House of Commons, and next to no recognition outside. "Solid, worthwhile, but apparently going nowhere," was the verdict of the newspaper most likely to be on his side, the *Daily Record*.[9] Another, more flattering profile of him, in December 1971, called him an "impressive committee man" and forecast that he could rise to be Scotland's chief law officer, the Lord Advocate, or even Secretary of State for Scotland. But the writer felt compelled to qualify this bold prediction with a warning that "these high promises can, of course, go terribly awry".

To be noticed, a new MP needs an issue which is interesting enough to make the news, without being so obviously important that everyone else has an opinion on it. John Smith found his in autumn 1972, when the government proposed to make members of the public pay to visit state-owned museums and art galleries. It offended the popular educator in him – he believed, as his father had, that knowledge must be available to the masses, whether they can afford to pay for it or not. There was a Scottish angle to it, too. The legislation was being drawn up by people who behaved as if they thought the world ended at Watford, and felt that the whole United Kingdom needed legislation to cope with the crush of tourists in central London. "It is one thing to impose charges at the Tate Gallery and the National Gallery in London, where there are more than a million visitors a year, but quite another to impose them on the smaller galleries in Edinburgh," Smith told the Commons. Finally, there were legal questions involved. The National Gallery of Scotland had two valuable collections of paintings left by wealthy benefactors, on condition that they were exhibited to the public free of charge. The government was having to grant itself the power to alter the trust deeds, which to John Smith was "nothing less than legal vandalism".[10] In November 1972, during Prime Minister's Questions, he demanded that the Paymaster General, Viscount Eccles, should be sacked for "going round to the public-spirited men who serve as trustees of our galleries in an attempt to blackmail and frighten them" into imposing admission charges. Edward Heath rebuked him for his "extravagant language".[11]

The issue dragged on. A year later it was the Secretary of State for Education, Margaret Thatcher, who was having to fend off another parliamentary assault from John Smith – about the Turner Collection in the National Gallery of Scotland. His attacks were all the more effective for the fact that he had his backers on the Tory side. In particular, one of the new Tory MPs, Jeffrey Archer, thought it a good cause to take up. The combination of a future Labour leader and a future millionaire fiction writer was more than the government could bear, especially when an election was not far away. At the end of 1973, when Norman St John Stevas was appointed a junior education minister, his first move was to give way, by promising unconditionally that all the receipts from admission charges would be kept by the museums, not the Treasury; that the museums' managements would have the right to have "free days", at their own discretion; and that there would be no admission charges for old age pensioners. This campaign was not forgotten. Five years later, when John Smith was elevated to the job of Trade Secretary, the *Sunday Telegraph* grumpily acknowledged that the Labour government had "doubled the number of Cabinet ministers who really care about the arts".[12] (The other art lover, in their estimation, was Harold Lever.) There is no doubt whence Smith derived his interest in art in general, and Scottish art galleries in particular: from Elizabeth Smith, although she was not yet an eminent figure in Edinburgh's art world.

Amid this welter of mundanities, there was suddenly an issue on which it was impossible to avoid taking sides and making enemies.

Edward Heath had succeeded where all previous Prime Ministers for over a decade had failed, and struck a deal to take Britain into the Common Market. Now he had to persuade the House of Commons to accept it. His own party was profoundly split on the issue, with Enoch Powell heading the opposition. John Smith's old acquaintance Teddy Taylor resigned his job as a Scottish minister to begin what would be a lifetime on the back benches, obsessively harrying his own party on the issue. The Tories' internal problems were so intractable that when the crucial vote came, on 28 October 1971, the government whips were called off, allowing Conservative MPs a free vote. The number of right-wing

Tories, led by Enoch Powell, who joined the Labour Party in the No lobby was easily large enough to have defeated the government, had Labour been united.

Heath was saved, and Britain's entry into the Common Market was secured, by sixty-nine Labour MPs led by the Party's deputy leader, Roy Jenkins, who defied their own three-line whip to support the government. John Smith was one of the sixty-nine. It was the only time in twenty-two years that he deliberately disobeyed the party line. Rebellion was not in his nature. In the years to come, he would serve loyally under leaders for whom he had little respect, and keep his own counsel on party policies with which he sharply disagreed. On this one occasion, though, he refused to let loyalty be his guide. The politician who had never done anything more risky than demand that the public be allowed into museums free of charge was willing to stake his career on this one. It was a risk, but in the long run it undoubtedly paid off.

Late the previous summer, the Commons had set aside an entire day to debate the issue, giving John Smith a chance to set out his position. The case he put forward was the polar opposite of what Tony Benn and other left-wing anti-marketeers have proclaimed for twenty years. To them, the EC is an institution created to preserve the privileges of private capital and curb the powers of elected left-wing governments. John Smith believed it could rescue Britain from economic decline, and be a force for social progress. In his view Europe was the gateway to new technology, which British industry desperately needed, and on which it would depend whether Britain was in the Common Market or out. Without it, the gap between the run-down industrial regions and the prosperous South would widen. He also took a singularly optimistic view of the future role of Brussels bureaucrats as defenders of economically depressed regions like west Scotland, policing the multinationals. "I cannot see how it will be possible for us to control the international companies that will increasingly dominate the economic scene if we are all working within a nation-state framework," he argued:

> "At bottom, this is a question of sovereignty, and many honourable members are reluctant to give up some of the sovereignty which is held dear in this country. . . . A sovereignty which is not real is not worth having. . . . I am willing to give up some national sovereignty to gain a sovereignty which will be able to do something about controlling the international companies of the future. . . . The Commission, derided so much, can be the instrument to stand up to and control the international companies. As a democratic socialist, I believe that the fundamental of democratic socialism is that economic forces must somehow be brought under popular control and be fashioned towards

> social and political ends which the people determine. If we do not enter Europe we shall not be in a position to control and achieve those economic, social and political ends. . . ."[13]

There was not a word here which could embarrass the future Labour Party leader, but then what was notable about the speech was not what Smith said, but the political background against which he said it.

All through 1971, there had been a steady drift of opinion among Labour MPs towards opposition to the EEC. Initially, all the Shadow Cabinet, even including Tony Benn, supported entry, with varying degrees of enthusiasm. Harold Wilson certainly believed in British membership: when he was in Downing Street he had tried to negotiate Britain's way in, but had run up against an immovable obstacle in General de Gaulle. Subsequently, when he was Prime Minister once again, he led the campaign to keep Britain in. Opposition to the Market, therefore, spread upwards from party activists, who were just beginning to display the disrespect for their leadership which would traumatize the Party ten years later, on to the back benches of the Commons, and into the leadership – fired all the time by the fact that Britain's quarter-century of economic growth and low employment was ending, and any opportunity to weaken an unpopular Tory government was not to be missed. In January 1971, 132 Labour MPs declared themselves anti-marketeers by signing a motion which was printed on the Commons order paper. That implied that there was already an anti-EEC majority on the back benches. As the summer approached, first Jim Callaghan, then Denis Healey, then Harold Wilson reminded themselves of Britain's historic obligations to New Zealand farmers, the owners of West Indian plantations, and others who would find new trade barriers between them and the British shopper. A three-line whip ordered all Labour MPs into the No lobby to oppose British entry. Wilson, Callaghan and Healey led the way. Naturally, most of the new MPs, including Neil Kinnock, Gerald Kaufman and John Cunningham, followed.

What was left was a group of Croslandite social democratic intellectuals and an assortment of stubborn right-of-centre individuals, whose political friendship, for the most part, would be of no long-term use to John Smith. More than a third of them later broke away to become the high command of the Social Democratic Party. Only five were still in Parliament as Labour MPs when Smith assumed the party leadership twenty-one years later, and three of those – Tam Dalyell, Andrew Faulds and Bob Sheldon – were veteran backbenchers with no real standing in the Party. Smith's hero at that time was Tony Crosland, who was then looked upon as a future party leader. When Crosland ran for membership of the

National Executive, Smith did his bit by inviting him to North Lanarkshire to secure his constituency Party's vote. "I felt, I think, much closer to him than to anyone else, but the younger MPs tended to do that. Tony was seen as the dashing figure. He had got a bit of style." But to the intense disappointment of some of his admirers, Crosland refused to join the pro-Common Market rebellion. The one rebel besides Smith who was a substantial figure in the Labour Party throughout the 1980s was Roy Hattersley, who recalls:

> "I think it was, in an unpleasant way – and it is unpleasant sometimes – democracy in action. We had a series of parliamentary party meetings in which it was more polarized than I have ever known it be. I mean, I have never known party meetings in which major figures debated with each other, and were booed and hissed and applauded. I can remember an old man called Lawson[14] actually taking his shoes off and beating on the desk like Khrushchev in support of Jenkins. I can remember Tam Dalyell trying to shout Willie Ross down over some strange issue like the processing of shale; those two would have an argument like that. I think Wilson and Callaghan were a bit frightened by the strength of feeling in the Party, and that is what made them vote against."[15]

This was not the kind of atmosphere which suited John Smith's temperament. Right-wing rebels held fervent meetings in the deputy leader's office, deciding who was on their side and who was wavering. Hattersley was sent off on a vain mission to win Crosland round. Bill Rodgers, later of the SDP, was assigned to Denis Healey. A delegation even had to be sent to woo David Owen, who was considering abstaining. "The prime mover was Jenkins. Roy liked the idea that he was making a bid for the leadership. It gave Roy a certain cachet, a sort of daring quality: he was the crimson pirate," says Hattersley. But Smith was unmoved: "I wasn't a great admirer of Roy Jenkins, I just saw him as one of them, one of the leadership." He was content to say his piece in Parliament, vote on the night, and be quiet.

It took a steady nerve to stay with the minority. Feelings in constituency parties were running high. Smith could be grateful now that he had failed to be selected for East Stirlingshire, because Dick Douglas came close to being deselected by his local Party for being one of the rebels. He would later say that this public row with his local Party contributed to his defeat by the SNP in 1974. In the case of one of the rebel MPs, Dick Taverne, relations with his local Party in Lincoln broke down altogether, and he resigned and fought a by-election, returning briefly to the Commons as an independent. He was beaten in a subsequent general election by one of the new breed of tough left-wing activists, a researcher from party head office named Margaret Jackson – now better known under her married name, Beckett. Yet Smith never wavered:

> "I thought about it quite a lot, because I'm an instinctive party man. I considered abstaining, but I thought that really wasn't right on a matter like this. What really swung me was that it was the biggest issue, I thought, that would come up during the time that I was likely to be in Parliament, and I felt strongly about it and I really had to do it. But I was not happy about being on the wrong side of the camp, as it were, against the majority of the Labour Party; but I thought their policy was wrong, so I swallowed hard and did it."[16]

The Labour Party's official policy had already switched once: from being pro-Market to being anti-. When Labour was back in government, it would be pro-Europe again. In opposition, the Party would first commit itself to pulling Britain out, and then become more European than the Tories. As Smith became party leader, Europe once again became the biggest political question of the day, with anti-EC sentiment in the Party on the rise. At a time like that, there was something to be said for a leader who made up his mind when first confronted with the issue, and stuck to it no matter what went on around him.

5
The Oil Minister 1974–76

To this day, John Smith believes that rebellion over Europe held up his career by keeping him off the opposition front bench. If so, the punishment did not last long. By the beginning of 1974 Edward Heath's prices and incomes policy had come unravelled, provoking the second miners' strike in two years. Coming from a constituency studded with pit villages, Smith was able to warn the government, from direct personal observation, that the overtime ban was solid, and government claims that it was being masterminded by the Communist Party would get them nowhere. "Among the membership of the NUM will be found all sorts of political opinion, including Conservatives as well as Communists, and all are behind the miners' claim and solidly support the overtime ban. That does not seem to have got through to Tory members, who believe that the miners are stupid sheep led by a few rabid militants," he said, adding: "People such as property speculators should not be allowed to flourish in a society where men such as coal miners, working in extreme dirt, danger and difficulty, are required to make a sacrifice."[1]

A few weeks later Labour was back in government, and the newly returned MPs were waiting anxiously for the call from Downing Street which would tell them whether they had a ministerial job or not. When the call came for John Smith, it was disappointing. He was being offered the post of Solicitor General for Scotland. In his own opinion he was too well qualified for it, being both a Scot and a lawyer, and he saw a future opening up for him in which he would become Parliament's foremost specialist in Scottish law, but nothing more. For the second time he risked angering Harold Wilson, and wrecking his future, by turning it down. "It would have parked me into a legal byway, so I said no thanks. I thought: That's torn it, that's me fixed."[2] He was at once proved right on one point: there was no need for the post to go to a mainstream politician. For the rest of the time Labour was in power it was occupied by a Scottish QC named John McCluskey, who was not an MP, but was made a life peer. Besides, Smith was not entirely left out in the cold. Willie Ross, a stern Presbyterian conservative and a feared political operator who had run

Scotland as his personal fief in 1966–70, had been reappointed Scottish Secretary of State, and picked Smith to be his Parliamentary Private Secretary (PPS). There was no pay to go with the title, but it gave him a status and a foothold in government. On the other hand, it left him as free as any backbencher to choose the subjects on which to speak, including nuclear disarmament.

In summer 1974, the small but growing unilateralist wing of the Labour Party had been roused by a press leak that Britain had secretly tested one of its new Polaris missiles. Typically, John Smith tried not to take a hard line in what promised to be an emotive argument, but to locate himself midway between the Labour left and the Tory right, saying: "There are hawks who think that no cuts should be made and doves who want to make cuts for the sake of cuts. I do not know what species of bird is halfway between a hawk and a dove, but I fancy the posture of that bird." As a "dove", he wanted defence spending tailored to what the economy could afford. As a "hawk", he defended the highly controversial decision to resume testing Polaris. "There is not much point having them if we do not test them, develop them, and keep them in a credible state of readiness."

In passing he delivered a rebuke to one of the "doves", who had just been "advancing the argument of unilateral disarmament". Who should this be but the young red-haired MP for Edinburgh Central, Robin Cook – who would manage John Smith's leadership campaign eighteen years later. Cook had joined CND in his teens, and it was to fight that cause that he first joined the Labour Party. He accused the government of "MIRV-ing" Polaris – that is to say, of giving them a pinpoint accuracy which would allow them to be used to destroy enemy missile sites. This technological improvement would have meant that Polaris ceased to be simply a deterrent, aimed at Soviet cities to prevent a Red Army invasion, and became an offensive weapon, capable of being used to facilitate a NATO invasion. Smith was unimpressed. "I do not believe that nuclear disarmament by Britain would enhance our security or lead others to follow suit," he asserted – an interesting comment, given that for nearly a decade he would himself be part of a Shadow Cabinet which accepted collective responsibility for a policy of unilateral nuclear disarmament. "There is no evidence that nuclear disarmament by this county would affect the policies of other countries."[3]

On defence, as on Europe, Smith was consistent all his life, whether what he believed was party policy or not. Later, during the years when Labour was committed to unilateral nuclear disarmament, more than one Tory MP would attempt to draw him out on the subject, only to encounter his talent for finding a middle way between evading the question on the one hand, and answering it on the other. He said his piece once, and that was it. He never made another speech in the Commons on defence policy during his first twenty-two years as an MP.

In October 1974 the Labour government was returned with a majority just large enough to see it through five years in office, and John Smith had his second summons to Downing Street. To his surprise, he was congratulated by Harold Wilson for rejecting the previous job offer – "though I still don't know if he was having me on"[4] – and this time he emerged with a job he could take seriously: Junior Minister for Energy, with a salary of £5,500 a year, £1,000 more than he was paid as an MP. It might have given him a moment's pause that he was succeeding a younger man, his contemporary Gavin Strang, who had become a minister at the age of only thirty, and was already moving on to his second assignment – but probably not; unlike so many other politicians, John Smith was too emotionally secure to waste his mental energy worrying that someone else was getting ahead faster than him – and it would, indeed, have been a waste of mental energy being envious of Strang, whose career had already peaked.

Energy policy was a more exciting topic then than it is now. The department was Britain's newest ministry – set up by the Tories on 19 January 1974, in the heat of the miners' dispute, and staffed by 1,155 civil servants, including a former *Guardian* journalist named Bernard Ingham, as its Director of Information. "It was a good ministry to be in," he says. "It was all new. The oil companies were developing the North Sea, and we were developing a regulatory regime in the North Sea."[5]

It was just a year since the Arab states had sent out the biggest tremor the Western economies had suffered since the war, multiplying the price of oil by a factor of five. The politics of oil was the stuff of everyday conversation: motorists had experienced queues at petrol stations and shoppers had watched horrified as the price of anything remotely based on oil, including the plastic bags in which they took their purchases home, rose inexorably. At first, the price rises appeared to be nothing but a disaster for Britain's faltering economy; but with the price so high, the cost of extracting oil from under the North Sea had become economic. Immense wealth was there for the taking: a £500 million market was opening up just for the engineering firms who built the rigs, John Smith told the North West Industrial Development Association in one of his first public speeches as a minister; keeping them supplied with hardware and spare parts could be worth £5,000 million. It would have to be high-quality, skilled work, because when drilling for oil cost £15,000 a day, "reliability becomes more important than price".[6] Four months later, he was able to boast that half the £800 million a year of business already being generated from the North Sea was going to British firms.[7]

It was an exciting job for a young politician. There was an occasion when he had to take the lift downstairs to meet Sheikh Yamani, the Saudi Oil Minister who was one of the world's powerbrokers. Lord Balogh, a Hungarian-born economist who was Smith's immediate senior in the department, was in the same lift, but was so excited that "his English went into pig and whistles". The overheated peer shot out through the revolving door as their guest came in, and Smith was left standing alone in the reception area as the sheikh advanced towards him, saying, "Good afternoon, Lord Balogh."[8]

It was also demanding. On 5 December, seven weeks after Smith had begun the job, duty required him to be at the dispatch box in the Commons at 2 a.m., defending the government's decision to invest £7 million developing sites for offshore oil production, and again twenty-two hours later, to speak on energy conservation. Now that fuel had suddenly become expensive, that too was a matter which directly affected ordinary members of the public. A government order introduced by the Tories the previous December had imposed a 50 mph speed limit on all roads except motorways, where it was 60 mph, banned the use of electricity for advertising by day, and set the maximum temperature in offices and other buildings at 68 degrees Fahrenheit. John Smith had to decide whether to continue the order, or make himself popular by scrapping it. He renewed it for a year. In the same busy week, he had to deal with the opening stages of a government Bill intended to deal with the farrago of legal complications thrown up by the unprecedented situation of a multi-million-pound industrial operation out at sea, and its inevitable impact on those living on the nearby coast. On the opening day he was on his feet to speak for the first time at about 4.30 p.m. and for the last time at 2 a.m. The complexities were such as to boggle the mind. At one point, on a subsequent day, he was explaining why the government was opposed to one of the many amendments to the Bill: "The mere designation of an area as a designated sea area does not affect the interests of a harbour authority because no action flows from the designation order, and no subsequent action within a designated area can be taken without involving the harbour authority and giving it the opportunity to express views. . . . "[9] The Labour MP to whom this was addressed, Dr Dickson Mabon, thought it was an "admirable reply", and withdrew his amendment.

As a minister answering questions in the Commons Smith was, as before, invariably well informed, witty and able to think quickly on his feet. The even-tempered ruthlessness with which he ridiculed political opponents warned others that it was best to be well-informed and careful what they said when they tackled him. Some of his most contemptuous barbs were reserved not for the Tories but for the Scottish Nationalists, who unfailingly irritated him. To him, they were people who made trouble without risking the responsibility of making decisions. Hence his almost flippant reply to Gordon Wilson, who had taken a Dundee seat from Labour, who wanted "our oil reserves conserved more productively and positively". How, Smith inquired, could anything be "conserved productively"? The SNP was claiming that all proceeds from North Sea oil belonged to Scotland. "It suggests that oil found 100 miles or so to the east of the Shetland Isles, where I would think few Scotsmen have ever been, must be apportioned only to one part of the UK," Smith replied.[10]

Occasionally, he would go for a backbench Labour MP such as Nigel Spearing, who presumed to ask how much a new European energy research programme would cost, when the figure had already been published in documents issued by Brussels. Stung by this ticking-off, Spearing accused Smith of not listening to his question, but the Minister replied relentlessly: "I took careful note of what my Honourable Friend asked. He will see in Hansard that he asked how much it cost. . . . "[11] He was right, of course. He seems, though, to have given himself a reputation for having a sharp tongue. The exchange was given its edge by the fact that Nigel Spearing, then and ever since, has been an untiring, obsessive opponent of the Common Market. It was the issue at the forefront of everyone's mind. The referendum campaign was on, and the Party was split again. John Smith's previous isolation was eased by the fact that since being returned to power, Harold Wilson and most of the Cabinet had rediscovered the virtues of the Market, and were campaigning for a "Yes" vote. He was embarrassed, though, by the behaviour of Roy Jenkins and Shirley Williams, who threatened to quit politics if the vote went against them. He had no time for people who talked like that. Never in his career did John Smith ever use a threat of resignation or desertion to get his way.

Since he was confident throughout that his side would win the referendum, his main concern was that the Labour Party should hold together, despite the gap between party policy and government policy. His contribution to the referendum campaign was to be one of five ministers, three of them anti-marketeers, who signed a letter to the Party's General Secretary, Ron Hayward, warning him off allowing full-time party staff or the Party's resources to be used to help the "No" campaign. It would "result in bitterness and intolerance in our "ranks" and "cause confusion among party workers whose loyalties will inevitably be increasingly strained," the signatories claimed.[12]

The referendum campaign had a more personal impact on John Smith after it was done than while it was on. For eight months he had been working for the smoothly right-wing Eric Varley, who was trusted by the oil companies and was close to the Prime Minister. Suddenly, he had a new boss of a very different calibre. In the summer of the previous year, John Smith had warned in his *Daily Record* column that "This week and every week until the general election there will be a new bogeyman – Tony Benn."[13] It was Benn who had pushed the government into holding a referendum, and had led the unsuccessful campaign for a "No" vote. Newspapers were clamouring for him to be sacked, and Harold Wilson, who loathed him, was happy to oblige by making Benn and Varley swap places. It was a drastic demotion for Benn, but it guaranteed even livelier times at the Department of Energy, which now had camera crews and press photographers crowding its doorstep to snatch pictures of the new Secretary of State arriving for work. For the next four years, according to Bernard Ingham, life in the Department of Energy was never happy, but never dull.

Two years of working with Tony Benn demonstrated one of John Smith's strengths: his ability to get on well with people with whom he had profound ideological differences. He could be at ease in the company of people well to his left, and would state his position when the occasion demanded, without setting off waves of mistrust or hostility. Benn's voluminous diaries, littered with unflattering remarks about a large number of Labour politicians, say nothing bad about John Smith. There were, for example, the Tuesday office lunches for energy ministers and advisers – beer, Coke, a plate of sandwiches and convivial conversation. On one occasion the economist Lord Kaldor was invited, and gloomily diagnosed that the economy was in such bad shape that it might be better if Labour lost an election and dumped the problem on the Tories. Benn guiltily admitted: "Part of me feels the same", but John Smith would have none of it. He thought "the Party would never forgive us for quitting and running away, they would never elect us. He is right really," Benn recorded.[14]

When Lord Balogh, who was seventy, was retired in December 1975, it had been Harold Wilson's intention to replace him with another peer; but Benn, who was thoroughly suspicious of the Prime Minister's business friends, fought hard to have John Smith as his Minister of State instead.[15] He would not have succeeded if Smith had not been so different from his boss. When Benn asked for Michael Meacher, an ideological soulmate, as his PPS, he was refused. It was an important promotion which established that Smith was on the way up. It was true that the ambitious David Owen had reached the level of Minister of State sooner, at the age of only thirty-six; but at thirty-seven Smith was not far behind. He owed Benn a debt of gratitude which he never forgot. It helps to explain the absence of personal hostility between the two men, despite the ferocious factional battles in which they were invariably on opposite sides. Smith, of course, did not make the pretence that he would vote for Benn when he first ran for the party leadership in 1976, or in subsequent campaigns; but in 1992 Benn voted for him, and spoke very warmly of him. "He is a very nice, very competent Scottish lawyer. I have always found him extremely agreeable. I like him very, very much," he said.[16]

The main task on which Benn and Smith were engaged together was establishing the British National Oil Corporation, the state company which owned 51 per cent of North Sea oil. Its headquarters were in Glasgow, but there was a London branch occupying 2,000 square feet, topped by a penthouse flat on the third floor for the company chairman, Lord Kearton, the former head of Courtaulds, best known for having fought off a takeover bid by ICI. Lord Balogh was his part-time vice-chairman. Smith had to fend off the nitpicking criticisms of the cost of the London office – which was trivial for a firm with an initial turnover of almost £500 million a year, he argued; of the age of BNOC's executives, some of whom, he claimed defensively, were "quite young"; of the alleged underrepresentation of Scotland – there were three Scots on a ten-man board; and of the absence of women directors – to which there was no answer.[17] He flatly refused to answer repeated questions from Tory and Labour MPs who wanted to know how much BNOC's top executives were paid.

The company was established under the curiously named Petroleum and Submarine Pipelines Bill, the first piece of legislation which John Smith regarded as truly his own. "Those were swashbuckling times. Benn was boss of the North Sea and I was a sort of crown prince. By the time I'd finished working on it, I knew every oilfield," he later claimed.[18] Tony Benn, he says, liked the grand sweep of policy, but left the details and the wheeler-dealing with oil companies to him. There was plenty of detail to be dealt with. The Petroleum and Submarine Pipelines Bill first went before Parliament in April 1975, and was then referred to a committee for line-by-line examination. The committee sat for fourteen hours a week through May and June, coming up against what John Smith described as the "repeated and dogmatic opposition of the Conservative Party to any notion of public enterprise or the extension of public enterprise in any shape or form".[19] Neil Kinnock, a Labour member of the committee examining the Bill, praised John Smith for being the "soul of patience" during its proceedings,[20] but patience ran out, and Smith went to the Commons to request that its timetable be guillotined. The Tories, of course, objected, but on the whole the argument was a friendly one until a Tory MP, John Peyton, accused Smith of being "complacent". That was a strange comment, the Minister retorted, coming from one "whose attention to Parliament is so detailed that he wandered out of the Chamber when he had finished his speech and returned only at the end of the debate". Mr Peyton did not take that sitting down. He complained: "That is the kind of conduct that my right honourable and honourable friends have had to endure from the Undersecretary throughout the committee stage of the bill. I can assure the honourable gentleman that he is doing his reputation no good."[21] Despite that contretemps, the Bill had wound its way through both Houses of Parliament by November.

"He was very competent," says Sir Bernard Ingham.

> "He was quite a robust and lively Minister of State. It was recognized that he would be a Cabinet minister. I doubt whether anybody thought that he would lead the Labour Party, because the conventional wisdom was that you had to be of the left, or to have good trade union connections like Callaghan. He lacked the credentials. He was clearly there to watch Wedgie on behalf of Harold Wilson, just as Balogh was put there to watch Eric Varley. There was this ludicrous system of checks and balances. But he was very good, and he gave me one of the best pieces of advice I ever had from a minister."[22]

Ingham turned to John Smith for help as his relations with Tony Benn deteriorated to a point where the two men were scarcely on speaking terms. The Director of Information wondered if he should ask for a transfer, but he feared it might give him a reputation in the service for being irascible and unprofessional in his handling of ministers. When he asked Smith what to do, the Minister reputedly said, "Have a row with him. Wedgie doesn't like rows."[23] Apparently, it worked. Another civil servant who came to know Smith well slightly later was Jim Ross, an undersecretary at the Scottish Office. "He was very, very good – an excellent, efficient minister and very straightforward. The last word you would apply to John Smith is 'eccentric'."

At the time when Smith was helping to create BNOC, state ownership of industry was still nominally the intellectual foundation stone upon which the Labour Party had been built. John Smith has never been bashful about calling himself a socialist, but when he uses the word it has a different sense to the one found in dictionaries, or the one used by such people as Keir Hardie or Aneurin Bevan. Bevan, for example, was quite clear that a socialist was one who believed in public ownership, though towards the end of his life he confided to a journalist friend that the Labour Party "isn't really a socialist party at all".[24] Smith's definition would be similar to the one given by his former idol, Tony Crosland:

> The Socialist seeks a distribution of rewards, status and privileges egalitarian enough to minimise social resentment, to secure justice between individuals

> and to equalise opportunities; and he seeks to weaken the existing deep-seated class stratification with its concomitant feelings of envy and inferiority, and its barriers to uninhibited mingling between the classes.[25]

The main line of attack against a class-ridden society, said Crosland, was through the education system, rather than nationalization. Smith's early pronouncements indicate that he thought so too.

John Smith believed in a mixed economy. He believed that common sense could determine which industries were best left in private hands and which should be run by the state. As ever, he planted himself midway between two poles: the free-market ideologists in the Tory Party, and those on Labour's left who believed that all the commanding heights of industry should be nationalized. "It has always puzzled me that Conservatives think that it is non-dogmatic and non-doctrinaire to oppose the extension of public ownership in any shape or form and yet that it is doctrinaire for the Labour Party to propose any extension of public ownership," he told the Commons. "The truth is that Conservatives are concerned to defend private rights and private property at every conceivable opportunity. They do not believe in a mixed economy."[26] This is very different from the classical socialist belief that no economy based on private ownership of capital can function without wage labourers being exploited, the vulnerable being pushed to the margins of society, and the innate rights and creativity of human beings being stifled. "We are socialists because we believe that these rights cannot be fully realised in any society under capitalism, which, as in Britain now, has entrenched by law the power of Capital over Labour and subordinated human values to the demand for profit," wrote Tony Benn.[27]

Smith's pragmatic belief in a mixed economy, moreover, did not automatically put him on the same side of the barricade as workers in their struggle. He appeared at the ceremonial opening of Britain's first offshore pipeline, built at a cost of £60 million, at Seal Sands, Teeside, on 21 October 1975, to draw in the first pint of oil from under the sea; and while he and Norway's Minister for Industry, Ingvald Ulverseth, and attendant officials enjoyed a champagne reception, 1,200 workers outside were holding a one-day strike because, as their union spokesman explained: "They are spending more than £100,000 on a glorified booze-up when we can't get canteen facilities or a proper first aid centre."[28] John Smith was too hard-headed to suppose that if he refused to behave in the manner expected of a government minister, it would improve the lot of workers in any measurable way.

When considering energy as a distinctive branch of the economy, however, John Smith was no less "socialist" than Bevan or Benn. He believed that energy supplies should be controlled by the state, because they are vital to the well-being of every individual member of society; because consumers rarely – if ever – have a real choice of where to buy their energy supplies; and because it is an industry which cannot be efficiently run by private firms required to show an annual profit for their shareholders. Any new project – be it a colliery, an oilfield or a power station – requires ten years from design to completion; consequently, energy supplies are uniquely subject to long-term planning. "BNOC was a great success story," he claimed, some years later. "It developed quickly as Britain's new public sector oil company and earned hundreds of millions of pounds for the British taxpayer. It pioneered a new and imaginative relationship between the public and the private sector of industry. Above all, it was a security for the British national interest in the North Sea."[29] When it was broken up, and its profitable section was incorporated in BP after the 1979 election, it was because Britain now had a government which could not bear the sight of a state-owned enterprise which worked well, he claimed.

6
The Devolution Minister 1976–78

Nothing has ever taken up so much parliamentary time to so little effect as the proposal to bring home rule to Scotland. No fewer than forty-seven days on the floor of the House of Commons – equivalent to nearly a third of one year's worth of legislative time – were devoted to a topic of no relevance whatsoever to the economic crisis lapping at Britain's feet. In fact, its great virtue, in the eyes of a beleaguered Prime Minister, was that it "helped distract parliamentary attention from a morbid preoccupation with the state of the economy".[1] Not since India was granted independence had so much time on the floor of the House of Commons been devoted to one topic. "Today," one observer wrote recently, "devolution seems as dated as kipper ties, Ally's tartan army and the Bay City Rollers – and, for many, marginally less alluring",[2] but at the time it was the talk of the talking classes. It came to grief through the indifference of the general public.

Oil, more than any other single factor, had revived Scotland's dreams of independence. The Scottish Nationalists could offer a superficially attractive and viable future for the country as a little, oil-rich state independent of England and the Common Market. There was some doubt as to what else the Scottish National Party stood for – whether it was a left-wing party, competing for Labour's vote, or a group of "Tartan Tories". Their most celebrated convert was the mega-rich Glasgow industrialist Sir Hugh Fraser, owner of the *Glasgow Herald*. In the column he wrote occasionally for the *Daily Record*, John Smith wondered aloud how an SNP MP like George Reid, a convert from Labour, could sit comfortably in the same party as such a man: "Labour Party plans for fairer distribution of wealth and public ownership have no attraction to Sir Hugh – and we wouldn't want him."[3] The SNP optimistically projected itself as a new kind of party which could transcend the old notions of right and left, and in 1974 that appeared to work. The SNP took 11 of the 71 seats in Scotland, mostly from Labour. That was enough to convince Harold Wilson that he ought to be seen to be doing something for devolution.

The change of policy was forced through a reluctant Scottish Labour Party at a special conference called on Wilson's orders in Glasgow, in August 1974. It was a sour occasion which left behind a lot of unhappiness. Alex Donnet and his opposite number in the TGWU, Alex Kitson, loyally cast their block votes in favour of devolution. Kitson, who had been instrumental in winning over Labour's National Executive in London, actually believed in the policy. Donnet made no bones about it: he was motivated by a desire to maximize the chance of returning Labour to power. Smith's speech to the conference was not the best of his life. As we shall see, it gave his audience the impression that the man who would soon make his reputation as the Devolution Minister was opposed to devolution.

In his more expansive private moments, when he is not feeling that his public position requires him to be modest, John Smith is apt to say that just two people kept the Callaghan administration afloat. One was Walter Harrison, the former Labour MP for Wakefield, a backstage operator who never spoke in any of the dozens of debates because of his position as a government whip, but succeeded in rounding up reluctant MPs and getting them to go through the lobbies to save their government from countless threats of defeat. The other was John Smith, Minister of State in the Privy Council office, who did all the talking. Before he reached this position, there had to be a new Prime Minister. Harold Wilson's resignation in May 1976 was so unexpected and inexplicable that it took some politicians hours to recover from their astonishment and begin plotting who his successor should be. There were six candidates in the opening ballot, but it soon came down to a contest between James Callaghan and Michael Foot. Smith had no hesitation about where he stood. On day one he volunteered himself as a Callaghan supporter, and had a frantic week lobbying MPs, totting up the numbers, and seeing if there were any waverers to be talked round: "I remember we used to swap notes with the other side, about people who had said to both sides they were voting for them. We uncovered a few. I had no doubt Callaghan was the right man. And I couldn't understand why there was any speculation about who would win in the end, because I thought he was bound to."[4]

Harold Wilson had been behaving as if he wanted to be seen to be sympathetic to home rule without allowing any power to slip away from 10 Downing Street. Back in 1968 he had referred the question to a royal commission, a classic Wilson delaying tactic. By the time Labour returned to office, the egg had hatched. It was known officially as the Kilbrandon Report, after the commission's chairman, and unofficially as the Kil-devolution Report. It proposed that when Scotland was granted an assembly, the Cabinet post of Secretary of State for Scotland should be abolished, and the number of Scottish MPs at Westminster cut down. The second of these two proposals was a recipe for ensuring that Britain never had a Labour government again. Meanwhile, the two Cabinet posts central to the devolution question were held by anti-devolutionists. Willie Ross, Smith's old boss, was still Scottish Secretary. The idea that his job was to be abolished did nothing to abate his long-standing opposition to home rule. The crucial job, though, was that of leader of the House of Commons and chairman of the Cabinet committee on devolution, which had been allotted to Ted Short, a Newcastle MP. Most northern English Labour MPs were hostile to Scottish devolution, fearing that it would suck regional aid from the depressed areas of the North-East and North-West into Scotland. At heart, Short was no exception.

By the time Callaghan became Prime Minister, the devolution question was too urgent to be evaded. To understand why, it is necessary only to look at the arithmetic of the House of Commons. Labour had been returned to government in October 1974 with a majority of just three. That vanished as four Labour MPs defected. The first were Jim Sillars and John Robertson, who left in protest at the way Wilson dragged his feet over devolution, to found the breakaway Scottish Labour Party. They were followed by John Stonehouse, who lost touch with reality, and Reg Prentice, who went to the Tories. And as the government's popularity slid, every by-election in a Labour seat was a potential nightmare. When Stonehouse quit the Commons, the resulting contest in Walsall North produced a record 22.5 per cent swing to the Tories – one of three disastrous by-election results on one day in November 1976. The following April, after David Marquand had decided to follow Jenkins into a job with the EC, Labour managed to lose Ashfield, in the Nottinghamshire coalfield, despite a 22,000 majority at the general election. Callaghan was therefore driven to make a pact with the Liberals, and to give the sixteen SNP, SLP and Welsh Nationalist MPs an incentive not to bring the government down.

Ted Short and Willie Ross were consequently dispatched to the House of Lords. The new Scottish Secretary, Bruce Millan, was more amenable to devolution, while the new Leader of the Commons, Michael Foot, was positively enthusiastic about it. But to steer a devolution Bill through Parliament was going to be horrendously complicated. By convention, because it was a measure which would alter Britain's unwritten constitution, the details could not be delegated to a committee of MPs in the usual way. The Commons had to be its own committee, and every tiny detail had to be thrashed out on the floor of the main chamber, in debates open to all comers. And on an issue such as this, MPs did not feel they had to defer to the opinion of experts. When it came to setting up a new elected legislature, they were their own experts.

Even if Foot had had the necessary legal training and fondness for detail to handle such a complex Bill, he would not have had the time. Every mildly controversial piece of legislation needed careful piloting, given the government's precarious hold on Parliament. He needed a reliable deputy. It was time to send for a Scottish lawyer who had proved his ability to cope with complex legislation. The summons to see the Prime Minister came during a meeting of an advisory committee on the North Sea oil. John Smith says he never guessed what was coming his way. He told his private secretary that he would go as soon as the meeting was over; but the civil servant came back with an anxious look, saying that Downing Street insisted, and if the Minister was not going to leave at once, he had better ring them himself to explain why not. "On my way out, Jimmy Milne, who was the General Secretary of the Scottish TUC and a member of this committee, said to me, 'I hope you get a good job, John.' It was the first time it registered with me that it was about an appointment. It never crossed my mind that I would not be doing energy."[5]

In the car to Downing Street, still not knowing what he was to be offered, Smith was weighing up whether he could risk refusing a job offer for the second time in just over two years. It was soon obvious that Callaghan was not looking for a volunteer. His administration's survival depended on the devolution Bill getting through somehow, and Smith was told to find a formula which would placate the Nationalists without splitting the Labour Party.

There was some confusion in the minds of his fellow Scots over where the new minister stood on devolution. In his *Daily Record* column in May 1974 he warned that the price tag attached to devolution, as set in the Kilbrandon Report, was "too high" to justify the experiment.[6] He made the same point in his speech to a highly charged Glasgow conference later that year, adding that anyone who claimed that Scotland could have an assembly without losing its Secretary of State and some of its Westminster MPs was "being dishonest".[7] On a different occasion, he warned: "I also take leave to doubt the effectiveness of an Assembly which does not have any real control over financial policy and trade and industrial policy in Scotland. . . . I doubt if a voice without power would be heard and I am even more suspicious of representation which does not carry responsibility."[8]

Since these were the contributions Smith made when devolution was the main talking point in Scottish political circles, they were the ones which stuck in everyone's mind. In fact, his contribution to the debate on Scotland had earned him a blast of disapproval in *New Left Review* from

Tom Nairn, the most prominent of several Marxist intellectuals drawn to the breakaway Scottish Labour Party. Nairn likened him to Sir Walter Scott, who was romantically nationalistic about Scotland's past, and more conservative than an English Tory in his defence of the British constitution. "The Labour Party . . . has become the ultimate repository of this dour devotion," Nairn claimed. "No speeches conjure up the old Unionist *Geist* nowadays more relentlessly than those of William Ross and John Smith."[9]

Smith himself, however, denies that he was ever against devolution in principle. So does his old friend Donald Dewar, one of the leaders of the pro-devolution camp. Brian Wilson, then a radical journalist and a prominent opponent of home rule, also credits Smith with long-standing consistency on the subject. And directly after the October 1974 election, he urged that there should be no delay in establishing the Scottish Assembly. "During the election it was suggested that Labour might backtrack on this pledge if they won. The cynics are wrong. Labour will set up an Assembly with effective powers over Scottish affairs," he predicted.[10] Jim Ross, the civil servant in charge of devolution at the Scottish Office, says: "A lot of ministers at the time were extremely sceptical about it, but I didn't see any sign in him of any lack of enthusiasm for it. But that doesn't necessarily tell you anything. John was the sort of minister who would have put his guts into whatever he was given to do."

At the time when Smith spoke to the Glasgow conference he was, of course, Willie Ross's right-hand man, and may have spoken out of character through loyalty to his boss. Whatever the reason, he had to endure taunts from all sides about an apparent *volte face*. Norman Tebbit suggested to him on one occasion that as a lawyer he could be hired to say anything his client wanted him to say – a view which Smith thought unfair on lawyers. Eric Heffer was another who challenged him to explain how he had come to emerge as the country's leading devolutionist. "Frankly," said Smith, "I changed my mind."[11] Characteristically, he found a middle ground between two extremes, wherein dwelt sensible people like himself. Speaking at the Commons dispatch box for the first time in his new capacity, he forecast: "We shall no doubt be opposed by blinkered unionists and blinkered separatists, but I believe we shall beat them both."[12] Two exhausting years later, he used almost exactly the same words when he complained to the Edinburgh branch of the Institute of Directors that the legislation had been "bedevilled by two sets of extremists – separatists, who want to break up Britain, and diehard and blinkered unionists who resist any move at all to decentralise decision taking to Scotland".[13]

Actually, the "separatists", or SNP, were the least of his problems. Their contributions were often annoying – barely worth answering, in John Smith's none too humble opinion. Jim Callaghan suspected that when the government ran into trouble with the Bill, the SNP "wept crocodile tears but in reality they were delighted, believing they could ascribe the defeat to English obstruction and so sweep Scotland into their camp".[14] But in the lobbies they were more reliable than Labour's own Scottish MPs, and in public debates they provided John Smith with a convenient threat to the United Kingdom, against which he could proffer his Bill as the Union's best defence. "It is my firm judgement", he told the Commons, "that the unity of the United Kingdom will be strengthened by recognising the diversity of its different parts."[15] On another occasion, he argued: "Our unity does not have to depend on enforced conformity from the centre. It can rest on recognising the diversity within our system."[16] And he told Edinburgh business leaders: "I believe the Assembly will act to underpin the essential unity of the kingdom."[17] All in all, he claimed, it was "an exercise of tremendous constitutional conservatism".[18]

The idea of Scotland seceding from the United Kingdom was not as fanciful then as it seemed a decade later. While the rest of Britain wallowed in economic crisis, the north of Scotland was in the first flush of an oil boom. John Smith may have believed his own claim that a Scottish Assembly would be an antidote to separatism. But with hindsight, those who believed Scotland would stay in the Union anyway can say they were proved right; and there was substance to a charge laid against John Smith at the time, by the Tory MP Julian Amery, that he was doing "something rather improper" by relying on the votes of Scottish Nationalists to support a Bill supposedly intended to prevent Scotland from quitting the UK.[19] His real problems were with the "diehard and blinkered unionists", who came in all shapes and guises. They included Queen and Country patriots on the Tory right, such as Julian Amery, Sir Nicholas Fairbairn, Teddy Taylor and Norman Tebbit. There was Enoch Powell, now Ulster Unionist MP for South Down, who could be relied upon to marshal long, learned and meticulously constructed arguments against any proposition which might interfere with the sovereignty of the British Parliament. Smith might have been able to ignore them, but the government's position was so precarious that even the votes of Ulster Unionists could be important.

Official Tory policy was to support the Scottish Assembly – until December 1976, just as the Scotland and Wales Bill was about to begin its progress through the Commons, when Margaret Thatcher performed her famous U-turn, setting her face against devolution in any form, and provoking resignations from her front bench, including that of the ambitious young Edinburgh MP Malcolm Rifkind. From then on, John Smith had to do battle with the Tories for every clause in his Bill, even against newfound opponents like George Younger – then the most eminent Scottish Tory and later a long-serving member of Thatcher's Cabinet, who had previously appeared at public meetings on the same platform as John Smith, arguing the case for devolution.

When it became known that the Tories would try to block the Bill, the Cabinet made one important concession to its own backbench critics by deciding to hold referendums in Scotland and Wales before it became law. This decision was made in a rush, on a Thursday morning, and slipped out almost casually during John Smith's speech in the Commons in the afternoon. Doing it that way, rather than through a formal ministerial statement, spared the government from having to answer questions. The problems he had had with the Tories were mild, though, compared with what John Smith had to tolerate from his own side. Even without Ted Short, there was intense opposition to the proposed Scottish Assembly from northern English MPs, now led by Eric Heffer.

Sending Willie Ross to the Lords had similarly weakened – but not eliminated – opposition from the Scots MPs. The young Robin Cook continued to believe, as Smith had once done, that the creation of the Assembly would be used by the Tories as an excuse to cut the number of Scottish MPs at Westminster. It helped Smith's case that the Tories themselves denied having any such plan. Whether their denials were sincere is another matter. Then there was Tam Dalyell, Labour MP for West Lothian. Like so many of the principal players in the drama, Mad Tam had begun by believing one thing, before being fanatically converted to the opposite. In October 1974, one day after the general election, he not only called for devolution but demanded legislation within two years. Unfortunately, as he later explained, he had been so exhausted by the election campaign that he had not actually read the White Paper on devolution, which had been published in September, the day before the campaign began. Three months later he read it, and then: "I really tumbled to what was up, because I and others had not realised until that time that what was involved was a Scottish Prime Minister, a Scottish Cabinet, and all the rest of it."[20] This proposal to give Scotland the full trappings of self-government was not what had been agreed by the Labour Party conference in August 1974, Dalyell claimed. He accused Geoff Bish, the head of the Labour Party's research department, of having rewritten the White Paper at the last minute[21] – as, indeed, he had. Bish, who held the post until 1993, says: "It was all done in an incredible rush, because we knew an election was approaching. I can understand why Tam felt a bit sore about it, because in a sense the Party was bounced into it."[22]

With incredible obstinacy, Tam Dalyell made it his one-man mission to block devolution. His main argument against it was that it would produce an absurd situation in which a Scottish MP like himself would have no influence over how Scottish secondary schools were run, when that matter had been devolved to the Scottish Assembly, but would be able to vote on how England's schools were organized. It was not his only objection, but he repeated this particular one so insistently, in so many ways, that Enoch Powell nicknamed it the "West Lothian Question". "The point cannot be made too often," Dalyell declared grandly on one occasion; whereupon John Smith's voice was heard muttering on the front bench: "Yes, it can." "No, it cannot," Tam persisted. "If this Bill comes into law there will be diverse subjects which I can raise in Down, South but which I cannot raise in my own constituency. The Minister of State may sigh in irritation, but he has not answered this point, because there is no answer."[23]

The Minister did more than sigh in irritation. At various times, he accused Dalyell of being "infantile and absurd"[24] ". . . boring . . . far from constructive . . . totally absurd and simplistic . . . He rises to give us lectures, advice, exhortation and visions of doom."[25] "He says the Scots are fractious. I take the view that we are no different from people in any other part of the UK. I suppose that he absorbed that sort of idea when he was at Eton and Cambridge. Fortunately, I had a Scottish education . . . " This particular outburst, condemning Dalyell for his pedigree, prompted Sir Nicholas Fairbairn, Baron of Fordell, to chip in with a claim that John Smith's Scottish education had taught him to be "unctuous", whereupon the Minister testily replied that if he ever needed his unctuousness refreshed, the likes of Fairbairn and Dalyell would be his models.[26]

In vain would Smith deny Dalyell's claim that Scotland was to have its own Prime Minister, and try to brush off the "West Lothian Question" as being scarcely worth an answer. "It implies that there should be a logical symmetry post-devolution and that every MP in the House of Commons should be responsible for the same thing," he protested.[27] The "West Lothian Question" refused to go away. The Labour whips soon gave up any attempt to keep Tam Dalyell under control. By his own admission, he voted against a three-line Labour whip on more than a hundred separate occasions.[28] One morning at 5.45, after a sitting which had gone on for fourteen hours, just seven MPs were still on hand to vote against the government. One was Tam Dalyell. For every vote, the indefatigable Walter Harrison had to find another Labour MP prepared to hang around all hours of the night, to support the government and cancel out Dalyell.

The plans for a Welsh Assembly were so much less controversial – since Wales was to be presented with a talking shop virtually without any powers – that it might be supposed no one would be strongly against the idea. In fact, Wales had its own version of Tam Dalyell in the obstreperous MP for Bedwellty, Neil Kinnock. There was no obvious political mileage in Kinnock's lone stand, but he saw the Assembly as a waste of time and money which had no real support among the Welsh working class, and would do them no real good. His exchanges with John Smith were never as bad-tempered as Dalyell's, but there was an occasion when the Minister objected to being barracked by his future leader, and commented archly: "If he will refrain from interrupting me from a sedentary position, we might make some progress."[29]

In his first speech introducing the Scotland and Wales Bill, John Smith warned that it had to be "formidably complex", because it cut across a string of other measures that were on the Statute Book. Education, health and housing were the three main concerns being devolved to the Scottish Assembly, which meant, potentially, that every Act previously passed by Parliament which affected any of these areas was up for amendment. Trying to keep the Bill short and simple would produce "not simplicity but shambles – anomaly, absurdity, vagueness and a permanent field day for litigation", he cautioned.[30] On that encouraging note, MPs settled down to days and months of pettifogging arguments, every one of which John Smith was required to answer on the government's behalf. Those who witnessed this parliamentary marathon agree that he displayed an almost heroic patience, and a masterly command of detail.

There was a long technical argument about whether the government was devolving "powers" or "sovereignty". To a lawyer like John Smith, this was more than a semantic argument; it was the heart of his claim that the Bill would bind the United Kingdom together. Hence his rather cross reply to a Tory MP who claimed that "sovereignty" was being devolved. Sovereignty, by definition, is something which cannot be taken away by a higher authority. "Powers are devolved – indeed substantial powers are devolved," said Smith; but what Parliament had given, it could take back. The devolution Act could be rescinded, and the Scottish and Welsh assemblies abolished, if that was Parliament's wish. "Sovereignty is not devolved. . . . This Parliament will remain the only sovereign Parliament."[31]

There were inevitable arguments over precisely what should be devolved. Scotland's schools and new towns were to be controlled by the Assembly, but its universities by Westminster. The SNP fought unsuccessfully for control over Scotland's electricity, coal, gas and oil. There was a debate over whether Scotland should have its own Forestry Commission and a fierce argument over abortion law, in which Jo Richardson, Labour's foremost campaigner for women's rights, found herself voting with the anti-devolutionists. She feared that the Scots would impose more draconian abortion laws than the English, opening up the prospect of desperate women travelling south for abortions, only to be interrogated about their Scottish accents when they arrived. Occasionally, the arguments were so detailed as to be plain silly. "Are you saying that the power to erect omnibus shelters is not to be devolved. If so, I am utterly shocked and dismayed!" Neil Kinnock exclaimed one day. There were also such questions as what to call Scotland's new Assembly, how often it was to be elected, how many members it should have, where they should meet, how it would be financed, and what would happen if there was political confrontation between it and the British Parliament.

John Smith refused to see the last question as a difficult problem, since the British system had coped often enough with clashes between the Commons and the Lords. Ah, but that was different, countered Neil Kinnock. There was no danger of unelected peers whipping up popular opinion for a showdown with MPs, but such a thing could easily happen if the Scottish or Welsh Assembly decided to take a stand against English interference. A closer analogy, he said, would be a clash between an elected council and central government. This was a more contentious prospect, because of the recent memory of little Clay Cross urban district, whose councillors were disqualified and personally surcharged for defying a government order to increase council rents – except that a confrontation between Parliament and a national assembly could be much more serious than the Clay Cross case, because "they ostensibly embody a national determination and will – and if they have to succumb to the supremacy of Parliament, will do so with great resentment". John Smith replied, a little impatiently, that it could never happen in Wales, because the Welsh Assembly was not to be granted any legislative powers.[32]

By implication, therefore, it could happen in Scotland. In the government's White Paper, it appeared that Westminster would be able to deal with a rebellious Scottish Assembly exactly as it did with Clay Cross – by a direct order, followed by disqualification and legal retribution for assembly members who disobeyed. John Smith could see an unnecessary recipe for conflict, and decided to have a sort of arbitration system written in. The Judicial Committee of the Privy Council – the Law Lords, sitting in different dress – was to be given the task of interpreting the law whenever there was a dispute over whether the Assembly had strayed beyond its devolved powers. If this system had ever come into effect, it would have shoved Britain's senior judges into political controversy. "There had been eternal arguments about that: should it be settled politically, or should it be settled in court? My view was that the judicial committee was the perfect answer, and my view prevailed," Smith says.[33]

This was more than an argument among lawyers. The SNP would obviously make it their aim to control the Scottish Assembly. If they achieved that, they would probably seize their chance to pick a fight with the government, and push it to a point where ministers had to choose between capitulation and heavy-handed intervention. A Labour government might ultimately have been forced to disband its own creation. The SNP leader, Gordon Wilson, hinted at this when he asked Smith: "What would happen if the Scottish Assembly, in exercise of the sovereign will of the Scottish people, refused to accept either the decision of the Privy Council, over which it had no control, or any decision from Westminster?" Eric Heffer, in fact, jumped in at this point to suggest that the whole experiment be called off, since the SNP plainly intended to wreck the Assembly. In his pragmatic way, though, Smith refused to be thrown off course by a crisis which had not yet happened. He, of course, was not going to be drawn: the government needed those eleven SNP votes too much. He airily replied that there was no such thing as a "sovereign will of the Scottish people", and left it at that.[34]

Finally, there were endless arguments over the two referendums – mainly over the dates on which they were to be held, the wording of the questions, and who would be eligible to vote. So far as John Smith was concerned, since the issue concerned Scotland and Wales, it would be decided by people on the electoral register in those two countries, and no one else. There was clamour from the Tories for the English to have the vote as well, or for it at least to be extended to Scottish and Welsh expatriates. Why, Sir Julian Amery demanded to know, should a Bangladeshi living in Scotland be allowed to vote, but not a Scot living in England? (He then rather spoilt his own case by saying that he had once met a Fijian chief who claimed to have Scottish blood, because his grandfather had once eaten two Scottish missionaries.)[35]

By February 1977, it was plain that the Scotland and Wales Bill was doomed. After four days debating the original White Paper, four days on the second reading of the Bill, and ten days of the House sitting as a committee, the Commons had ground its way through the first three clauses. There were 112 to go. At this point Michael Foot made a desperate attempt to salvage it with a so-called "guillotine" motion, which would have limited the Bill to another twenty days in committee – more time than Parliament had spent on any Bill since the First World War, except for the Government of India Bill. He was unable to get Parliament to accept his timetable. The Tories, the Liberals and a handful of rebel Labour MPs combined to block the guillotine.

Callaghan and Foot then faced the choice of either abandoning the whole idea, or winning over the Liberals. What exercised the Liberals most – then as now – was the fact that the millions of votes they attracted each general election gave them only a tiny number of seats. David Steel knew that there were some Tory and Labour MPs who individually supported the case for proportional representation. He was keen to know how many, and was offered a way of finding out: if he co-operated in getting the devolution Bill through, there would be a free vote in the Commons on whether the new Scottish and Welsh assemblies would be elected under a system of PR. Consequently, the show went back on the road in November 1977. John Smith had been given a break of several months in which he was under instructions to redesign the Bill to please the Liberals, without making any more enemies on the Labour side. Callaghan acknowledged that "it was a tall order but John Smith was equal to the task".[36] Behind him, Smith had the invaluable Michael Foot, who may have been uninterested in the minute details of the Bill, but certainly understood the ways of Parliament, and maintained a wry, gallows humour as the government narrowly escaped one crisis after another. On one occasion, when Smith consulted him on how to sell a particularly doubtful clause to the sceptics, Foot advised him, with mock gravity: "In politics, you should never neglect the possibility that you might have to fall back on the truth."[37]

This time the legislation was divided into two parts, and a timetable was imposed on day one, against vigorous protests from the Tories. Between November 1977 and July 1978, the House of Commons spent 97 hours and 55 minutes of its time, stretched over 18 separate days, and the House of Lords a further 11 days, just on the Scotland Bill. There was also a Wales Bill, which occupied 11 days in the Commons. There was a free vote, as agreed, on PR, which was rejected by the Commons. The Lords inserted it into the Bill, against the government's advice, but the Commons took it out again, without sundering the agreement between Labour and the Liberals.

One last guillotine motion guaranteed that for better or worse it would all be over in three days. On the second to last day, as that end-of-term feeling was starting to spread, John Smith was interrupted yet again by Tam Dalyell. As he sat, and Dalyell stood, a bag of horse manure came flying down from the public gallery, narrowly missing Dennis Skinner's head to splatter over Dalyell. Two young demonstrators, one of them the daughter of the Prime Minister of Malta, were making their protest against conditions in Northern Ireland's Long Kesh Prison. If Smith had been on his feet, he would have caught the whole load. As it was, he received just a small helping on his lapel. "There was a kerfuffle in the gallery, and I saw the thing coming through the air. It burst. Tam got full frontal, right in the face." Under Commons rules, business must carry on as if nothing had happened, and Smith – a little smellier now – stood up to reply, but Dalyell protested that he could not sit down, because his place on the green benches had turned brown. As the Speaker cleared the House, one of the wigged clerks – who never speak in the House except to give legal advice, and then only in a whisper – muttered to John Smith that he had just experienced a "close encounter of the turd kind".

By the end of July 1978, both bills had become law. While it lasted, the great devolution show had filled the Scottish and Welsh media, guaranteeing the government the backing of three of the minority parties. It was a long breathing space. John Smith's hard-earned reward came in the Queen's Birthday Honours list: he was made a Privy Councillor, on the same day as Gerald Kaufman. Now he was the Right Honourable John Smith, and a grateful Jim Callaghan was looking for the chance to make him a Cabinet minister.

Though it all came to nothing, and the devolution debate seems now like an arcane debate from long ago, it is almost certain to return. Every political party but the Conservatives is committed to the principle of a Scottish assembly. When the Tory government eventually falls, as one day it must, the "West Lothian Question" will stalk Westminster again.

7
Inside Trade
1978–82

Promotion came to John Smith sooner than he could have expected. Labour's Trade Secretary, Edmund Dell, had been offered a job in the City, and in November 1978 he resigned. It was a bad sign for the Callaghan government that a Cabinet member should think of jumping ship, and irritating for the Party. Benn, for one, thought it was a "scandalous betrayal", although he was pleased to see the back of a colleague whom he regarded as "more right wing than the Tories".[1] Scandalous or not, it was a lucky break for John Smith. Until now, his best hope had been that Labour would somehow scrape through the election, and he would then be the natural candidate to replace Benn at the Energy Department. Suddenly, with Michael Foot's fulsome backing, he was at the top table.

He had done well. He was only just forty, and the first and only member of the 1970 intake of Labour MPs to become a Secretary of State. Reaching the Cabinet only eight years after entering Parliament was rapid progress by any standards: John Major rose through Tory ranks at the same speed in the following decade, but he started slightly later in life, and was forty-three when he arrived. There were older men who might have thought themselves better qualified to take on the job awarded to Smith, but Jim Callaghan had already come to terms with the prospect of defeat and a period in opposition. For that reason, he had promoted a trio of younger ministers – Hattersley, Owen and Smith – to be the backbone of a Labour Cabinet in the mid 1980s. The three were bracketed together by Michael Jones of the *Sunday Times*, on the day after Smith's elevation, as "possible contenders for leadership of a future Labour government".

Jones shared the honour of being the first journalist to tip Smith as a future Labour leader with the *Sunday Mirror*'s political editor, Victor Knight, who pointed out that "thirty one years ago, another rising star became the youngest member of the Labour cabinet. Harold Wilson was appointed President of the Board of Trade – exactly the same job now taken up by John Smith."[2] The following morning's *Daily Mirror* was less kind – "Some will say that the unknown is following the unknown, now that John Smith has replaced Edmund Dell" – while *The Financial Times* hailed him as "another of the Great White Hopes who have their eyes on No 10". A week later, even the *Sunday Express* caught on to the "coming man of Labour politics": "A twitch of unease runs through the younger members of the Cabinet. A collection of distinguished noses is put firmly out of joint. Mr John Smith has arrived."[3] The prize for prophecy, though, must go to the *Evening Standard* diarist, who wrote: "Who knows, by the 1990s it could be Smith on the Right versus Neil Kinnock on the Left for the Labour leadership, with Varley and fat Hattersley a bit over the hill. And whatever happened to Owen?"[4]

Smith's Tory opposite number, John Nott, also paid tribute to his "high parliamentary reputation", which had made him "respected on both sides of the House", but warned him to keep watch over his two "bored and frustrated" junior ministers, Stanley Clinton Davis and Michael Meacher. Meacher, especially, was attracting controversy. In his first ministerial job, he had upset the civil servants by querying every document put in front of him before he would agree to sign it. Now he was convinced that the Labour government was guilty of a loss of nerve in the face of powerful vested interests, and needed its backbone stiffening. He had calculated that Callaghan would retire after the next election, and was organizing behind the scenes to have Tony Benn elected as his successor. But Smith, having spent the past three years deputizing for left-wing Cabinet ministers, had no intention – characteristically – of allowing this to interfere with the smooth running of his ministerial team.

No doubt he did allow himself some quiet pleasure at being the object of so much flattering attention in the national media. But he was too sensible to forget that the history of politics is littered with the names of people who have been tipped at one time or another as future party leaders and Prime Ministers, and for more than a few it has been the first step on the road to ruin. Today's potential Prime Minister is tomorrow's target for jealous intrigue, and the day after that he is the person whose meteoric career has taken a downturn. As we have seen, John Smith's great strength was his patience. He was never tempted to make a dash for glory, like David Owen. More than thirteen years after he was first tipped as a possible Labour leader, he was still there.

Besides, being back in economic work after three years buried in constitutional niceties reminded him how serious Labour's problems were. Callaghan had forgone his chance to call an early election, and faced a winter of strikes at the head of a deeply divided Party. At his first Cabinet meeting, three days after his appointment, Smith witnessed a furious argument between Denis Healey and Tony Benn over whether Britain should join the proposed European Monetary System (EMS). A campaign against was being orchestrated on Labour's back benches by Bryan Gould. Healey wanted to sign up both to the EMS and to the more controversial Exchange Rate Mechanism (ERM), but Callaghan had already decided that the Party would not wear it – at least, not before an election. These were problems which were to reappear in John Smith's life. For the moment, he had a miscellaneous department to run – by his own recollection he was "partly an economic minister, partly a City regulator, and a bit of a transport minister as well" – and three big problems to tackle: Britain's ever-worsening trade balance, scandals on the stock market, and a long-running argument over whether employees should have representatives on company boards.

The previous year, a few mild proposals on industrial democracy had been set out in the government's Bullock Report – a lot milder, certainly, than ideas which Michael Foot and Tony Benn had been pursuing in Cabinet. The hostility from Britain's managerial class was encapsulated in a *Sun* headline which dismissed it as "A load of Bullocks". The captains of industry were not in the least impressed by the argument that industrial democracy had helped Germany to achieve an economic miracle: German trade unions were disciplined branches of the industrial process, whilst Britain's workers were looked upon as the willing dupes of militant shop stewards, and industrial democracy was a recipe for allowing Reds into the boardroom. The CBI had let Edmund Dell know that it would oppose any workers being placed on any company boards by any form of legislation, no matter how much it was watered down. Dell's advice to the Cabinet was that it had no choice but to give in, because if multinationals believed their freedom to make investment decisions was being put under any form of trade-union supervision in Britain, they would simply move their assets abroad. The Employment Secretary, Albert Booth, by contrast, believed that trade unions should have a legal right to nominate directors. A Cabinet committee chaired by Shirley Williams had tried – but failed – to reconcile these conflicting views.

Such a situation cried out for John Smith to apply his special brand of homespun common sense. The centre between two polarized positions was where he naturally belonged. His approach to industrial relations was typified by a story he was fond of telling: some years earlier a company manager had phoned him to appeal for help in settling a three-week-old strike which was threatening the very future of a plant in North Lanarkshire. Smith knew the relevant trade-union organizer, and arranged a meeting between the two sides. "After an initial flurry, it was decided to get down to negotiations. I acted as chairman and I arranged for each side to have discussions with one another and then individually." Six hours later, they emerged with a two-year pay agreement. "It is not possible to draft an Act of Parliament or create a court or some other machinery to enforce good industrial relations: it cannot be done," he warned[5] – but goodwill, solid negotiation, and a forum where minds could meet could achieve a great deal.

On his first day as a Cabinet minister, which happened to be a Sunday, Smith evidently got straight down to the business of talking off the record to lobby journalists. Two pieces appeared in Monday morning's newspapers which bore that distinct look of having come direct from the minister's mouth. "The CBI can expect a rougher ride from Mr Smith," forecast Simon Hoggart in *The Guardian*. "Mr Smith has told friends that he is impatient with the attitude of the CBI and hopes to persuade it rapidly to adopt a much more positive line on industrial democracy." And similarly, in *The Financial Times*, Elinor Goodman predicted "a somewhat less sympathetic hearing" for industry, "when arguing against the government's proposed legislation on industrial democracy".

First, there was the less controversial business of tightening up the law on share dealing. The main purpose of the Companies Bill which Smith presented to the Commons a week after taking office was to make insider share dealing a criminal offence. Insider dealing was the special form of sharp practice made famous by the Boesky case in the USA, and the resulting Hollywood movie *Wall Street*. It was already banned under Stock Exchange rules, but only recently had it been taken seriously enough for legislation. Even then, there were Tory MPs who defended the practice on the grounds that there was nothing wrong with making money out of being well informed. However, neither this nor the various other clauses in the Bill, which altered the definition of a public limited company and tinkered with the ground rules, faced serious opposition. Smith evidently believed he had an agreement with John Nott to allow the Bill to be hurried through Parliament before the election – in which case he could have claimed credit for being the minister who made insider dealing a crime. But as time ran out, the Tories put a stop to it, then within eighteen months introduced their own Bill, which was identical to Smith's in every important respect. For years John Smith had to face taunts from Tory ministers that they had made insider share dealing illegal after the Labour government had done nothing about it. It is open to question, however, whether the new law, which produced a grand total of seventeen convictions over the next eleven years, ever made much difference. "It was regarded as a pretty bold thing to do at all, but I don't think there has been much energy and vigour put into enforcing it," says Smith. A week later he was steering another uncontroversial piece of legislation out of dry dock. The Merchant Shipping Bill contained measures to limit oil spillages and similar accidents at sea, such as making it an offence to be drunk in charge of an oil tanker.

Another side of Smith's job was to boost British exports. He was plunged straight into the highly complex set of international trade talks known as the Tokyo Round. And when the Labour whips were satisfied that they could allow a minister out of their sight for a few days without risking the immediate downfall of the government, he was able to travel. In January 1979 he made a whirlwind tour of Singapore, Malaysia and Thailand with John Chalmers, head of the Boilermakers' Union. The *Daily Mail* claimed that he also went accompanied by a joke book which his mother-in-law had given him, because his speeches were just not funny enough, but the story is apocryphal, says Smith: "My mother-in-law, who is dead now, wouldn't know a joke if it sat up and bit her."[6] In March it was Czechoslovakia. In April it would have been Egypt, but by then the country was deep into an election.

The government's chances of survival had worsened by the day, as the combination of price rises and wage restraint produced the wave of strikes known as the Winter of Discontent. In January 1979 John Smith was forced to admit to the Commons that British exports appeared to have fallen by a third because of stoppages at the ports. At about the same time, he warned the Cabinet that Margaret Thatcher would probably call for harsher laws to curb strikes, including a ban on secondary picketing.

The devolution legislation which he had so meticulously guided through Parliament fell apart in February. Its destruction was attributable to thirty-four Labour MPs, backed by the Tories, who had inserted a last-minute clause into the Scotland Bill the previous spring, against John Smith's objections, laying down that at least 40 per cent of eligible voters must endorse devolution for the Act to become law. Scotland's referendum produced a majority for devolution, but on a small turnout. The Act which had absorbed so much time and effort was wiped out. It was this failure which motivated the Scottish Nationalists to vote with the Tories when the tottering Callaghan administration faced a vote of "no confidence" at the end of March 1979.

The final days of the Parliament had their farcical side. The vote was clearly going to be close, making every uncommitted MP from the political fringe a potentially valuable convert. Two Northern Ireland politicians who normally rallied to the government – the SDLP leader Gerry Fitt and Frank Maguire, the independent member for Fermanagh and South Tyrone – had had enough, and resolved to abstain. On the big day, 28 March, John Smith, Roy Hattersley and Ann Taylor, a government whip, made a desperate effort to make good this loss by shutting themselves away in a private room with two wavering Ulster Unionists, hoping to cajole them into supporting the government. They complained about the price of food in Northern Ireland. Roy Hattersley, who was Secretary of State for Prices and Consumer Protection, offered a government inquiry, which they accepted. But they wanted the promise in writing. John Smith settled down to type out the agreement on the spot, while Ann Taylor provided the pen to sign it. Unfortunately, she had a penchant for keeping pens of an unusual colour in her handbag and, as luck would have it, this one contained green ink, which was not a good colour to put before an Ulster Unionist. Luckily, another pen was found. It is a verifiable fact that in the "no confidence" vote eight Ulster Unionists – including Enoch Powell, Ian Paisley and James Molyneaux – voted with the Conservatives, but John Carson, from North Belfast, and Harold McCusker, from Armagh, backed the government. One more vote, and it really would have been a historic piece of wheeler-dealing. Instead, it was just not quite enough. The "no confidence" motion was lost by one vote, and the country was pitched into the election which, as everyone knows, took Margaret Thatcher into Downing Street.

This defeat was less traumatic for the Labour Party than others which followed. On the whole, they had seen it coming. They now expected to see the Thatcher government dragged into the same economic morass which had sunk theirs, and to be back in power in four or five years. Their confidence was borne out by opinion polls showing Mrs Thatcher as the most unpopular Prime Minister since records began. It is often forgotten how poor the Tories' chances of survival looked in the three years before the Falklands crisis.

The elections to the Shadow Cabinet gave no hint of the internal upheaval which lay ahead, with Denis Healey topping the poll and Roy Hattersley in fourth place. Tony Benn caused a surprise by deciding not to stand, but when he heard the news John Smith probably reacted as David Owen did – by thinking that it improved his own chances of success. Indeed, it was decisive. Combined with the fact that Shirley Williams had lost her seat in the Commons, it created just enough room for Smith to slip in, coming twelfth in the contest for twelve places. So he began an extraordinary record of being elected to the Shadow Cabinet for thirteen consecutive years. After 1987, he and Roy Hattersley – who, as the Party's deputy leader, did not need to stand for re-election – were the only survivors of the original twelve.

Smith was told to keep his portfolio as principal spokesman on trade and combine it with prices and consumer affairs. He went straight back into action, arguing the same case with the same courteous persistence, but from the opposite side of the aisle. Very soon, he had two major issues before him. One was British Airways. The Conservatives had not said that they proposed to privatize it, either in their manifesto or during the election campaign. Smith's deputy, Stanley Clinton Davis, had none the less forecast that they might, and was denounced in the *Daily Mail* for telling a "dirty lie". Late in July 1979 – just before the summer recess, and on a Friday morning, when fewer MPs are about – John Nott arrived in the Commons to announce that the nation's airline would be sold off.

When the legislation began its journey through the Commons in the following November, John Smith took what would be a familiar Labour line as one privatization followed another. Assets owned by the public were to be put up for sale cheap, by a government "motivated by an attitude of malevolent spite to the public sector".[7] It was a "fraud on the public", an "outrageous and monstrous proposition".[8] No doubt many of the speculators lining up for their cheap shares imagined they would be able to resell them at a huge profit when Labour renationalized the airline. Well, John Smith had news for them: "The Labour Party intends to reacquire those assets, because it believes in the public ownership of a national airline. Those who bought the shares should not expect compensation for unjustified capital enrichment at the expense of the British taxpayer. It is only fair that a proper warning should be given."[9] Actually, the privatization was held up by the airline's massive losses, which it took until 1983 to turn into a profit, and an awkward anti-trust suit facing it in the American courts, which President Reagan quashed in 1984. The sell-off was still a live political issue when Smith became trade spokesman again that year, but by then Labour was no longer greeting each privatization with a pledge to renationalize without compensation.

The Conservative manifesto had also said nothing about abolishing the Price Commission, the only formal government instrument for keeping any control over the price of food and other necessities while inflation was rampant. By law, large firms had to notify the Commission of any planned price increase, and the Secretary of State had the power to delay those which he thought unjustified. Sally Oppenheim, the Tory spokeswoman on prices, had had a bad moment partway through the campaign when she was directly asked, on television, whether the Commission would be abolished, and plainly did not want to answer. In July 1979, as inflation climbed to 16 per cent, came an announcement that it was being abolished. This led John Smith into one of the most inaccurate predictions of his life. The disappearance of the Commission would be a "milestone", he told the Commons, adding: "As prices soar in the unchecked scandal which their policies promote, so will the justified resentment of the public increase to a stage at which they will speedily sweep this government from office."[10]

This was not as laughable when it was uttered, in July 1979, as it sounded three years later. When the Bill abolishing the Price Commission came before the Commons early in 1980, John Smith itemized the dire effects which the arrival of Conservatism had had on the lives of ordinary consumers: inflation up from 10.1 per cent to 17.2 per cent in eight months; VAT up from 8 per cent to 15 per cent; the mortgage rate up from 12 per cent to 15 per cent, domestic gas prices scheduled to go up at least 27 per cent, and other huge increase due in rates, council rents, charges for school meals, school buses, and NHS prescriptions. "The situation is rather like one in which the fire brigade arrives at the blaze . . . and instead of pouring water on the flames, it pours on petrol. . . . The government are deliberately increasing price inflation."[11]

The Bill which abolished price controls was – incidentally – called the Competition Bill, it being the government's strategy that over the long term, competition in a free market would reduce inflation. However, when *The Times* and *The Sunday Times* were bought in 1981 by Rupert Murdoch, who already owned Britain's biggest-circulation national and Sunday newspapers, it was John Smith who was left arguing the case for more competition. He wanted that sale and Lonrho's subsequent acquisition of *The Observer* referred to the Monopolies and Mergers Commission, one of whose tasks, in theory, was to limit the concentration of media ownership. "One wonders what is the point in having on the statute book any purported system of control it is so easily avoided," he complained, in a letter published in – of all places – *The Times*.[12]

Then, the Shadow Secretary of State for Trade, Prices and Consumer Protection went quiet. In December 1980, his standing in the Party was still high: he came eleventh, with 112 votes, in the Shadow Cabinet elections when David Owen created a vacancy by refusing to stand in protest at Labour's rapid drift to the left. Neil Kinnock slipped in at twelfth place. One of Scotland's newspapers forecast that Smith would be party leader by the time he was fifty – that is, by 1988 – "not because he is the man most people want, but as the man who has no enemies".[13] The following year his vote dropped by just one: to 111. He could, perhaps, begin to be grateful that so many Labour MPs remembered he was there at all. After February 1981 John Smith made just two speeches to the Commons: one opposing the government's decision to abolish the registry of company names; the other a subdued appeal to them to give up the idea of privatizing British Airways. That was on 16 November 1981. The next time he spoke in a Commons debate was on 14 December 1982 – an unprepared speech made just after he had been given a new job, as Shadow Energy Secretary. It was the only occasion in the whole of 1982 when he involved himself in a Commons debate.

Apart from that, the man whose whole reputation was based on his formidable performances in Parliament would turn up on the fortnightly occasions when the Trade Secretary, John Nott, faced questions in the Commons; he did his constituency work, occasionally submitted written questions, and was on hand for the important votes. But if Parliament was missing him, the Scottish courts were not. In other years he did court cases only in August and September, during the long summer recess, just to keep his hand in. In the early 1980s he took on much more. In December 1982, for example, he and Ross Harper flew to Germany to defend two British airmen facing court martial. The case was almost tragic – one man had had a close brush with death; but since he escaped unhurt, it was more like a rollicking farce. The lawyers must have had a tough time keeping a straight face.

In the course of their duties in Germany, the pilots and navigators from RAF 92 Squadron were required to take their Phantom fighter aircraft out on mock exercises, hunting German airspace for military aircraft. When they spotted a target, they were expected to sweep down on it and, at the right moment, press the firing button, and take an instant photograph. Every aircraft correctly captured on film counted as a "kill". However, a new commander decided that it was time for his men to train with live missiles. The safety manual, or "Noddy Guide", said that there should be safety devices attached to the missiles, and a piece of red masking tape over the firing button to remind the pilot that his aircraft was equipped to kill. Unfortunately, it was technically impossible to fit safety gear in a Phantom, and at the last minute catch-22 came into operation: the store at the RAF base was completely out of red tape.

Flight Lieutenant Roy Lawrence and his navigator, Flight Lieutenant Alistair Inverarity, had been in the air for only ten minutes when they spied a passing Jaguar. The "kill" took only a matter of seconds. Alas, in that short time the pilot quite forgot that his aircraft was loaded, and with a cry of "tally-ho", he pressed the button and fired a live sidewinder. Thus it was that a fellow British pilot was making his way peaceably back to RAF Wildenrath, his day's exercises done, when a sudden seismic jolt went through his aircraft, knocking it off its path and sending it careering downwards, its radio and controls dead and its instruments going berserk. Under the circumstances, he followed the training manual and ejected. As he floated through the air on the end of his parachute, seven million pounds' worth of metal and high technology met the ground and exploded. When the shaken pilot had limped back to the mess, he was greeted by the men who had almost killed him with the words: "What can we say? We're desperately sorry." With that, they bought a barrel of beer.

The RAF did not see it as a matter for celebration, and court-martialled the two crewmen. Smith, as defence counsel for the pilot, put heavy emphasis on the piece of tape which should have masked the firing button. (Incidentally, in a court martial a civilian lawyer acting for the defence is temporarily given the same rank as the prosecutor; consequently, he was Group Captain John Smith for a month.) His client was found guilty of negligence, which was a mark on his record but need not seriously affect his military career. It could have been a lot worse.

By now Smith was no longer acting as a junior counsel, but was virtually doing the work of a QC, without collecting quite the massive fees a QC can command. Generally, it takes longer for a Scottish advocate to become a QC than it does for an English barrister. In Scotland, ten years is fast, fifteen is about average, and there are no "political" QCs, as there are in England: politicians who practise law have to prove themselves in the courts like any other advocate. Smith took silk in April 1983, sixteen years after he was first called to the Bar. The cases he handled usually involved a corpse found in a Glasgow street, and a murder charge, but without the mystery of a detective story or the sordid glamour of organized crime. Typically, a fight would have started over some trivial insult after too much alcohol had been consumed on a Friday or Saturday night; someone was dead, but of the three young men on murder charges, only one struck the fatal blow; Smith would be trying to prove that his client had not been "art or part" nor "acting in concert". This was the routine end of criminal advocacy. One case which might have made interesting reading had it come to court was a libel claim against the now defunct *Sunday Standard*, which had accused the Scottish Labour Party's General Secretary, Helen Liddell, of planning secretly to defect to the SDP. Donald Dewar offered to be her solicitor, and lined up John Smith as her advocate, but she decided not to take the financial risk of going to court.

As a QC, Smith cost more but took fewer cases than he had taken as an advocate. His new status, though, allowed him a part in the biggest gangland murder trial in Scottish legal history. There was a terrible irony that the writer Bill Forsyth had just completed a gentle, funny film called *Comfort and Joy*, about guys fighting over pitches to park their ice-cream vans, when the real ice-cream war burst into the news. Nine members of a family named Doyle were asleep at 29 Bankend Street, in the east end of Glasgow, one night in April 1984, when hoodlums doused their door with petrol and set it alight. The father, three brothers, a sister and her eighteen-month-old baby died in the fire. At the time, it was the worst single crime the Scottish police had ever had to investigate; only once, in the case of a serial killer who picked off his victims at different times, had anyone in Scotland ever been charged with so many murders. The police were able to make a relatively quick arrest, because so many people in Glasgow knew who was behind the trouble involving the Doyle family. A gangster named Thomas "T.C." Campbell – who denies the crime to this day – was sentenced to life, with a recommendation that he serve at least twenty years. An associate named Joseph Steel also drew a life sentence.

These murders were the climax of three violent years, during which T.C. Campbell and his gang had used threats and occasional criminal damage to drive other ice-cream vendors off the territory which they were claiming for themselves. Campbell's operators, who included most of his relatives, had the added advantage that they were able to sell their ice-cream at below the normal price, which must have helped him to keep public opinion on his side. He had worked out that an ice-cream van was a good point from which to deal in drugs, stolen liquor and cigarettes, and launder hot money. In 1982–83 Campbell's team drove rival vans out of the Carntyne and Haghill districts of Glasgow. The city's biggest ice-cream van operators, the Marchetti Brothers, claimed that they had lost £15,000 worth of business, and that eighteen of their forty drivers had been threatened. In 1984 the situation promised to get worse: the gangsters moved into Garthemlock district, where George Marchetti had started up his business twenty years earlier. Determined to stand their ground this time, the Marchettis decided to increase the number of their vans in the area from two to three, and hired an eighteen-year-old, Andrew "Fat Boy" Doyle, to drive the third. The youth must have had steady nerves. His presence was a direct affront to Campbell's reputation as the hardest thug in Glasgow. He endured a series of threats, including bullets fired through the windscreen of his van, before meeting a horrible death in the fire which engulfed his parents' home.

John Smith's client at the subsequent trial was T.C. Campbell's brother-in-law, Thomas Lafferty, known as "The Shadow" for the devoted way he hung around his leader. He was not implicated in the arson attack, but was charged with attempted murder of Doyle and a fifteen-year-old girl who had been in his ice-cream van on the occasion when shots were fired at it. Lafferty had had a criminal record since the age of nine. He and Campbell had been tried but acquitted in 1980 on a charge of aiding the escape of three Glasgow gangsters who broke out of the top-security Barlinnie Prison. Smith's line of defence was to build up a picture of Lafferty as a chronic drunkard who was too unreliable to be used as a hit man by any self-respecting gangster. It worked quite well: Lafferty was acquitted of attempted murder, convicted of the lesser charge of "assault with intent to endanger life", and sentenced to three years.

Defending murderers and other such villains did not bother Smith. The case which caused him the greatest personal anxiety, curiously, was one in which he liked the defendant and believed he should be acquitted:

> "I remember defending a boy of eighteen, who was charged with quite a serious offence, and was just on the edge of going to university. He had been involved in a fight. He had been in a school party, and they stopped at a place in North Lomondside, and the local crowd just jumped on the children. In the course of the struggle, a guy attacked him with a steel knife. He took the knife off his assailant, but got back with it and quite seriously injured him. He was charged with this quite serious offence. He was a terribly honest boy, and he wasn't a great witness either, but actually he got acquitted. I remember worrying about that case more than any other, because it was a very heavy responsibility."[14]

There is, of course, a simple explanation of the fact that John Smith, the advocate, was so busy at this particular time, while the politician was doing so little. These were the years of Labour's civil war.

8
Troubled Times 1979–83

The bitter warfare of 1979–83 spilled over from the old familiar battle-grounds of state ownership, nuclear weapons, Europe, and the alliance with the USA into a new, fiercely fought and still unresolved dispute over how the Labour Party should organize its own affairs. The concept of the Party as a machine designed to win elections and soften capitalism's hard edges by using ready-made state machinery was being challenged. There was a long battle over whether party policy should be the preserve of its establishment – its MPs and municipal leaders, and trade-union officials accustomed to settling their affairs over beer and sandwiches at Downing Street – or whether the street politics of militant shop stewards, CND marchers and diverse pressure groups should have a share in decision-making.

The new left was quite different from traditional Tribunites like Michael Foot and Neil Kinnock. Foot may have been an old rebel who went marching from Aldermaston at the weekend, but during the working week he believed absolutely in the sovereignty of Parliament. He recoiled from the idea that an elected government, even a government as unpopular as Margaret Thatcher's, should be challenged and defeated outside the House of Commons. And since most MPs felt as he did, the Bennites introduced a number of strategic changes to party rules, each intended to weaken the influence of the parliamentary Party and strengthen the political activists on trade-union and constituency party committees. The two biggest reforms were mandatory reselection, under which sitting Labour MPs effectively had to reapply for their jobs, once a Parliament, to the general management committee of their local Party; and the new system for electing the party leader and deputy leader, through an electoral college of trade unions, with 40 per cent of the vote, and MPs and constituency Parties, with 30 per cent each. Another, which caused less comment but was no less important, was to keep the Party's National Executive in control of the contents of the election manifesto.

During a hiatus at the end of 1980 – when the Party had been committed to holding a special conference to revise the rules, but before the celebrated Wembley Conference had taken place – Jim Callaghan resigned, so that his successor could be chosen by the Parliamentary Labour Party alone. Since Tony Benn refused to participate, it came down to a contest between Michael Foot and Denis Healey. Though he was fond of Foot, Smith threw himself into the Healey campaign. But it was a symptom of the demoralization of the Labour right that even when the vote was restricted to MPs, the older, weaker and less experienced candidate won.

The intellectual weakness of the right and the new organizational muscle of the left both arose from the apparent collapse of the economic theories of John Maynard Keynes. Since the thirties, it had been assumed that recession and unemployment could be overcome by an increase in public spending. When Labour had come into office in 1974, however, Britain was already gripped by a previously unheard-of combination of falling output and rising prices, made far worse by the oil crisis. Under the conditions of the IMF loan, in 1976, the government had no choice but to turn on its own natural supporters by imposing public spending cuts and holding down pay awards. There had been other left-wing rebellions against the Labour Party leadership, most notably in Aneurin Bevan's heyday in the 1950s, but in those days the leader could always rely on the block votes of big unions to keep the Party's annual conference and National Executive under control. In the late 1980s a number of big trade unions like the TGWU and NUPE had come into direct conflict with the Labour government, and willingly cast their block votes with the left. In addition, the Party suffered a haemorrhage of its traditional social democratic support. At the top, the right-wing leadership split between those like Callaghan, Healey and Hattersley on the one hand, who believed they had no choice but to arrive at some form of compromise with the left to hold the Party together, and David Owen and his allies on the other, for whom any deal was a sell-out. During 1981, four former Cabinet ministers and twenty-six sitting Labour MPs boldly went to break the mould of British politics by forming the Social Democratic Party. During that year, the Liberal–SDP Alliance overtook Labour in the opinion polls. At one point, seemingly, half the voters in the land were Alliance voters.

The founders of the SDP had been John Smith's natural allies. Their sense of their own existence as a distinct group originated from the rebellion over EC membership nearly ten years earlier. Smith had more in common with them than with most of the MPs who remained in the Labour Party, but he was never tempted to join them, and was never asked. "I was scandalised by their behaviour," says Smith. "Dreadful and disloyal."[1] "My fulminations could be heard before they got near my room."[2] At the time he rubbished the idea, dear to David Owen, that the

SDP was a new force in politics, distinct from the Liberals. They were, he claimed: "An appendage of the Liberal Party . . . packaged to try to attract Labour votes."[3] Like the Bennite left they were also, in his view, an English phenomenon. The overwhelming view in Scotland's right-wing Labour establishment was in favour of staying and fighting.

Smith also denies that he ever consciously considered throwing up politics altogether to take up the quieter and more lucrative profession which was available to him as a Scottish QC. The signs are, though, that the thought could not have been far from the back of his mind. January 1981, when the special Wembley Conference erupted in factional warfare, was the lowest point of his political career:

> "I remember walking away from the Wembley Conference with my heart in my boots. I am normally a fairly optimistic practical sort of chap, but I was really quite dismayed by the fights within the Party. Some colleagues enjoy them, but I don't, seeing the overall damage that they do. I don't think I made a conscious decision to withdraw from politics. Trade was not a terribly demanding portfolio. But the Party was in such a mess. I may have done that subconsciously."[4]

In addition to the thousands lost to the SDP, there were many others who either quit, or wound down their political activity as John Smith did. Another example – which went unnoticed because it was further down the pecking order – was Peter Mandelson, a researcher at the House of Commons and Lambeth councillor, who went off for three years to be a television producer. Despite these losses, however, the number of paid-up individual party members appears to have increased between 1978 and 1981, in so far as it could be measured accurately.[5] Recruits flooded in from the left, from the Trotskyite groups formed with such high hopes during the Vietnam marches of the late 1960s, whose members were now passing thirty and less convinced of the imminence of revolution; from the feminist movement; from the anti-fascist campaign of the late 1970s, more recently from CND; and from an assortment of causes and single-issue campaigns. Two well-known individual examples were Tariq Ali, the 1960s student leader who applied to join in 1981, but was barred after the NEC had intervened; and Peter Tatchell, a gay rights campaigner who joined in 1978, and was the candidate in the disastrous Bermondsey by-election of 1982.

Tony Benn gave the left its most intelligent and determined parliamentary leader since Bevan. In April 1981 Benn decided to test the new rules by running for the deputy leadership of the Party against the incumbent, Denis Healey. The contest dominated the news for six months. "Terrible", Smith calls it, although once it started, he became involved again as a leading organizer of the Healey campaign. Once again he found himself embroiled in an argument with Tam Dalyell, who owed Benn a personal debt for an earlier act of kindness and was insisting that he would discharge it by voting for him. Smith, too, could never bring himself to dislike Benn, and was also in his debt, but to vote for him was another matter. "Don't you realize he could win!" he exclaimed – but to no avail. Dalyell's mind was made up.

Healey's narrow escape is usually seen as the moment when the advance of the Bennite left was halted. It was more a stalemate than an outright win, though. There was a more significant development a year later, when a group of trade-union fixers organized by the MP John Golding used the block vote to recapture control of the NEC. They removed Benn from his power base as chairman of its Home Affairs Committee, and took him out of Parliament for nine months by ensuring that he was consigned to a marginal seat after the 1983 boundary changes. Effective leadership of the "extra-parliamentary" left, as it was occasionally known, then passed to civic leaders like Ken Livingstone, and to Arthur Scargill. As a movement, it was finally defeated in 1985 when the miners went back to work and the GLC gave up its threat to defy the law by not setting a rate.

Even if he had agreed with every line of the manifesto – which he certainly did not – Smith's star would have been eclipsed anyway in the stormy years 1979 to 1983. The activists' democracy which the Labour Party almost became simply did not suit his temperament. Sometimes duty required him to speak to crowded mass meetings of excitable party supporters. Those who heard him for the first time on one of these occasions would have been astonished if they had been told they were listening to a future party leader. It was not the content of his speeches – he could always find enough to say to avoid offence to his own conscience and to his audience; it was the manner of his delivery which was out of place. Perfect for Parliament or the courtroom, it was a dampener at any rally. Tony Benn, Neil Kinnock, Michael Foot and Denis Healey were crowd-pleasers in their different ways, who knew how to project their voices and use repetition, crescendo, arm gestures, and jokes to keep their audience bubbling. John Smith would deliver his lines in quiet, unflamboyant phrases, his body stiffly to attention, his remarks factual and sensible, his sentiments moderate and unexciting. The most he would ever do by way of emphasis was to raise his eyebrows, making his eyes look enormous behind his spectacles. This was a man who would let the Revolution pass him by.

There were times, inevitably, when he could not avoid direct questions about some of the nooks and crannies of Labour Party policy which he was reluctant to acknowledge. In Parliament, as a frontbench spokesman, he could stick to energy policy and leave others to deal with nationalization, or Labour's intention to remove Britain from the Common Market. In long interviews it was harder to ignore contentious issues; consequently, he gave very few in this period. However, a small left-wing magazine, now defunct, was able to record Smith's thoughts on Labour's defence policy three months before the 1983 general election. His answers are worth quoting in full. On being asked whether he thought unilateral nuclear disarmament was a vote-winner, he replied: "The proponents on both sides will probably become even more strongly convinced of their cause, but the effect on the marginal voters I find very difficult to predict. I *do* feel, though, that on this issue above all others, politicians should decide their policies on what they think is right rather than on what they think is popular." Was that an endorsement of one of Labour's central symbolic policies, or not? Answers, as they say, on a postcard.

Smith was also asked whether he believed a Labour government really would go ahead and clear Britain of nuclear weapons, as promised. He replied that it would, as a move to trigger "more general disarmament" by the superpowers. He added: "There is no great moral gulf between a unilateralist and a multilateralist if they are both genuine disarmers. What is needed is good timing so that a unilateral initiative has the maximum multilateral effect." He gave President Reagan's hawkishness and the "increasing sanity" of the Kremlin's elderly leadership as reasons why the timing might be right. "What everyone in the Labour Party is agreed on is that we must take some risks for peace. I myself believe that Britain cannot afford to be, nor is there a good reason for being, an independent nuclear power."[6] The overall impression is of a man struggling to put the best gloss he can on a policy he would not have chosen to defend.

John Smith's North Lanarkshire seat was far removed from the seething centres of socialist radicalism. This was just as well for Smith, because there were English MPs well to his left who were deselected by their local parties for being too middle-of-the-road. The story goes that the controversy raging over black sections in the mid 1980s, surprisingly, was raised at a party meeting on John Smith's patch. There, white racism was not as immediate an issue as the divide between Protestants and Catholics in Airdrie and Coatbridge. Someone suggested that if the Party was to have black sections there could be orange and green sections too, and the discussion got no further. It was a different world from Hackney.

An old dispute which had refused to go away was over the deselection of the former Education Secretary, Reg Prentice, by his local Party in north-east London in 1975. The case had attracted weeks of intense media coverage, which included exposure of the personal life of one of the constituency officers. It became the first big test case in the battle over whether Labour MPs should be answerable to their local parties, or to the whips' office. At a crucial point in the dispute, Prentice's local Party was sent a letter signed by 180 Labour MPs, including a dozen Cabinet ministers and thirty-five other ministers, praising his achievements in government. John Smith, of course, was one of the signatories. However, Prentice did a singular disservice to those who had defended him by joining the Tory Party, returning to the Commons as a Tory MP in 1979 and becoming a minister in Thatcher's government. As relations between MPs and their local parties reached crisis point, Prentice served as visible, living evidence for those who wanted the opinions of active party members to be taken more seriously. It was, says Smith, "appalling behaviour".

A publication much talked about in party circles at the time was *How to Select or Reselect Your MP* by Chris Mullin, editor of *Tribune*, a lay members' guide to the complicated rules for reselection. What gave it notoriety was an appendix which encouraged party members to find out how their MPs had voted on ten occasions when the Labour Party had not been united, because there had been either a free vote or a rebellion. The authors did not lay down what was the right or wrong way to have voted, but the guide was received as a rough-and-ready guide to the ideological correctness of individual Labour MPs. The Chief Whip, Michael Cocks, was – to put it mildly – furious.[7]

The pamphlet is one way to measure how correct Smith was on issues like Europe, defence spending, wage restraint, the House of Lords, the Labour government's decision to expel the journalists Philip Agee and Mark Hosenball, sanctions against Rhodesia, the Prevention of Terrorism Act, and abortion. The answer is: not very. Some allowance has to be made for the fact that he was a government minister, and consequently had to support the Labour government when there was a whip. Discounting those occasions, he achieved a correctness rating of one out of five. In May 1980 he was one of 142 Labour MPs who turned out to vote for a Bill, introduced by the backbench MP Jeff Rooker, to abolish the House of Lords – which, of course, was quashed by the Tories. Inside the Cabinet, he had sided with the left on this issue against Callaghan, who refused to include it in the 1979 election manifesto. Otherwise, almost everything Smith had ever said or done could have made him a suitable target for deselection. Instead, he was faced with a painless choice between two safe seats. Boundary changes introduced on the eve of the 1983 election had carved up his North Lanarkshire seat and neighbouring Airdrie and Coatbridge, creating Monklands East, which took Airdrie, a bit of Coatbridge, and mining villages nearby; and Monklands West, based principally on Coatbridge. (By the way, there is no such town as Monklands, though in ancient times the area had more than its share of monks.)

Labour's Scottish headquarters was keen to rearrange Lanarkshire's political map so that each new seat was allocated to a sitting MP. James Dempsey, the long-serving MP for Airdrie and Coatbridge, had recently died, and his place had been taken by Tom Clarke, who was born and bred in Coatbridge and had served on its council for almost twenty years. The logical outcome was that he inherited Monklands West, while Smith took over Monklands East. It was fractionally less solidly Labour than Clarke's seat, but Smith won with a 9,799 majority and over 51 per cent of the vote, even in the disastrous 1983 election.

He was also protected from controversy, to some extent, by Michael Foot's decision to appoint him Shadow Energy Secretary in December 1982 – part of a last-minute reshuffling of Labour's economic team. The Party had got itself into a position where it was committed to an election manifesto to which a majority of the Shadow Cabinet and the NEC were now opposed. Its economic section – which included plans to renationalize everything the Tories had privatized, to introduce planning agreements, to promote co-operatives and to extend state ownership – had been drafted when Tony Benn chaired the NEC's Home Affairs Committee, and endorsed by party conference at the same time as the right, under John Golding, took over control of the NEC. The industry spokesman then was Stan Orme, a member of the Tribunite "soft left", whom Foot had insisted on appointing, in preference to Roy Hattersley. With an election drawing near, and Labour's support perilously low, Foot was persuaded to introduce the more reassuringly right-wing Merlyn Rees, the former Home Secretary, as co-ordinator for trade, industry and energy over Stan Orme's head. (At the same time, Solidarity members in the Shadow Cabinet ganged up to prevent Neil Kinnock from joining the economic team as employment spokesman in place of Eric Varley.)

The move suited Smith. It put him in a slightly more senior post, handling a subject he knew exceptionally well – rather better than the government's new Energy Secretary, Nigel Lawson. It was also one area where he happily agreed with the Labour left that coal, electricity, gas and oil should be owned by the state, and consumer prices should be kept down to a level at which even the poorest could afford to pay their fuel bills. With complete conviction, he could berate the government for increasing electricity prices by 84 per cent in three years, causing 100,000 homes a year to be disconnected; for forcing up gas prices and compelling the gas board to sell off its North Sea oil interests; and for dismembering the British National Oil Corporation; and he could earn the applause of the left wing while he was about it. After a long absence he came back in style, catching Nigel Lawson out for making two mutually contradictory statements in the same month over a sum of £30 million which had been moved from one account to another during the process of breaking up BNOC. Lawson's deputy, Hamish Gray, tried to come to his rescue by pointing out that what he had done was permitted under John Smith's own Petroleum and Submarine Pipelines Act, a remark which produced a withering reply: "Because Parliament gives power to a Minister, Parliament is presumed to have endorsed all the stupid uses of the powers that ministers will get up to. That is a bald proposition, even from a Minister of State."[8]

Later, he was to be heard at full throttle attacking the sale of state-owned oil interests as "public asset-stripping on a scale never seen before", and the ministers behind it for being motivated by "an obsessive need to ingratiate themselves with the Prime Minister by privatising anything within reach". As for Lawson, Smith claimed: "He has left our oil policy in ruins through the wicked, stupid, senseless destruction of the British National Oil Corporation."[9] He had another advantage, besides his safe seat in rural Scotland: he was a highly thought-of member of a well-organized group in the Parliamentary Labour Party. The Manifesto group, formed by pro-Common Market MPs in the 1970s, and its adjunct outside Parliament, the Campaign for Labour Victory, fell apart because of the rift between those who planned to leave to form the SDP, and those who proposed to stay; but while it lasted, it had been highly effective in getting its approved list of candidates, like John Smith, elected to the Shadow Cabinet. Its successor, Solidarity, was launched in January 1981, with Roy Hattersley and Peter Shore as co-chairmen. Shore, in contrast to Hattersley, was a lifelong anti-marketeer – a sign that Solidarity was agnostic about the issue which had divided the Party more than any other six years earlier. At this stage it was possible, indeed, to be a member of both CND and Solidarity, whose function was to combat the advance of the left in the constituency parties, and protect MPs from deselection.

Apart from doing his bit to secure Denis Healey's re-election as deputy leader, there is no evidence that Smith became deeply involved in Solidarity. Fortunately for him, he was not called upon to get his hands dirty. Solidarity immediately accepted him into its ranks on the strength of his reputation as a parliamentary performer, and put him straight on its slate for the 1981 Shadow Cabinet elections. It was worth being on. Despite what was happening in the Party outside, Solidarity dominated the parliamentary Party by being better organized than any corresponding group on the left. As late as 1986, ten out of fifteen elected Shadow Cabinet members were from the Solidarity slate. Roy Hattersley says:

> "One of John's great strengths, and one of John's tactics, has always been to be on the right side, but not deeply involved in the right side. He was always on our slate for the Shadow Cabinet. We naturally thought of him as one of us. I can't remember whether he was on the committee of Solidarity. If he was on the committee of Solidarity, he either didn't come very much or didn't say anything that I remember."[10]

In June 1983 a much-depleted collection of Labour MPs came limping back, shattered by their worst general election defeat in half a century. Their numbers, which had already fallen by fifty at the previous election, had now dropped by another sixty to 209, the lowest figure for either of the main parties since the Second World War. Considering that Labour's portion of the vote had plummeted to less than 28 per cent of the total, they could consider themselves lucky to have so many MPs. The immediate question was not whether Labour could ever win a general election again, but whether it could survive as the official opposition. Within what remained of the Party, however, the Solidarity group was proportionately stronger. Its strength was generally in old Labour heartlands like Scotland and the North-East of England, which had turned out to vote Labour regardless of what the rest of the country might do. Proportionately, the left had sustained more losses than the right – including Tony Benn, who was out of Parliament for nine months, and therefore out of the running when Michael Foot's resignation set off another leadership race. With Eric Heffer as the Bennites' standard-bearer, there was not a chance that they could even put up a serious challenge.

In fact, Solidarity went into the leadership race, which opened in June, with high hopes of success. Denis Healey, who was now sixty-five, was persuaded not to stand, but to nominate the younger Roy Hattersley. This time, John Smith was to be at the centre of events as Hattersley's campaign manager. When the leaders of two of the three biggest trade unions, the AUEW and GMBATU, came straight out in his support, Hattersley was convinced that he had won. But as everyone knows, he was in for a rude disappointment. The "soft left", which had played a rather sad piggy-in-the-middle role in the Healey–Benn contest, had gelled this time behind a much tougher and more appealing candidate. Neil Kinnock, only forty-one years old, had the look of a winner untainted by any association with the failings of past Labour governments. He conveyed a sense that the Party had a future as well as an unhappy past, and looked like a man for all factions who could bring the bitter disputes of the past four years to an end.

The outcome was an overwhelming victory for Kinnock, in all three sections of the electoral college. The trade unions, MPs, and constituency Labour Parties all gave a Hattersley a clear second place, but a long way behind the winner, and then made him the convincing winner of the deputy leadership contest. Both victories were decisive enough to give the Kinnock–Hattersley ticket a solid legitimacy which saw it through eight and a half years. On the whole, the partnership worked. Despite their initial rivalry, the underlying friction between them never became open enough to be a serious problem for the Party – largely because the leader's gradual shift to the right wiped out their political differences.

It might not have worked out so conveniently. When he stepped into the race, Roy Hattersley intended to win. He wanted to be Prime Minister, not deputy to a man who was ten years younger and had none of his experience in government office. In the previous three unhappy years, he had spoken often enough to Denis Healey about the miserable time he was having as Foot's deputy, and had repeated, time and again, how much brighter the Party's future would have been under Healey's leadership. The idea that he could look forward to four or five years of having John Smith or Gerald Kaufman similarly commiserating with him did not appeal at all. And in the Hattersley camp there were people who looked upon Neil Kinnock as a half-reformed left-wing troublemaker, only marginally more acceptable than Tony Benn. Moreover, Gerald Kaufman, who had topped the poll in the previous autumn's Shadow Cabinet elections, was mulling over the idea of running on the Solidarity ticket as Hattersley's deputy. In the deputy leadership stakes, however, the Campaign group was running Michael Meacher, who was a more popular and respected figure than Eric Heffer within the fast-disintegrating Bennite left, and was also – to Heffer's disgust – pitching for the centre vote by promising to vote for Neil Kinnock and be a more loyal deputy to him than Hattersley could ever be.

Despite Hattersley's optimism, John Smith read the runes correctly, and saw very early on that disaster was heading in Solidarity's direction. Kinnock's campaign had been kick-started by a public endorsement from the doyen of centre–left trade-union bosses, Clive Jenkins of ASTMS, and he was collecting support from a number of leading MPs who had voted for Benn in 1981, including Robin Cook and Frank Dobson, who were managing his campaign. There was a real possibility that Kinnock would win the leadership, and the deputy leadership would be a run-off between Meacher and Kaufman. That result would have been hard to predict. It was Smith, with John Golding, who then brokered the deal by which Kinnock and Hattersley emerged in tandem as the so-called "dream ticket". Step one was to persuade Neil Kinnock to stand for the deputy leadership, as well as the leadership, as his way of saying that he would be willing to serve under Hattersley. That part was easy. Kinnock was already confident that he would win:

> "I looked at the line-up of the votes straight away and saw that I was going to get the preponderance of the unions' votes, and CLP votes, and our target therefore amongst the PLP was to try to get a hundred. I thought: Right, I'm going to win, and I've got to conduct myself entirely on that basis. The important thing was that the whole contest should prove the point that after all the self-inflicted damage of the previous years, you could have a contest for the leadership and in the course of that, do good for the Party. I thought that the Labour Party needed bonding more than it needed anything else, and wisely – and, as I later came to understand, typically – Roy Hattersley then adopted the same attitude."[11]

Talking Hattersley round required a little more diplomacy:

> "There was about a month at the beginning of the campaign when it looked as if I was the favourite. There was a good deal of thought that the PLP wouldn't vote for Kinnock, which was wrong, because he got a majority. It was clear after the TGWU came out for him, without balloting their members, that he was going to win. Before it was clear, Neil announced that he wanted to be deputy – or that he would stand for deputy – and I remember John Smith coming to my house with John Golding, and John saying: 'It's a good ploy, it's emollient, he looks like a party servant, and you have to announce you're going to do the same.' And I said: 'I don't want to be deputy.' But Smith said: 'You're not doing it to be deputy – you're doing it to scotch this idea you only want the top job and Kinnock is a nice man who'll serve the Party in any capacity.' That's how it happened. Then, gradually, it became clear that Neil was going to win, and win substantially, and Smith talked to Cook, and Smith and Cook agreed that the best thing for the Party would be if we established the idea right from that moment onwards that it would be the two of us – whichever way round it was going to be, it was going to be the two of us. That was worked out between Cook and Smith."[12]

Says Kinnock:

> "I thought it was commendable at the time. What I didn't realize then, because I only came to know him in the course of our working together, was that Roy is a man of very generous spirit, and he was making a typical response. It meant that, though we had never sat down and discussed it together, his objective in getting the maximum amount of unity as a basis for the development of the Party was the same as mine."

Being a kingmaker does not necessarily bring rewards. Robin Cook fell out with the new leader in less than a year, and was never allowed to hold a politically sensitive job in the Shadow Cabinet until after Kinnock had gone. For John Golding, who switched to the Kinnock campaign after a few weeks as Hattersley's fixer, the pay-off was even smaller. He was attached in some undefined capacity to Kinnock's private office for a time, and given a second-rank job on the front bench, before he quit Parliament in 1984, angrily blaming Hattersley for his failure to do better.

John Smith, too, might have wondered whether his future was secure. For the first time, he had tried his luck by running for the National Executive. However, he was competing for one of the seven places filled by nominees of local constituency parties, whose delegates were still overwhelmingly from the Bennite left. The left swept the board, with Tony Benn topping the poll as usual. Smith's vote – 23,000 – was so insultingly small that he never tried his luck in an NEC election again. Then, on his first day back in Parliament later in the month, the new Energy Secretary, Peter Walker, who had been Edward Heath's campaign manager against Margaret Thatcher in 1975, warned him: "When I last took part in an election campaign in my party, I failed and was sacked from the Shadow Cabinet within twenty-four hours."[13]

The simple answer to that was that when Margaret Thatcher beat Edward Heath, she had scored an ideological victory for the Tory right. Kinnock had deliberately not set out to inflict humiliation on the social democratic right of the Party. His campaign theme was that democratic socialism had once been threatened from two sides: by the social democrats and by an intolerant, doctrinaire left wing. Since the social democrats were now outside the Party, Kinnock's argument implied that the only enemy within was the Bennite left. Former Bennites like Michael Meacher might hope that he would forge a new left-wing coalition which would finally rout the right, but he had no intention of even trying.

9
Union Matters 1983–84

As they surveyed the wreckage of the previous four years, John Smith and those like him on the right of the Party found they need not despair. The Labour Party had been badly hit, but it was already displaying an inner resilience given to it by thousands of active members who never thought of giving up, even after the worst election result they could ever remember. Within the damaged hulk of the Labour Party, the right's position was certainly better than at its nadir two years earlier. John Smith emerged from the leadership election as a more influential figure in the Labour Party than anyone who had been on the winning side. Up to now, his authority had been confined to the narrow fields which he had made into his own specialities – North Sea oil, or devolution. He soon became part of an informal inner group within the Shadow Cabinet who controlled economic policy, and steered the Party away from its dream of massive state intervention in industry.

The right had lost none of its vital trade-union base, despite the schism with the SDP. Even the electricians' union, the EETPU, which was soon to be expelled from the TUC, remained a Labour Party affiliate, delivering its block vote for the right. Other unions whose delegations had occasionally wavered, like the AUEW and NUR, were back under right-wing control. The power base of the Labour Party right was intact. The rise of Thatcherism was a threat to them, as to any other part of the left, but they were at least in a better shape to deal with it than the SDP, or the Bennite left.

The SDP's problem was that its overwhelmingly new and inexperienced membership had signed up believing they were going to be very successful, very quickly. In 1981, David Steel had told the Alliance to "prepare for government". Then there were twenty-nine SDP MPs; after the election, there were six. Psephologists studying voting patterns and polling evidence were still predicting that the Alliance had "broken the mould" of British voting habits, turning Labour into a "failed ghetto party",[1] but old hands experienced in practical politics sensed that the SDP was like a firework which had given its spectacular display and was now rapidly burning out. Margaret Beckett, for one, was convinced that it would never last, having witnessed the rise and fall of Dick Taverne's organization in Lincoln. Taverne's followers had been attracted by the prospect of rapid success, and melted away after their first defeat, whilst the Lincoln Labour Party had its core of dedicated activists who drudged onwards, undismayed, whatever the political weather. For every Labour Party member who defected to the SDP, there may have been three or four more who toyed with the possibility; but after 1983, the flow ended. Later, those who regretted leaving began to trickle back.

Within the Labour Party, the left was breaking up. It had been an uneasy grand coalition, shoved together in the late 1970s by a shared feeling that the Party was badly organized, and the government was letting down those who elected it. The Bennites were harder hit by the defeat of 1983 than any other faction in the Party, because it was their manifesto on which the campaign had been fought. They had a final fling when Smith's former boss, Eric Varley, left Parliament, creating a vacant Labour seat in Chesterfield. The local Party defiantly selected Tony Benn. Like most of the Shadow Cabinet, John Smith made an overnight visit to Derbyshire, to be seen to be doing his bit to secure Benn's return to the Commons. When that was accomplished, it turned into an anticlimax. It was almost the last important victory for the Bennite left in Parliament, or even within the Labour Party organization. Thereafter, they would spend years trying vainly to defend positions taken before 1983.

The "Kinnock" wing, or "soft left", meanwhile, was certainly gaining ground. The Shadow Cabinet elections produced a small shift to the left. Out went six members of Solidarity, through defeat or retirement. Two younger Solidarity members, John Cunningham and Giles Radice, were elected; the other four vacancies were taken by MPs who had all voted for Tony Benn in 1981, with varying degrees of enthusiasm. Only one, Eric Heffer, refused to be part of Labour's drift to the right. He lasted for only a year. The other three – Robin Cook, Michael Meacher and John Prescott – were now all Kinnock supporters. Even so, Kinnock was perched on an alarmingly small political base. The first time he entered the Shadow Cabinet room as leader of the Party, he found himself surrounded by fellow MPs of whom ten had voted for Hattersley in the leadership election, compared with five who had backed him;[2] they included an alarmingly powerful group – John Smith, Gerald Kaufman, John Cunningham, Giles Radice – sponsored by the GMBATU, whose General Secretary, John Edmonds, described Kinnock as a "T&G man surrounded by the GMB". All of them except Robin Cook were older than the new leader, and almost all had more experience in government. The Solidarity slate had taken the top four places in the Shadow Cabinet poll, and

Kinnock had no alternative but to allocate the main positions on his team, including all the main economic portfolios, to those who had been on the losing side in the leadership election.

John Smith had his best result yet in the Shadow Cabinet poll, coming fourth behind Denis Healey, Gerald Kaufman and Peter Shore. For the next nine years he never failed to make the top five, despite the notorious unpredictability of the contest. Of those in front of him, Denis Healey was not happily settling into an elder statesman role, while Peter Shore, who had unwisely contested the leadership and been humiliated, was beginning a rapid downward slide. It was the trio of Hattersley, Kaufman and Smith who wielded formidable influence in the next few years while the new leader found his feet. Similarly, on the twenty-nine-member NEC, elected the day after Kinnock's victory, there were eleven Bennites who continued to operate as a bloc until late in 1985, a Solidarity group of about twelve or thirteen, and a loose little "Kinnock" group of at most half a dozen. All the important committees were chaired by members of Solidarity. The crucial Home Affairs Committee, which had drawn up the 1983 party manifesto, was now chaired by Syd Tierney, the little-known president of the shopworkers' union USDAW. The committees which handled party matters were run by even less well-known union fixers: Ken Cure of the AUEW and Charlie Turnock of the NUR. Roy Hattersley remembers:

> "Up to 1987, there was on my side of the Party a great deal more coherence than there was thereafter. After 1987, we all became Kinnockites. Up to 1987, there were people – Charlie Turnock, Ken Cure, John Smith, me – who had all been together in previous campaigns, in Solidarity, in the leadership campaign; and we worked together much more closely than any group I have worked with since. In those days, a right-wing NEC group used to meet separately, so if John and I wanted something, we worked it out with them."[3]

Under the circumstances, it is not surprising that Labour should have said goodbye to the manifesto on which it had fought the previous election, and begun its long march back to the centre of politics. What is surprising in some ways is how little distance was covered before 1987. While the right held the strategic positions in the leadership, they were keen to conciliate. It took Roy Hattersley's principal supporters two years, at most, to discover that Neil Kinnock was a better party leader from their point of view than anyone from Solidarity could have been. His combative personality, supreme skills as a party manager and left-wing past enabled him to repress the Bennite left much more effectively than the right could ever have done.

Having started out with the look of a captive leader surrounded by older, more experienced and better-organized rivals, Neil Kinnock was subsequently able to use his management of Labour's internal affairs to achieve a dominance within the Party which would have been the envy of any of his predecessors since the 1950s. As he rose in influence, the right wing of the Tribune group, which included ambitious young members of the 1983 intake like Gordon Brown and Tony Blair, rose with him, until they were plainly in control. John Smith was almost the only luminary of the Solidarity group to survive the changeover.

By that time, the Labour Party's centre of gravity had shifted so far into the centre ground of politics that there was no discernible difference between the general political views of old Solidarity members and those who had come up through the Tribune group. John Smith's and Gordon Brown's views on economics, for example, are so close that it would be impossible to slide a sheet of paper between them. Indeed, the most drastic revision of the party programme, which did away with major symbolic policies like state ownership of strategic sections of industry and unilateral nuclear disarmament, came in the post-1987 policy review, when all the key people involved, except John Smith, were from the vastly expanded Tribune group. The difference between the groups was in their attitudes to party organization. Solidarity was staffed by a generation of politicians whose attitude to the Labour Party machine was that it was there to be called upon at election time, and should otherwise be entrusted to the guardianship of the massive block votes of right-wing trade unions. The new Kinnock-style politician took seriously the idea that the party membership must be nurtured.

John Smith's remarkable survival was aided by two qualities vital to a democratic politician: his excellence as a parliamentary performer, and sheer good luck. One crucial piece of luck was that the first job given to him by Neil Kinnock, Shadow Employment Secretary, lasted for only a year. At the time, he was pleased to be given it and even considered it a compliment. New laws to clobber Britain's trade unions were almost an annual event under the Thatcher government. That year's piece of legislation was a particularly noxious one from Labour's point of view, and Smith was glad of the chance to lead the opposition to it. What he did not know when he took up the appointment, in November 1983, was that the ideological struggle which he had hated so much while it occupied the Party was now transferring itself to the unions. Those who despised Labour's incurable "parliamentary cretinism" could take heart from the fact that there were major trade unions prepared to defy the will of Parliament, as they had done – successfully – when the Tories were in power in the early 1970s.

In Warrington, the owner of a small newspaper group, Eddie Shah, sacked six of his workers in order to avoid giving the print union, the NGA, a presence in his firm. Hundreds – indeed, thousands – of people converged on his plant every week for several months, until he went to court to have the mass picketing declared illegal. When the NGA refused to pay the first £50,000 fine, more followed, until the union was almost bankrupted by fines totalling over half a million pounds. It fell to Smith to plead in vain with government ministers to step in and make an attempt to settle the dispute. In a foretaste of the way the miners would be treated, the government acted exactly as if they wanted the dispute to escalate, so that the NGA would put itself outside the law, and the unions and the Labour Party would be tainted by some of the ugly scenes on the picket lines. Whenever Smith raised the possibility that they might conciliate, he was told he should be condemning the pickets. His line was that of course the opposition deplored violence and sympathized with its victims, but "if the government expected unbalanced, divisive and discriminatory legislation to be accepted without difficulty, they must have had a curious notion of how that legislation would be applied to industrial disputes in the real world".[4]

A few months later, Britain was embroiled in one of the longest and most contentious strikes in its troubled industrial history. Since the miners' strike was primarily a dispute over how the country should maintain its energy supplies, it fell mainly to Stan Orme, who had succeeded Smith as energy spokesman, to deal with its political ramifications; but as employment spokesman Smith was drawn directly into issues such as the government's decision to take a slice out of the social security benefits for miners' families. Anyway, the sheer scale of the social and political battle being waged outside Parliament sucked in the whole Parliamentary Labour Party, whether they liked it or not.

The party leadership had no problems with the NUM's demands on the government, since the union was simply trying to preserve an agreement made when Labour was in power in the late 1970s. Even more than other members of the front bench, John Smith utterly opposed the Tories' destruction of the coal industry. When Ian MacGregor was first appointed head of the Coal Board, Smith had warned that it would be "provocative, divisive and not in the coal industry's interest".[5] One of the first pits closed by MacGregor was Cardowan Colliery in Smith's old North Lanarkshire seat. The miners who lost their jobs included friends and colleagues he had known for more than ten years. At a rally to protest at the closure, at the height of the 1983 election campaign, he promised that a Labour government would keep the colliery open. In principle, he – and, indeed, the entire Labour Party leadership – supported the strike.

The way the strike was led was another matter. Backed by militants in the union's middle ranks, Arthur Scargill resolved not to ballot the NUM membership but to use mass pickets to try to shut down the pits in Nottinghamshire, where miners were refusing to strike. This tactic failed, and provided a pretext to involve the police and the judges. Rather than surrender to a law passed by the Tory government, the NUM leader and those closest to him set up a bizarre paper trial to try to put the union's sequestered funds beyond the reach of the courts. It was an implicit challenge to the legitimacy of Parliament. Plainly, in Scargill's conception of how the class struggle should be conducted, the Parliamentary Labour Party had only a supporting role. That was anathema to the Tribunite "soft left", as it was to Solidarity, but not to party activists on the Labour left. As they saw it, the miners were taking on the Tory Party in direct engagement, whilst the parliamentary leaders were asking them to wait for another general election. A visitor to the 1984 party conference who heard Neil Kinnock give his first formal address as party leader, and watched the debate on the miners' strike, could have been forgiven for thinking that it was Arthur Scargill's party.

While the strike continued, it was another element which weakened Neil Kinnock's authority as party leader. Even more than other Shadow Cabinet members, the Labour leader was deeply involved emotionally as a miner's son from a mining constituency, with members of his own extended family enduring the hardships of a long strike. As a younger man, he would have had no qualms about implicating the Party in the wider political agenda of the NUM president. Now he believed that the authority of Parliament and the laws it passed were unchallengeable, because Parliament was the instrument the Labour Party would use to defend those who relied upon it. "How do we help the miners? By one means. By getting a Labour government . . . that is the way to help the miners," he protested.[6] This dilemma made him the butt of jokes on the alternative comedy circuit, as the man who was welded to the fence.

After the strike was over, Kinnock demonstrated the sort of leader he would prove to be by deliberately marching into the thick of a dispute over whether Labour should promise an amnesty for miners penalized by the courts during the dispute. First, he put his own prestige on the line to cajole the NEC into rejecting the proposed amnesty, by a majority of only one. Then, contrary to normal procedure, he went before conference delegates to defend his stand in person, although he faced certain defeat. "It would be utterly dishonest now for this party to give an undertaking to anybody . . . that somehow people can come into conflict with the common law, and one day, sometime in the future, the cavalry will ride in in the form of a Labour government and pick up the tag," Kinnock told a hostile audience.[7]

One day earlier, Kinnock had executed an even more dramatic piece of political theatre with his ferocious and wholly unexpected attack on the leaders of Liverpool's Labour-controlled council. It was the start of the drive against Militant. Simultaneously, he had erected a perimeter on Labour's left wing and pronounced that anyone beyond it, like Derek Hatton, was a political enemy. He had demolished the reputation that was beginning to stick to him – that he was too nice and soft a man to control the Labour Party – opting instead to make himself a much-hated figure in parts of Liverpool and the Yorkshire coalfield. And he was making an emotive and quite painful break with his own left-wing past.

John Smith, by contrast, had no left-wing past to renounce. It was not his responsibility to sort out the Labour Party. He heartily disliked internal party feuds, and did not offer himself as a target. Therein lay the seed of a bitter complaint from within Kinnock's circle when Smith took over the party leadership: that Kinnock had been made to do the dirty work, while Smith benefited by inheriting a Party no longer racked by faction fighting.

Many of the activists who became involved in the miners' strike found it an inspiring experience, a huge social and political struggle pitting working-class families against the bourgeois state. Not Smith. He had no ear for the battle hymns of the class struggle. What he saw was a messy dispute, turning miners against each other and leaving trade-union bosses openly squabbling; and he was sure in his own mind who was benefiting from it all: the Conservative government. "They're not too unhappy when there's disorder, not too unhappy when there are disputes between trade union members and the leadership," he said. "It's all going along quite nicely, from their point of view."[8] In this sort of crisis, his special skills as a parliamentary debater were out of place.

Even the battle against the latest trade-union Bill, which was the purpose of his appointment, was being fought outside Parliament. This was a piece of legislation left behind by Norman Tebbit, who had recently moved on to greater things from his previous job as Employment Secretary. Trade unions wishing to maintain a political fund from which to make donations to the Labour Party were to be compelled to ballot their members about it once every ten years. If the members voted against, the union would be banned, effectively, from contributing to any political organization. Since 90 per cent of party funds came from the unions, the new law threatened Labour's capacity to carry on as the main opposition party. Against a government with an overall majority of 144, there was not the slightest chance of keeping the proposal out of the Statute Book.

Consequently, the only sensible defence was to accept that union members would have to be balloted eventually, and to fight hard and early for a "Yes" vote.

A campaign was set up by affiliated unions at about the time when Smith became employment spokesman. Early on, union leaders decided that the best way to save their political funds was to leave the Labour Party out of it. Instead of a grandiose campaign to save Britain's two-party democracy, they rather wisely chose to pitch their propaganda directly at their members' immediate interests. The full-time campaign organizer, Graham Allen (later Labour MP for Nottingham East), says:

> "The way we campaigned was to regenerate the unions' links with their members – a grass-roots campaign rather than a top–down media campaign. And in a sense, the campaign strategy was selling the negative. We were telling them: 'You have certain rights at the moment, because you and your trade union have a right to a political voice, which can be used in a number of ways' – and we gave examples – 'You have a voice, don't let them take your voice away'."[9]

In the circumstances, the Party did not need an employment spokesman to go barnstorming about the country decrying the threat to the Labour Party, but rather someone who could make a forensic attack on the civil rights implications of the latest Bill, as if it were a matter between the unions and the government in which Labour was only a sympathetic onlooker. At least that was the sort of job Smith did well. In his first parliamentary speech in his new job, he dived straight into a comparison between the organizational habits of the trade unions and of the Conservative Party: "It is a party in the internal process of which, as witnessed by the sickeningly deferential annual conference, democracy is only occasionally glimpsed, and yet it has the temerity to use the powers of the state to impose on the trade unions the Conservative Party's ideas of how they should be run internally."[10] Later, he compared the Tories' tender concern for Poland's free trade unions with their cheerful suppression of the rights of British workers.[11] Months later, a little to his own surprise, John Smith had cause to thank Norman Tebbit for introducing the legislation. His gratitude was dipped in irony, of course; but it was a surprising fact that the political fund ballots had turned out to be boons for Labour's trade-union affiliates. Despite early fears, based on opinion poll samples, that all but three or four unions might disaffiliate, every single one turned up at least three-to-one majorities in favour of keeping their political funds. One union which had never had a fund held a ballot, which was won by a similar margin, so the new law actually improved the Party's finances.

Once that task was accomplished, there was not much else for Smith to do. There was a fundamental argument to be had with trade-union activists over whether or not they should comply with the laws imposed on them by a hostile Tory government, but Smith was not the right man to conduct it. He believed unions should have the right to recruit members and hold strikes, and that the rules of engagement in industrial disputes should not be deliberately loaded against them. He accused Margaret Thatcher, during an eloquent denunciation of the banning of trade unions at the GCHQ intelligence centre in Cheltenham, of seeing them as "intrinsically malign".[12] As in everything else, he sought to be the voice of reason, leaning neither to one extreme nor to the other. His arguments would carry weight within unions naturally sympathetic to him, like the GMB; but in front of an audience like the National Union of Seamen, who would soon have the full force of Tory legislation thrown at them in a bitter dispute over union recognition on cross-Channel ferries, he was apt to sound like a lawyer lecturing them. The job was better done by someone who had been a shop steward, and could say that militancy had not delivered the goods. As it happened, there was John Prescott, who had started his working life as a ship's waiter and had been deeply involved in the notorious seamen's strike of 1966, who was cut out for the job.

Meanwhile, a personnel problem had developed further up the ladder. As a morale-booster, Labour decided to treat elections to the European Parliament in summer 1984 as if they were a miniature general election. There was, of course, a difficulty about persuading voters of the importance of electing Labour Euro-MPs when Labour was committed to pulling out of the Common Market, which was why campaigning in the previous Euro-elections had been desultory. This time, silently, almost imperceptibly – the policy altered. By the next election, Britain would have been in the Common Market for fifteen years, and withdrawal was no longer a realistic option, the new line went. Thus John Smith, who had been out of line with party policy in 1972, back in line in 1975, and out again in the early 1980s, found that finally he was back in the fold.

The Party's trade and industry spokesman, Peter Shore, and his deputy, Bryan Gould, had had the same experience. They were both Keynesian socialists who, through all the twists in the party line, believed that EC membership would permanently prevent the British government from intervening to reverse the country's industrial decline. For a time they had been in tune with party policy, but no longer. Three candidates had been considered for the trade and industry post in Kinnock's original Shadow Cabinet line-up: Peter Shore, John Smith – who, of course, was being tipped by the Scottish press[13] – and Robin Cook. Shore was the one Kinnock least wanted. Indeed, he did not especially want him in the

Shadow Cabinet at all. Apart from the fact that Kinnock had made up his mind that opposition to the EC was a lost cause, there was personal rivalry between the two. Shore had imagined that he was Michael Foot's right-hand man and natural successor; he had not enjoyed being supplanted by someone younger and less experienced, and was not attempting to disguise his opinion that Kinnock was not up to the job.

In 1983, however, Kinnock was in too weak a position to humiliate someone so senior. He therefore gave him two jobs: as Shadow Trade and Industry Secretary and Shadow Leader of the House – privately hoping, no doubt, that he would screw up at least one of them. A year later, Labour was planning an ambitious campaign to promote itself as the party which could revive industry and effect a dramatic drop in the unemployment figures. Even Shore's former allies in the Solidarity group could not fail to see a problem with having the campaign fronted by an old anti-marketeer who did not believe that economic regeneration was possible whilst Britain was tied by the rules of the Community. Shore obligingly dropped to sixth place in the Shadow Cabinet elections, giving Kinnock the excuse he needed to sack him from his economic job. He carried on for another three years as Shadow Leader of the House, in an isolation to rival the Lady of Shalott's, until he was ignominiously voted off the Shadow Cabinet in 1987.

That did not automatically make the job Smith's for the asking. Robin Cook had just presided over the European parliamentary election and, as the man who had also organized Kinnock's leadership campaign, was expecting promotion. If the leader had been in a strong enough position, Cook probably would have got the job; but some rather heavy pressure was applied by Solidarity members, who emphasized that John Smith would be a reassuring face for the captains of industry, with relevant Cabinet experience, whereas Cook was an unknown with a left-wing reputation. Cook had queered his own pitch, anyway, by publicly opposing Kinnock on a party matter concerning the selection of parliamentary candidates. He was punished with what amounted to demotion. The left's only gain was that John Prescott became employment spokesman when Smith moved on to be Shadow Secretary of State for Trade and Industry.

At the very time when his friends were secretly rooting for him, a glowing piece appeared about John Smith in the *Daily Mirror*: "He could be described as the tortoise of Labour politics. For he has demonstrated to the seemingly faster hares that the race does not necessarily go to the swift – or the noisiest – runner."[14] It was the best write-up he had had since his days as a Cabinet minister. And his new job was his best break since then, because instead of restricting him to Parliament, it took him out and about among ordinary party and trade-union activists more than any other post he had held. Also, by chance, it gave him a unique opportunity to remind the Party and the country of his credentials as a first-class parliamentary operator.

10
Jobs and Helicopters 1984–87

In the leader's office and in the bowels of Labour Party headquarters some hard thinking had been going on about why the 1983 election result had been so spectacularly bad. One point on which there had been general agreement was that the Party was going to have to try to sell itself to an increasingly sceptical electorate. "The key problem with policy making is that it is done in a sort of vacuum," the head of research, Geoff Bish, warned in a private memorandum. "We work out what we think needs to be done, given the basic attitudes of the party conference, and then plonk it before the electorate, with our other policies, to take it or leave it as they wish."[1]

As a small-scale experiment the Party ran a campaign on the health service in 1983–84, with press launches, party political broadcasts and speaking tours. It worked. Their own polling evidence, supplied by the MORI organization, showed that health as a political issue featured a little more prominently in the public mind after the campaign was over than before it began. Though it might seem blindingly obvious, the idea that the Party must campaign to win votes was an exciting novelty to some of those who had worked for years within the self-styled natural party of government, planning how power was to be exercised without ever giving a thought to how it was to be obtained in the first place. Preparations began for the most ambitious campaign the Party had organized for as long as anyone could remember: around the central idea that Labour would tackle Britain's massive unemployment problem by using the revenue from North Sea oil to revive the country's industrial base.

When the Jobs and Industry Campaign was launched in spring 1985, it came as something of a surprise to journalists accustomed to amiable, bumbling amateurishness from the Labour Party machine. What they found was well-written, well-designed material, with a professionally designed logo and a uniform "house style" – a colour arrangement found on the leaflets, on the podium, on the desk at which Shadow Cabinet members sat, and on the backdrop behind them. Even the printed invitations sent out to political journalists bore the "Jobs and Industry" logo, in the campaign colours. It was the start of the rise of the image-makers, a phase in Labour Party history memorably debunked by TGWU leader Ron Todd: "The modernizers are in full swing . . . and Nye Bevan is spinning in his grave as the last vestige of controversy, of political opinion, of socialist content, is ground out of the election literature, in favour of glossy pink roses, a sharp suit and a winning smile."[2]

For those who were inclined to suspect that glossy presentation was but a camouflage for a retreat from socialism, ammunition was lying about, particularly in an internal memorandum, attributed to Smith himself and leaked to the *New Statesman*, which warned:

> Labour has lost the economic argument. People do not believe that our policies will work. The Keynesian argument has been tried before and failed. . . . We should not promise too much too soon. In particular, the term "full employment" may now appear nebulous and over-ambitious. There is abundant evidence that voters know that Labour had promised to reduce unemployment but did not believe that we could deliver, and saw unemployment as the main issue, but did not believe that there was any solution. The Jobs and Industry Campaign will present a set of clear images conveying the idea that Labour believes there is a political solution to the recession and is preparing the foundations of a credible policy. If these images are retained in people's minds, then at the next General Election we will avoid the suspicion that Labour is putting forward a vote catching formula behind which there is no real thought.[3]

The promise made in 1983 – to eliminate long-term unemployment altogether in just five years – was indeed on the way out. Instead, the centrepiece of the 1987 election campaign was to cut unemployment by one million in two years. Half the new jobs were to be in the construction industry, through a government-generated boom in housing, hospitals, schools, transport and sewers. It scaled down Labour's jobs programme to a size which made it easier to sell to a sceptical public, but it was still a lot more ambitious than what would be on offer five years later.

The 1983 manifesto had also vowed that a Labour government would renationalize everything the Tories had privatized, and nationalize a good deal. While the government held the commanding heights of key industries, others would be subject to planning agreements drawn up between company managers and a national ministry for economic planning. All that was whittled down, but without a dramatic break with the past. The more time the government had to organize the sale of public assets, the more expensive it became to take them all back. On those purely practical grounds, successive party conferences were persuaded to learn to live with the idea that some of what the Tories had sold would stay in the private sector. Even so, the list of assets which were to be bought back, wholly or partially, included British Telecom and Mercury, British Aerospace, and –

should they be privatized – gas, water, electricity, British Leyland, Rolls-Royce, and Royal Ordnance. The famous Clause Four of the party constitution was not to be revoked.

The real attempt to break with the past was the promise that the way state industries were managed would be radically changed. There would be a system which Roy Hattersley called "social ownership". The old model of large, remote and frequently inefficient nationalized industries was to give way to more modernized, democratically run and consumer-friendly public companies, along the lines being pioneered by Sweden. A policy statement drawn up in 1986 admitted: "Socialists have frequently focussed upon the question of ownership and neglected ways to ensure that socially-owned industries or services are democratically and efficiently organized."[4] In short, Labour wanted to change the image and operational efficiency of the nationalized industries, not drop them from the programme. Similarly, Hattersley and Smith regarded the scale of intervention in industry implied in Labour's policy on planning agreements as too great. This involved a battle of wills with John Prescott, who tried to revive interest in the issue via a Jobs and Industry Subcommittee which he chaired. He failed because the main trade-union leaders were simply not interested in fighting to preserve the policy.[5] What remained of the old policy was a promise that trade unions would have a right to inspect a company's books and obtain other relevant information, to be consulted, and to be represented on boards of management.

The manner in which policies were arrived at was haphazard and informal. "It was worked out in little groups of us," says Roy Hattersley. Even so, the end product was principally the work of Roy Hattersley, John Smith, and their union allies in the right-wing bloc on the NEC. "John is supremely good at that sort of situation, the 'Let's not be stupid about it, it can't be done' situation. John was absolutely crucial in all this."[6]

After the first Jobs and Industry launch came a series of others, each worked out by a committee which met regularly in the Commons, with John Smith in the chair. There was a "local enterprise charter", which Smith launched in Liverpool in July. Each region was then presented with a Jobs and Industry booklet of its own, with a title like "Yorkshire and Humberside Can Make It". Each booklet had its set-piece press and TV launch in its appropriate region, usually starring John Smith, who would spend a large part of his day's visit on local radio or television, or being interviewed by regional newspapers.

There were also booklets on different industrial sectors – like *Labour and the Motor Industry*, launched by John Smith in Birmingham at the end of May 1985. Its content included no dramatic departure from traditional industrial policy since British Leyland was then state-owned, and Labour intended that it should remain so. There was a promise of a dramatic 50 per cent increase in output, and a veiled warning to foreign multinationals operating in Britain that if they wanted government assistance they had better manufacture the entire car in their British plants rather than use them for assembly only.

What was unusual about these booklets was their attractive design. They were markedly different from older Labour Party publications, in which professional researchers wrote for people from their own educational background. A car worker could have dipped into *Labour and the Motor Industry* in his lunch break. On the back cover, he would have read: "Now it's up to you to discuss the ideas you have just read . . . " While this was going on, campaign material was raining down upon local parties, accompanied by exhortations to elect their own local Jobs and Industry organizers, have a Jobs and Industry meeting, then leaflet their locality. For the true devotee, there were Jobs and Industry badges, pens, T-shirts, mugs and writing-pads, the chance to take part in a John O'Groats to Westminster Jobs and Industry sponsored cycle ride, or even get hip and go to a Jobs and Industry rock concert.

The Jobs and Industry music tour owed its success to the radical folk singer Billy Bragg and his manager. John Smith, who was just about young enough to have caught the beginning of the Elvis Presley phenomenon – had he been that sort of teenager – was informed midweek that Billy Bragg was prepared, free of charge, to front a campaign to encourage the young to vote Labour. Sensibly, he said nothing until he had had a chance to go home and consult his daughters. On the Monday morning, he returned to London fired up with the enthusiasm of a recent convert. Later, he told cheering delegates at that autumn's party conference: "Billy Bragg has pioneered concerts from one end of the country to the other. And when we sent Billy Bragg out to concerts from one end of Britain to the other, we sent Labour MPs as well so that they make direct contact with our young people. . . . "[7]

In this period, "campaigning" became a buzz word in Labour's inner circles. There were those who were for "campaigning", and those who were against – either because they thought it used up too many resources for too little results, or because they suspected it was being used to camouflage an organized retreat from socialism. Certainly, it became an instrument by which Neil Kinnock got a grip on the Party.

Nominally, the Party's staff worked for the NEC, but ten years of splits within that body and between it and the Shadow Cabinet had reduced effective managerial control almost to nothing. The staff had decided that a lot of time and money would be devoted to trying to involve the ordinary party membership in the Jobs and Industry Campaign. In part, this was done to overcome the estrangement between party activists and MPs. It was also a strategy for overcoming the right-wing bias of Britain's press. As the leaked Smith memorandum put it: "The party can never rely on the media for sympathetic coverage, nor do we have the resources to mount major publicity campaigns. But we do have a unique resource: the party membership and affiliated trade union membership. And if we can mobilise this resource, we can get our message across."[8]

Mobilizing a few hundred thousand unpaid volunteers scattered about the country was easier said than done, and there was a lot of mumbling that the results did not justify the effort. The sponsored bike ride, particularly, lingered in the Party's memory because of the time it took to organize. John Smith went along with this strategy, but never really agreed with it. One morning he was overheard having a very angry exchange of words with Tony Manwaring, the head office researcher who was the main driving force behind the campaign, over the time politicians were expected to spend on little events involving small numbers of party members. That all ended when a new post, Director of Campaigns and Communications, was created. Its first incumbent, Peter Mandelson, who held the job for four years, acquired a reputation as a political magician who "created a viable opposition by turning a crazed gang of fissiparous ideologues into a solemn army marching behind a designer rose".[9] In reality, Mandelson had only limited contact with "crazed ideologues", but he had an extraordinary impact at party headquarters. He was the agent through whom Neil Kinnock stamped his authority there. The campaigns which followed Jobs and Industry were less anarchic and more closely controlled by him, with less emphasis on involving constituency parties and more television photocalls, opinion polls, and professionally designed advertising. The Mandelson strategy for dealing with press bias was to rely on radio, television, and a superabundance of photocalls.

Another job thrown up by the new enthusiasm for campaigning was that of Campaigns Officer for the Parliamentary Labour Party. It went to David Ward, a charity worker who was also the Party's candidate in Chelsea. Robin Cook, now the Shadow Cabinet's campaigns co-ordinator, likened his appointment to a heart transplant: the organism threatened to reject the new heart. No one had really worked out what Ward's job was to be, but it obviously ought to involve working alongside members of the Shadow Cabinet. Each of them, however, already had a full-time researcher with a vested interest in keeping out intruders. Theirs was not always a secure trade. Annually, when the Shadow Cabinet elections came round, one or two researchers might find themselves on the dole. In between, they were dependent on the goodwill and approval of one employer, with no tribunal to appeal to if things went wrong.

John Smith had been lucky in the first researcher he hired, in 1980. Murray Elder, a Scot from Kirkcaldy, was then a junior official at the Bank of England, who wanted to take up politics. He spent his weekends hundreds of miles north of London, in Ross, Cromarty and Skye, where he was Labour candidate in 1983. A year later he moved back to Scotland permanently, as researcher in Labour's Scottish Office, and subsequently as General Secretary of the Scottish Labour Party. He continued to be part of Smith's circle of personal friends. Without him, things were not quite so happy in the Smith office. An advertisement in *The Guardian* soon sent a nervous shiver through the little community of frontbench researchers: "Senior Labour politician requires a full time researcher and speech writer. . . . Must be a member of the Labour Party, be able to relate well and easily with politicians – cv to include 500 word essay on 'privatisation' . . . "[10] Smith's young researcher, who is now out of politics, laughed along with all the others at the grim jokes being cracked in the canteen about which of them was being lined up for the sack. He stopped laughing when he found out that the "senior Labour politician" who had placed the advertisement was John Smith. It was not quite a sacking. A group of sympathetic industrialists had been so impressed by Smith that they had clubbed together to provide the money for an extra researcher. The incumbent, though, took the hint and went job-hunting.

The applicants for the new post were all warned that it would last only about two years. Interestingly, Smith seems to have operated on the assumption that Labour would lose the coming election. He did not try to tempt applicants with the prospect of a job in government in 1987, and indicated to one of them, who was in his early twenties, that it would not be very good for someone of his age to be a Shadow Cabinet researcher for six or seven years. Bill Jones, who got the job, stayed for two years.

Here was an opening for David Ward to step in and make himself useful. He soon discovered that constituency parties had responded remarkably well to the call from headquarters to launch their own Jobs and Industry initiatives. He found a mountain of unanswered letters from constituency secretaries asking for a visiting speaker to address their Jobs and Industry event. Most wanted Neil Kinnock, with or without musical accompaniment from Billy Bragg. John Smith often featured as second choice. In their absence, another frontbench politician might do; but frequently there was no one suitable to offer. Smith himself was already rushing about the country from one speaking engagement to another. He had ideological differences with his talented deputy, Bryan Gould, which would grow in the coming years. Other names on offer aroused no enthusiasm at all from local parties. Plainly, Smith needed someone to be his understudy.

Gordon Brown at once emerged as the obvious choice. Brown had made a striking impression in his first two years in the Commons, as a member of the Select Committee on Employment. He had also been very well known and well thought of in the Scottish Labour Party ever since his days as Scotland's foremost student politician. To offer a frontbench position to someone so new to the Commons was unusual then, but not unprecedented. Brown's friend Tony Blair had actually beaten him to it, having already joined the Treasury team. Consequently, David Ward found himself walking up and down the corridors of the House of Commons conducting three-way negotiations with Smith, with the leader's office, and with Gordon Brown, which resulted in the appointment of a new Shadow Minister for Regional Affairs. In that capacity, Brown was able to meet some of the demand for visiting speakers.

Another person who stepped in and volunteered to be part of the Smith operation was Jenny Jeger, a lobbyist with well-known family links to the old Gaitskellite wing of the Labour Party. She helped Smith find a good secretary, Ann Barrett, to work for him in the Commons full-time. She also devised an ingenious scheme to get business leaders to pay to listen to John Smith as part of the Jobs and Industry Campaign. In some regional capitals there were seminars to which local businesses sent senior managers, and paid a hefty entrance fee. In others, the local Chamber of Commerce organized a huge lunch, with Smith as after-dinner speaker. The first such event was a car industry seminar in Birmingham, in May 1986, for about twenty-five people, including the chairmen of all the motor companies and a team from the Department of Trade and Industry. There were similar events in Newcastle, Leeds and Manchester. In June, the Glasgow Chamber of Commerce was reported to have listened in "rapt attention"; but, according to the local paper, "the most interesting fact about . . . [his] speech was that he was invited to make it at all".[11] It was a sign that business leaders were starting to take the possibility of a Labour government seriously, for the first time in four years. Jenny Jeger claims: "They were absolutely intrigued, because nobody in the Labour Party had ever asked them to come and meet anybody in the Labour Party and be consulted before. Of course, it helped that it was John they were being invited to come and hear. Doing it with Robin Cook would be much harder."

The Jobs and Industry Campaign raised Smith's stock among constituency Labour Parties. It singled him out from other senior members of Solidarity, who seemed to want to wall themselves up in Parliament and take no part in the life of the Party. Even if Smith's politics were no more popular than before among predominantly left-wing activists, he was seen now as a party man and a hard worker. Then chance presented him with a unique opportunity to re-establish his reputation in Parliament.

A fall in world demand for civil helicopters had badly hit the little manufacturing firm of Westland, in Yeovil. In the latter part of 1985 its new management started hunting for a larger company or consortium to come to their rescue, with a cash injection in return for a minority shareholding. The government was involved because Westland also supplied helicopters to the military. In fact, the £750 million worth of defence orders it had had in the previous two years amounted to vastly more than the company's total value. The government's own advisers, the National Armaments Directors, insisted that Western Europe should have the capacity to supply itself with military helicopters. A four-nation consortium was put together, involving British Aerospace and its counterparts in France, Germany and Italy, with the backing of British Defence Secretary Michael Heseltine. Westland's chairman, Sir John Cuckney, met the Trade and Industry Secretary, Leon Brittan, in October, and was told that the government had commercial and political reasons for wanting the European deal to go ahead.

Two months later, what began as a straightforward and minor item of government business erupted into a scandal which nearly forced the resignation of the Prime Minister. A rival suitor had returned with an improved offer which interested Westland's directors: Sikorsky, part of the giant US conglomerate United Technologies. The boardroom battle between Sikorsky and the European consortium brought out latent conflict in the Tory Party over the deeply emotive questions of Britain's future in Europe, the special relationship with the USA, and the free market. Heseltine was a pro-European, and by Tory standards his views on the economy were interventionist. He accepted the argument that as the Cold War was ending and the possibility loomed that one day the USA might run down its military presence in Europe, Western Europe must be able to supply its own defence equipment. To Margaret Thatcher, that notion contained a hint of a future European superstate; this appalled her. Moreover, whilst Westland and United Technologies were private companies, the firms in the European consortium were state-owned. A minister was coming to her with a proposal for a marginal increase in the volume of British industry under state control.

This being a government of the free market, however, there could be no question of it having an official view, one way or another, on the respective merits of the two bids. That must be left to the directors and shareholders of Westland plc. So ran the public position, whilst behind the scenes Leon Brittan was set the task of stalling the European option and clearing the path for Sikorsky. It was a simple matter for Margaret

Thatcher to order Leon Brittan, who was her own creature, to execute an undignified about-face. However, Michael Heseltine, who considered himself her potential successor, was made of sterner stuff. Westminster was treated to the fallout from a battle of wills between the two strongest personalities in the Cabinet.

The Labour Party, of course, had no inside information about what was really going on in the government. They could rely only on hints and guesswork to tell them what line of attack to take. By mid December 1985, though, John Smith had gleaned enough to be able to tell MPs that there was a power struggle in the Cabinet, in which he singled out Heseltine as the good guy, "perhaps belatedly, but certainly vigorously" defending the national interest, while Brittan was doing as he was told by the Prime Minister. "As usually happens when the Prime Minister intervenes, party ideology has once again triumphed over the national interest," he added.[12]

It so happened that 15 January 1986 had been set aside in the Commons timetable as a day when the opposition could choose the subject for a full-scale debate. To devote hours of Parliament's precious time to a small firm in the West Country, where the local MP was a Liberal, was an odd choice; but that was what Hattersley and Smith fixed up over Christmas, while Kinnock was away on holiday in Spain. It was a calculated ploy which could easily have fallen flat. The Cabinet might have settled its differences, leaving Labour struggling to keep up a parliamentary attack with precious little to go on. In fact, the threat of exposure in the Commons made Margaret Thatcher increasingly determined to silence the incorrigible Heseltine, who literally walked out of the Cabinet, on 9 January, to tell his side of the story to the world. Even with Heseltine on the rampage, Labour was still mostly groping in the dark, trying to understand the significance of droplets of information seeping out from all over Whitehall. "It was a situation perfectly tailored to the skills picked up in the Scottish Courts, where by now John Smith could be earning probably four or five times his MP's salary," said an admiring newspaper profile the following month. "In particular, colleagues were stunned by the sheer speed with which he thought and spoke on his feet during the crucial Westland encounters."[13]

Whilst Heseltine valued his reputation with the Tory Party too much to give Labour any overt assistance, he shared their interest in prising the truth from ministers. Four days after his resignation, he asked Leon Brittan an innocent-sounding question in the Commons – had the government had a letter from British Aerospace? – to which the Minister answered that he had not. Plainly, something was afoot. Before the afternoon was out, Smith had found out at least part of the truth, and was back, interrupting another debate, to make a formal demand that Brittan be summoned to the Commons to explain himself. A letter from the chief executive of British Aerospace, Sir Raymond Lygo, had been delivered to 10 Downing Street that lunch time, though no one outside the government knew what it said. Brittan could, of course, take refuge behind the technicality that *he* had not had a letter from the company – the Prime Minister had. Even so, he had come perilously close to being caught telling an outright fib to the Commons, something the British establishment will not tolerate. He was made to come back to the House late in the evening to apologize.

The reason the government wanted its dealings with British Aerospace kept secret, it soon emerged, was that on the day before Heseltine's resignation, Brittan had met Sir Raymond to discuss Westland. The businessman went back to his board of directors to say that he had just been ordered by the Minister to pull British Aerospace out of the European consortium, because it was "not in the national interest". Sir Raymond's account of the conversation, which Leon Brittan hotly refuted, made a mockery of the Thatcherite claim that Westland's future was being left to its shareholders and the free market. "The Westland affair provides us with the clearest possible, most graphically illustrated, most thoroughly documented demonstration of how the government have sacrificed . . . public interest to their ideological obsession with market forces," Smith told the Commons.[14] While that was "important" enough, there was another facet to the affair which Smith designated as "sinister". This was the organized rubbishing of Michael Heseltine, which began while he was still a senior Cabinet minister, dragging civil servants into the Tory Party's family quarrel. Smith commiserated, after Heseltine had resigned: "We know how he has been cut down from behind, that he has had to face stories and gossip, and we know the way in which he has been prevented from putting his case."[15]

The most notorious incident, which forced the hapless Leon Brittan to resign, was the leak of a private letter sent by the Solicitor General, Sir Patrick Mayhew, to Michael Heseltine, politely warning him that he might have exaggerated the consequences for Westland if the European deal fell through. Sir Patrick, it later emerged, had been asked indirectly by Margaret Thatcher to write the letter. Selected highlights were leaked by an official of Brittan's department. In a final Commons exchange on the whole affair, after Brittan's resignation, Smith tried hard to pin responsibility on the Prime Minister, forcing her to humiliate herself by coming to the dispatch box repeatedly to assert her innocence. "If we accept the explanation that has been given to us, it is a sorry tale of woeful incompetence. If we cannot accept it, the whole integrity of this administration is suspect," he claimed.[16] In the end, the Commons had no choice but to take her word for it. The circumstantial evidence was against her, but the unmistakable proof was not there.

No sooner was the Westland drama over than the government presented Smith with another chance to prove himself. In February 1986 the new Trade and Industry Secretary, Paul Channon, announced a bold plan to get state-owned British Leyland back into the private sector – by selling most of it to US multinationals. In the original version, Leyland Trucks, Land Rover, Freight Rover and related overseas operations were to be bought by General Motors, the Laird Group was to take over Leyland Bus, and the rest of BL would be sold off as soon as practicable. Two days later, it emerged that the government was having talks with Ford about taking over Austin Rover.

For John Smith, the announcement was a gift. Sell off the prime parts of Britain's motor industry to foreign competitors, indeed! – here was a chance to speak for British industry, for British defence needs – since BL was almost the only British-owned supplier of military vehicles – and for several thousand workers and their families in parts of the country stuffed with marginal Tory seats. Better still, the whole enterprise unravelled almost as soon as it began. It was on 5 February 1986 that Labour whipped up controversy over the talks with Ford. They were called off the very next day. The battle over General Motors carried on for another eight weeks, with other companies trying to put in rival bids, and John Smith repeatedly accusing the government of having created an unfair competition by allowing the American car firm to get in eighteen months ahead of anyone else. The sale of Land Rover, which Smith denounced as a "sweetener" to get General Motors to buy less profitable parts of BL, attracted so much political controversy that the government tried to persuade GM to be content with Leyland Trucks and Freight Rover. Negotiations broke off at the end of March. It was, said Smith, "the collapse of a venture that was ill conceived in purpose, anti-British in effect and handled with almost unbelievable incompetence".[17] The final climbdown came in April, when the Minister finally announced that Land Rover and Freight Rover would stay part of British Leyland.

After a series of outstanding Commons performances by John Smith, the flow of speculation that he was a future Labour Party leader – or at least a future Shadow Chancellor – resumed. Later in the year, it won him the *Spectator* "Parliamentarian of the Year" award, which was worth a case of whisky, a lunch at the Savoy, and a great deal of prestige. (Recognition of a different kind came in the same day's mailbag, from a voter who promised him: "You'll not get my BT shares yet, you bald, owl-looking Scottish bastard. Get back to Scotland and let that other twit Kinnock go back to Wales.")[18]

Neil Kinnock was not so fortunate. He had to lead off the opposition day debate on 15 January 1986 on a subject which he had not chosen. Never one of the great parliamentary performers, he faced organized barracking and interruptions from the Tories, and simply failed to rise to the occasion. Michael Heseltine, who spoke next, reacted as if the Labour leader's uncertain touch had suddenly reminded him that what united the Tories was more important than the little things dividing them. "I do not believe the House has listened in a decade to a worse parliamentary performance than the one we have heard today," he claimed.[19] It was an occasion which would prey on Kinnock's mind, because he was not the type of person who could simply shrug off failure and forget it. It was the start of corrosive muttering on the Labour benches by MPs saying how much more effective Smith was in Parliament and how much they needed a leader who could perform well on the big occasions. Kinnock would have to endure this for six years.

Westland represented the high point of Labour's hopes of election victory. Later in the year, the government appeared to pull Britain out of economic crisis. Inflation, interest rates and unemployment all fell, at the beginning of the now notorious Lawson boom. Support for Labour began to fall away, as was brought home cruelly in March 1987, when the Party was forced to defend Greenwich, a seat it had held even during the 1983 debacle, and lost it to the SDP. On that miserable night John Smith was taking part in a live programme for BBC TV, and had to explain away a catastrophic defeat. He tried to blame it on tactical voting. The SDP voters were "only Tories", he said. "What, all of them?" exclaimed the astonished presenter, Robin Day. Smith was right up to a point, in that thousands of Tory voters had switched to the SDP to defeat Labour. However, Labour's vote had also gone down: to below even its 1983 level, in a foretaste of the bigger defeat to come.

There has probably never been a general election in which the two main parties painted such different pictures of what life in Britain was like. In 1983, there had at least been common agreement that the country was in crisis, although the remedies on offer bore almost no resemblance to each other. Four years later, a buoyant Conservative Party was telling electors that the country's problems were basically solved. Easy credit had created a boom. Wages and salaries were rising, property prices were soaring – so that homeowners added more to their nominal wealth by occupying a home than they did by going to work – interest rates were down, productivity was up, and even unemployment was falling from its peak. Conservative Britain was back on its feet. Labour's election manifesto, by contrast, described eight years of higher taxes, public service cuts, rising crime, meanness, and social divisions.

Labour's miscalculation was that more voters were in work, enjoying the benefits of the boom, than out. They preferred the rosier view coming from the Tories to the pessimistic warnings from the opposition.

11
Shadow Chancellor 1987–88

For the Solidarity group, another blow followed. Not only had Labour lost the election, they had lost their hold on the Labour Party. The new, expanded "Kinnockite" Tribune group moved up and pushed them out of the way. The point was dramatically illustrated by the Shadow Cabinet elections in July 1987, when the Solidarity contingent was cut by five. One, Denis Healey, had chosen to retire. The other four were swept away as the votes piled up for the Tribune slate, which took eight of the fifteen contested places, including the top three. John Smith came in fifth, behind Gerald Kaufman – his worst showing throughout the Kinnock years. Solidarity took the hint, and disbanded itself. Smith was the main speaker at its last rally, on the Sunday morning preceding the 1987 party conference.

As the Party's deputy leader, Roy Hattersley was immune from the vagaries of the Shadow Cabinet elections, but not from larger political events. During the postmortem on the election defeat, blame fell on him, as Shadow Chancellor, for the way the Party's taxation and public spending plans had been handled. The Conservative Party, aided by the *Daily Mail* and other right-wing newspapers, had run an effective campaign around a warning that the "real" cost of Labour's election promises came to £35 billion, which implied that the Party had secret plans to raise taxes to much higher levels than Hattersley had admitted. The Tory case was strengthened by apparent holes in the Labour programme. A policy document passed by the 1986 Labour conference, *Social Security and Taxation*, said explicitly that the married man's tax allowance was to be abolished. That was left out of the election manifesto, probably by Kinnock and Hattersley, giving credibility to the Tories' claim that Labour was trying to hide some of its planned tax increases. Also, on one disastrous day in the middle of the campaign, Kinnock conceded in a local radio interview in Welwyn that people earning less than £25,000 a year might be worse off under Labour's tax plans, Gould – at a press conference in London – denied it, and so did Hattersley, who went into a TV live interview in Cambridge unaware of what either of them had said.

It was an unhappy end to what had been shaping up as a brilliant campaign, and – rightly or wrongly – Hattersley took the blame. It was said of him that he had spent too much time on political manoeuvring, journalism and other pastimes, and not enough on his brief. Hattersley accepted the inevitable, and agreed to being shifted back to the job he had first held in 1980: Shadow Home Secretary. He was not so amenable, however, when he heard that Kinnock was considering Bryan Gould as his successor.

Gould had had an extraordinarily good year, which started when he was unexpectedly elected to the Shadow Cabinet the previous November. It allowed him to take over from Robin Cook as campaigns co-ordinator, when the approach of an election made it one of the two or three most sensitive jobs in the Party. Simultaneously, he was Hattersley's deputy in the Treasury team. Robin Cook, whose luck had temporarily deserted him, spent a year as John Smith's deputy.

Even before the election campaign began, politicians were talking about the incipient rivalry between John Smith and Bryan Gould. Previously, when there was speculation about who the next Labour Party leader might be, John Smith's was usually only one name mentioned. If he had found that embarrassing, now at least he could share his embarrassment with someone else. After they had both spoken in the debate which followed the 1987 budget, Nigel Lawson accused them, with an uncomfortable accuracy, of competing for "moderate candidature in the battle for the Labour leadership, which cannot now be long postponed", adding: "I shall give a word of advice to the opposition. Although [Gould] is undoubtedly flashier, I would go for Smith. He is very canny. He has seldom, if ever said anything. . . . [Gould] has said a great deal, most of it highly critical of the Labour Party and all of which we have kept on file for future use."[1]

During the election Gould held daily briefings for the London press corps, and was seen on television every day, but never said a word out of place. His performance made him a household name. Temporarily, he was the epitome of the new, acceptable face of Labour. In the Shadow Cabinet elections, he topped the poll with the highest vote ever achieved by any candidate during Labour's first twelve years in opposition. Later in the year, he succeeded in being elected to the NEC; it was the first time in over a decade that someone had managed to get himself on to the section controlled by the rebellious constituency delegates by upholding party policy. His other advantage was that he was closer to Neil Kinnock, then, than either Hattersley or Smith. Hattersley and Smith, however, were familiar with Gould's economic views. He was an unrepentant anti-marketeer, a protégé of Peter Shore. His solution to Britain's industrial decline was the one which the Tories turned to in desperation five years later: to devalue the pound by allowing it to float – or sink – in the money markets, in defiance of any arrangements arrived at within the EC. For Hattersley and Smith, who had once staked their political futures on a Europe which could bring order to the money markets, the thought of Gould rewriting Labour's economic policies was anathema.

Neil Kinnock himself denies that he ever intended to appoint Gould as Shadow Chancellor and says, moreover, that Gould never asked for the job. Hattersley, however, certainly thought it was a possibility. For the second time in three years, there was a covert operation by the Solidarity network to secure advancement for John Smith. It included a well-placed press leak.[2] Once again, it worked. John Smith became Shadow Chancellor, and Gould succeeded him as head of the Trade and Industry team. Smith assembled a formidable group around him. After the problems which Labour's spending plans had caused at the previous election, Kinnock wanted the second job in the Treasury team, that of Shadow Chief Secretary, to be taken by a member of the Shadow Cabinet, who would be given authority to inspect every policy document, every statement put out at a press conference by any other member of the front bench, to ensure that there were no rash promises which could be taken down and costed by researchers at Tory Central Office. To give the appearance of political balance, it was better if it was someone who had been elected on the Tribune slate.

That was an easy choice. The Tribunites included Gordon Brown, who had just arrived as the Shadow Cabinet's youngest member, at thirty-seven, after only four years in Parliament: the fastest rise through opposition ranks since the 1950s. As well as being extremely able, Brown was a team player, slightly shy and famously workaholic, without the brittle, sensitive ego often to be found in politicians. He could be trusted not to use the number two post in the team for some private enterprise to advance himself at his boss's expense.

A remarkable piece of evidence later came to light, showing the effect of Brown's supervision of Labour's public spending promises. His opposite number, the Chief Secretary to the Treasury, whose name was John Major, had sent a circular round to other Cabinet ministers asking them to get their civil servants to examine Labour's policies, estimate their cost, and send the results back to him. He was entitled to do that, because part of the function of the civil service is to examine and cost suggested alternatives to government policies. However, when the ideas are coming from an opposition party, there is an obvious danger of civil servants being sucked into party politics. What the minister wants to be told is that the opposition's ideas are ludicrously expensive, so that they can be rubbished in public.

A memorandum drawn up in the Department of the Environment in July 1989 and signed by the Permanent Secretary, Sir Terry Heisler, was leaked to Gordon Brown. The text revealed that there had been some friction between officials and the Minister's special adviser, a political appointee, who had been urging them to make assumptions about how Labour's policies would be put into operation which would justify hanging a very high price tag on them. Sir Terry's reply must have come as a severe disappointment. He concluded: "The Labour review document has been drafted much more carefully than on some earlier occasions. The promises do not readily lend themselves to precise costings. And in most cases the assumptions you have asked us to cost are vulnerable to counter-attack from the opposition."[3] How the rest of the exercise fared, no one knows. John Major was suddenly – unexpectedly – promoted to the job of Foreign Secretary, and the matter was shelved.

The rest of Smith's Treasury team was also drawn mostly from the ever-expanding Tribune group. The most unlikely appointment was Stuart Holland, a left-wing intellectual once closely linked to Tony Benn, who represented almost everything within the Labour Party to which John Smith was antipathetic. He was appointed as the only MP in town who understood the complexities of Third World debt. Dr Holland, who had never liked John Smith (he left British politics in 1989), was surprised to discover how easy it was to work with him as a team leader. Smith's style was to allocate everyone their tasks, treat their opinions with respect, and allow them to get on with it, without letting broader political differences get in the way.

The system by which economic spokesmen were serviced by advisers and researchers, and party policies were worked out, was overhauled and formalized. The rift between the NEC and the Shadow Cabinet had finally been sorted out. There had been a shift of power in the NEC towards the "Kinnockite" centre and the "soft left". The leading right-wing union fixers had either gone, or were on the way out, and had been supplanted by figures like Tom Sawyer of NUPE and the MP John Evans, who were closer to Kinnock. A new network of policy review committees, on which the Shadow Cabinet and NEC were jointly represented alongside a carefully picked selection of outsiders, was set up to supervise what turned into a huge exercise in political revisionism. Behind the scenes, an Economic Secretariat, made up of full-time advisers with degrees in economics, was established in place of the hotchpotch of friends and advisers who had worked with Roy Hattersley. They were supplemented by a network of high-powered economists, several of whom had previously believed that Britain should go it alone in a drive to expand the economy and reduce unemployment, but had now been won over to the stability and shelter of the European monetary system. They were co-ordinated by Andrew Graham, an economics don at Balliol College, Oxford. Others involved were Chris Allsop, of New College, Oxford, David Currie, director of the Centre for Economic Forecasting at the London Business School, and, from the City, Gavyn Davies of Goldman Sachs, Neil Mackinnon of Yamaichi and Gerald Holtham of Shearson Lehman Hutton.

The Labour Party had emerged from its shattering defeat in remarkably good heart, as if the shock had not yet sunk in. There was no anguished soul-searching over why the Party had lost. It was as if everyone already knew. Actually, there were two incompatible answers on offer: the left blamed the Party's retreat from socialism, claiming that the election could have been won on approximately the same manifesto as in 1983 if it had been promoted with real conviction; while the diagnosis accepted by those in the mainstream was that the Party had appeared to pay too much attention to the have-nots, such as the jobless, the recipients of state benefits and the ethnic minorities, and too little to the numerically larger affluent white working class. Neil Kinnock ordered a review of all party policy, to be conducted by seven separate groups set up jointly by the Shadow Cabinet and National Executive Committee, who had to produce their final reports within two years. They were told to find policies which would appeal to people who were – in Kinnock's words – "comfortable, secure, satisfied with decent conditions, and the best of British luck to them".[4]

John Smith's policy review group was "Economic Equality", which looked into tax, social security and related issues. Its interim findings, published in summer 1989, contained all the elements which were to be the centre of fierce controversy as the next election approached. There was the national minimum wage, for example, which the Tories would denounce one day as a supposed threat to millions of jobs. It had also long been a source of controversy inside the Labour Party. Opposition came from two sides: from right-wing craft unions like the EETPU and AUEW, who complained that it would erode pay differentials; and from left-wing unions like the TGWU, who saw it as a revival of the last Labour government's attempts to set pay policy instead of leaving it to collective bargaining. The case in favour was being pushed by unions with large numbers of low-paid, mostly female members, like NUPE and USDAW. It became party policy at the 1985 conference, but Neil Kinnock was still hostile to it while it brought him into conflict with the TGWU, and argued ferociously about it with the employment spokesman, John Prescott.

John Smith had always believed in a statutory minimum wage, as an act of simple social justice. While he was employment spokesman he laid out all the arguments in favour during a Commons debate on low pay, and rubbished the Tory claim that lower wages create more jobs. What they actually mean, he countered, is that taxpayers are forced to subsidize bad employers, and their employees are forced to undergo the humiliation of visiting social security offices to top up their pay. He forecast, nearly two years before the event, that Labour would adopt a policy of a national minimum wage.[5] On a separate occasion, he suggested to the Tories that they might want to apply the rule that lower pay means more jobs to some of their own supporters: for example, "If one divides a stockbroker's salary by five, there would be five more stockbrokers."[6]

The principle behind the policy review was that everything was up for revision. The policy of a statutory national minimum wage could have been scrapped if John Smith and the new employment spokesman, Michael Meacher, had not wanted it, but it went straight back in. The legal minimum, in 1989 terms, was to be set at £2.80 an hour,[7] which went up to £3.40 by the time of the election.

The other proposals which would feature centrally in the 1992 election were all also agreed with very little argument at the time. Income tax for the well-off was to be set at 50p in the £. There was also the hint that they would be hit by an extra 9p National Insurance on top of that. There was a hint – later to be dropped as Britain dipped into recession – that income tax for the low-paid was to be cut to below 20p in the £. In autumn 1987, Smith was hoping to set it at 15p for the lowest-paid compared with the current rate of 25p.[8] It was also made clear where a large part of this extra tax revenue would go. The previous election manifesto had promised an immediate increase in state pensions of £5 a week for the single pensioner and £8 a week for a couple; and a rise in child benefit of £3 per child per week. Robin Cook, now Shadow Social Security Secretary, and his deputy, Margaret Beckett, rather forcibly put it to the policy review group to consider whether they wanted to retreat on a promise to the nation's elderly. They did not. Labour committed itself to a pension increase "which would not be less than the manifesto commitment in 1987".[9]

Child benefit was a slightly more complex issue, despite its simplicity and the high take-up, because there are other ways to increase the income of mothers: through independent personal taxation. At the time, however, the Tories were allowing child benefit to wither by repeatedly refusing to increase it in line with inflation, and there was a real fear that it might be abolished altogether. This was no time for Labour to make their job easier by appearing to back down. Consequently, there was a promise of a "substantial" increase in child benefit in year one of a Labour government, with more later "as resources allow".[10] For better or for worse, the central idea of Labour's 1992 election campaign – a redistribution of income away from the highest-paid to the low-paid, the elderly, and mothers – was the work of John Smith and those most closely associated with his leadership: Robin Cook, Margaret Beckett and Gordon Brown.

While his mind was on other things, the new Shadow Chancellor – uncharacteristically – got off to a bad start in the House of Commons. Neil Kinnock had given his team their new jobs in July, expecting them to use the summer break to learn their subjects and come back properly briefed. Robin Cook, for instance, went into several months' purdah, emerging remarkably informed about the health service and social security system. But John Smith, perhaps, felt that after eight years as an economic spokesman he could get by on what he already knew. He knew the Chancellor, Nigel Lawson, quite well from the early eighties, when they had battled over energy policy. Then Smith had a subject he knew back to front from his days in government, and was able to make Lawson look like a novice. The Tory Minister was even goaded into admitting: "Unlike the Right Honourable Gentleman, I do not profess to know all the answers . . . "[11] Confident as ever, Smith reverted to an old habit, and spent two months at work in the Scottish courts.

He paid for it when he returned in the autumn. Nigel Lawson may not have been an expert on energy policy and may have been, in retrospect, a bad Chancellor, but economics had been his life. He was one of the most confident and knowledgeable politicians ever to have occupied the post, and he had behind him the fair wind of what seemed like impressive economic success. Pay was rising, unemployment was falling, interest rates had been cut to 9.5 per cent, homeowners knew that they could add more to their nominal wealth by sitting at home watching property values rise than by going to work. An ordinary-sized family house in London was going up in price at a steady £1,000 a month. Britain was enjoying a spending spree, and the government had never been so popular. The Tories had collected 43 per cent of the vote at the election. By the autumn their standing in opinion polls was at 50 per cent, and there it remained for a year, while Labour's hovered around 36–38 per cent.

In November, Lawson announced that because the government had collected more tax and spent less on unemployment and social security than forecast, government borrowing was below the original estimate, and there was to be more money for health, housing, education and the police. In the ritual Commons knockabout, Smith denounced this as a "confidence trick", adding: "He boasted in the first half . . . about how he was reducing public expenditure, while in the second half he boasted about how he was increasing it."[12] All the supposed increases were actually only an attempt to keep up with rising costs, because inflation was up by 1.5 per cent, Smith claimed. Unfortunately, he was wrong on the latter point – public spending really was being increased – and on the first point too, because what Lawson was claiming was that public spending was going up, but not as fast as incomes, so public expenditure as a portion of national income was going down. And so on. The Chancellor was able to dissect Smith's speech point by point, throwing up errors of fact mixed with arguments of doubtful strength. All in all, Smith had a bad day.

He had not even done well during the spectacular Stock Exchange crash of October 1987, when it looked for a moment as if the terminal crisis of capitalism, so long predicted by the Marxist left, had finally arrived. Obviously, there was only a limited amount the government of a capitalist nation could do to prevent wild fluctuations in share prices. One thing which Smith believed would help was if Britain were to sign up to the European Exchange Rate Mechanism which, by creating stability on the currency markets, would also help to soothe the stock markets. Lawson's succinct view was that it was "poppycock" to suppose there was that sort of direct relationship between fluctuations in currency values and share prices. Smith thought he could make his opponent regret saying that by the well-known technique of involving the name of a prominent public servant. He claimed that it was a "calculated insult" to the president of Germany's central bank, Karl-Otto Pohl. This was an unwise attack, because he had advanced into Lawson's home territory. The Chancellor knew Herr Pohl, and knew that he did have the opinion Smith imputed to him. After being challenged no fewer than nine times in a few minutes to prove his claim or apologize, Smith was forced to mumble defensively: "I believe that what I have said is correct and I stick to it."[13]

One side-effect of the stock market crash was that it made a fiasco of the next stage in the privatization of BP. All the big sales of state assets had worked on the principle that punters were given a unique chance to buy shares at less than their market value. Those who bought were grateful to the Tories for the profits they made, while the taxpayer did not feel a loss. BP was only partly state-owned. Shares were already on sale in the stock market before the government announced it was selling its stake at an attractive price of £1.20p a share. Unfortunately, come the day, BP's share values had dropped so much that they were much cheaper on the open market. The people who stood to lose most were the underwriters – City firms who, for a fee, agreed to buy, at the quoted price, any shares which the public did not want. They could end up having to buy the entire government holding at a loss of more than £1 billion. In past privatizations, the underwriters had agreed to being paid for doing nothing without complaint, but this time, naturally, they were at Lawson's door pleading for the sale to be cancelled at once.

Labour, of course, believed that BP should never have been lined up for privatization in the first place, so Smith, too, was calling for the sale to be cancelled. In the parliamentary exchanges which followed, he had to face Lawson's taunts that he was running a campaign to save the underwriters. However, when Lawson finally produced his solution to the BP problem, Smith was able to produce an off-the-cuff one-liner which helped to repair the damage to his parliamentary reputation. Lawson announced that the government would put a limit on how much the underwriters could lose by guaranteeing that for the next month or two, the Bank of England would buy BP shares from anybody at 70p each, and would hold on to them for at least six months, unless the price went above £1.20 before then. In effect, the government had intervened to ensure that BP share prices could not fall below 70p. It was, said Smith, "the first privatisation which has nationalisation built into it".[14]

More generally, an event which wiped millions off share values in a single day might be expected to embarrass the Conservative Party, as the party of capitalism. It did not bother Nigel Lawson, who decided to take action to avoid recession by cutting interest rates, which fell all the way to 7.5 per cent by May 1988; and the top rate of income tax, which he reduced from 60p in the £ to 40p in March 1988. For the well-paid, it was an astonishing bonanza. For a married man on £200,000, it meant an extra £33,314 a year, or £640 a week cash in hand, as John Smith pointed out afterwards, adding: "That is enough, I remind Conservative members, to keep open the hospital ward in Wales which the Queen Mother opened and which is now closing because of a shortage of funds." It was, he claimed, "immoral, wrong, foolish, divisive and corrupting".[15] It is now conventional wisdom that Lawson's action then caused the recession which descended on Britain two years later. At the time, though, Smith sounded a little like a Presbyterian preacher, as he expounded the case in favour of high taxes.

He rubbished the various arguments advanced by Tories to demonstrate that the whole of society benefited from anything which made the rich richer. One favourite was that the more the rich were taxed, the more they evaded or avoided paying; consequently, when the top rate of tax came down, receipts went up. Only a "fool" would believe that, said Smith. The government certainly did not, because they had officially estimated the cost of the tax cuts at £2 billion – money which should have gone to the NHS. As to the idea that the rich had more incentive to work hard if their tax rates were lowered, why was that principle never applied to the poor, and where was the "incentive" in Lawson's decision to cut inheritance tax? – "The only one I can work out is an incentive to get rid of rich relatives. . . . " He went on:

"One may have been blessed with good fortune which has given one brains, talent, energy, good luck or inherited wealth. Privilege, as well as ability, can contribute to one's income. When one has that income one should not want to get rid of one's obligations as the rich in this country almost seem to want to do; one should shoulder that obligation as part of one's citizenship and be proud of it."[16]

During the 1988 Labour Party conference, about a fortnight after his fiftieth birthday, John Smith's normal self-control momentarily left him: he walked out of a radio interview in a fit of bad temper. Even allowing for extenuating circumstances – that the temporary studio in a Brighton hotel was stuffy, a good breakfast was only a few feet away, and there had been two irritating days of unfriendly newspapers making hay from a TV interview by Roy Hattersley, which was being written up as if the deputy leader had committed the Party to sweeping away private education and private health care and hitting the rich with high taxes – for one so careful of his public image and so meticulously polite in private as John Smith, it was out of character. He had been up having a good time the previous night. He arrived a quarter of an hour late, then took exception to being asked: "Is it not the case that once in power as Chancellor you would bring in a wealth tax, abolish private health care and the public school system?" – because none of these was party policy, and even if they had been, two of the three would have been outside a chancellor's sphere of responsibility. "I don't know where you get these ideas from," he protested. The interviewer, Peter Deeley, persisted, until Smith bade him a curt good morning, and was gone.[17]

Back in his Edinburgh home that weekend, he complained of a headache, which was also unusual for him. His wife Elizabeth thought he looked ill, and persuaded him to miss the two o'clock flight back to London. She called in a doctor, who found nothing wrong but told him to go into hospital for a check-up. Even the registrar gave him a clean bill of health, after inspecting him with a portable cardiogram, and told him to get dressed. As he bent down to tie his shoelaces, John Smith tumbled into darkness.

"I came round lying on a trolley and they were opening my mouth and pulling at my clothes. That was a bit alarming. . . . I had never been ill in my life. I got injected with a thing which clears out your arteries and repairs the damage, 'the magic fluid', they call it."[18]

He had had a massive heart attack. Indeed, it is probable that if he had taken the flight to London, he would have been dead on arrival.

There was no deceiving himself about the cause. By his own admission, he had succumbed to the temptations that are notoriously open to northern MPs, who have to spend four nights a week away from their families: he had overeaten, drunk too much, and kept bad hours. He was a purely convivial drinker, with none of the disturbing or repulsive characteristics of people who depend on drink, whose personalities change as the alcohol flows: Smith under the influence was a more relaxed, expansive and funnier version of Smith sober. The most he might do after a long evening's entertainment was tell some off-colour jokes. Added to that, he had never allowed a night's celebration to be an excuse for slacking. One of his boasts was that he was always punctual about getting up in the mornings. He confessed:

> "My fatal weakness was an inability to say no to invitations. I was scrambling from one end of the country to another for things which didn't really merit all the effort. . . . I trained myself to keep on plodding even when I was terribly tired. I kept every engagement. I thought I was invulnerable."[19]

Now he had been given a shocking warning that it would have to stop. For the next three months he had no choice but to recuperate, spending the rest of the year at home, then taking a holiday in the Gambia. There had been some damage to his heart, but it had been minimized by his extraordinary good luck in having the attack in a hospital. He was advised that he could expect a complete recovery, and need have no fear of a second attack, provided that he took exercise and reduced his weight. Even so, there was the anxiety to cope with, as he had to learn to pace himself without despairing if he felt tired, and there was the nagging doubt about whether he would recover his self-confidence. It was a time for reflection.

A possibility which went through his mind was to give up politics altogether. He had never been one of those frantic souls whose position in the House of Westminster is the only thing which gives their lives any meaning. He had another profession to which he could easily return; he had a family and a home country a long way from London. "I wouldn't have been destroyed if my political career had been over," he said.[20]

> "I had a marvellous way out if I wanted to. And I decided I really did want to stay and I asked the doctors is it OK if I do this, because I am a father and a husband as well as a politician, and they said, if you want to, you can. I still take a little medication, Warfarin, which kills rats. I can't be a rat because I have survived."[21]

He was, after all, a pivotal figure in Britain's main opposition party, and his recuperation period was punctuated by messages and calls from Labour MPs anxious to see him come back in full health. "Just concentrate on parliament and television, that is what we want you to do," Sam

Galbraith, the brain surgeon turned MP, advised him.[22] All this concern had a keener edge to it because of the state of the Party in Westminster. Next, he had to consider how his own future would be influenced by the fact that virtually the whole country knew he had had a near-fatal heart attack. At the political level at which he expected to operate, anything could be used against him. Sooner or later, there was sure to be a headline like the one used by the *Sun* on the eve of his election as leader of the Labour Party: "He's fat, he's fifty-three, he's had a heart attack and he's taking on a stress-loaded job."[23]

Once John Smith had decided to return to front-rank politics, he had to demonstrate that even a heart attack can be turned to political advantage. Towards the end of the year, insiders became aware not only that the Shadow Chancellor had made a full recovery, but that a very skilful operation was being prepared to ensure that his comeback was a success. It was from this time that the legend of the Munros begins. The "Munros" are the 277 Scottish mountains over 3,000 feet high, catalogued by the Victorian eccentric Sir Hugh Munro in 1891. Smith had always been fond of country walking. In the early eighties, he and Murray Elder would organize weekends with old university friends like the television journalist Donald MacCormick, or with political contacts like the AUEW leader Gavin Laird or GMBATU's Scottish researcher Doug Henderson, who is now a Newcastle MP. These were long but not arduous strolls in the open air. Laird and Henderson would sometimes break off to ascend a Munro, then rejoin the party. Now, Smith needed to discipline himself to keep taking exercise; to give himself a purpose, he decided to see how many peaks he could conquer. Since then, it has been almost obligatory for those who write political profiles of him to say that on his office wall there is a map of Scotland, spiked by red-topped marker pins which record his progress.

If John Smith reaches Downing Street, we may be sure that the Prime Minister who walks the Munros for recreation will become as familiar to the British public as John Major's Brixton boyhood, Margaret Thatcher's manic refusal ever to relax at all, Harold Wilson's pipe and holidays on the Scilly Islands, or Harold Macmillan's grouse-shooting on the moors. However, stuffing a pipe in your mouth, or eulogizing your boyhood, is effortless. Munro-bagging is not.

When the opportunity arises John Smith sets out with ice axe, crampons, torch, tent, whistle and sandwiches, to reach another peak. He is not an expert climber; he is nowhere near to being in the same class as Chris Smith, the only MP to have bagged all 277, including the Isle of Skye's infamous Inaccessible Pinnacle. John Smith's expeditions involve walking uphill and down again, for about a six-hour round trip, often accompanied by Murray Elder, who survived a heart transplant, or by Gordon Brown, or the Kirkcaldy MP Lewis Moonie. Even so, it is a seriously healthy hobby. Doug Henderson says: "My description of him is 'tenacious'. He always keeps going, no matter how hot, how steep, or how much he is carrying." He set himself the target of bagging a hundred before the general election, and almost achieved it. By the time he became party leader, he had scaled 96. He conquered No. 100, Buachaille Etive Mor, at the entrance to Glencoe, in September 1992, on the day before his fifty-fourth birthday. Climbing was also an excellent way to counter the most formidable obstacle to his future success. It was now not enough for him to feel fit and well: he had to stop others from wondering about his health. Naturally, his formal announcement that he would return to work, on 23 January 1989, was preceded by a weekend photo opportunity featuring John Smith at the top of the famous 500-foot crag which dominates Edinburgh's skyline.

There were also political as well as physical advantages to losing weight. Health and diets are subjects which obsess the popular newspapers and magazines, so a feature on how an eminent politician has lost weight offers a new way of approaching an old theme. A week before Christmas 1988 the *Sun* gave over almost two pages to a feature on how the chubby Shadow Chancellor had taken four inches off his waistline, reducing his weight by two stone to 13st 5lb, by following a strict 1,000-calorie-a-day diet. "John's Tum-Trimmers" included Kellogg's All-Bran (120 cals per 1oz helping), Weight Watchers baked beans from Heinz (112), Findus Lean Cuisine (170) and Baxter's Consommé of Wild Game Soup (40). "Even a Shadow Chancellor can learn how to budget with calories," remarked admiring "*Sun* Slimming Editor" Sally Ann Voak.[24] Such a massive helping of positive publicity in the *Sun* was unusual for a mainstream Labour politician, to say the least.

Later, John Smith starred in a video by the Family Heart Association, and appeared at an FHA fringe meeting at the 1990 party conference alongside Barry Howard, a star of "Hi-De-Hi" and another heart attack survivor. He was even elected vice-president of the Ramblers' Association at their annual conference in Ormskirk in April 1992. By the time he was back at work, the physical change was truly remarkable. From being 42 inches round the waist, and weighing in at 15st 5lb, he was now down to 37 inches and 12st 12lb, and vowing he would always be this slim. It was an ambition he did not fulfil. By agreement, his calorie intake was to increase to 1,500 a day while he was working, but even with that concession, in the long run, dieting proved a harder test of will than walking the Munros. It is easier for someone of John Smith's temperament to steel himself to do something difficult than stop himself doing something simple. There were times when old colleagues accused him of being a slimming bore – as, for example, when he berated George Robertson, who had owned up to scoffing a bar of chocolate. "You could have had a steak and sorbet for that," Smith is reputed to have told him, after calculating his calorie intake – to which the reply came straight back: "Not behind the wheel of a car, I couldn't."[25]

One of the most frequent callers during his recuperation at home was, of course, Gordon Brown, who was having to stand in for him during his absence. This produced one of those debates which have gone down in the mythology of the Palace of Westminster as a great parliamentary occasion, when Nigel Lawson made his 1988 autumn statement on the government's spending plans. It was assumed that this would lead to an embarrassing duel, in which the heavyweight Chancellor would humiliate his inexperienced opponent. But with his solid command of detail and his rapid, confident delivery, Brown held his own. The MPs sitting listening were impressed. Later in the month, Brown rang Smith to convey to him, in a half-apologetic tone, the results of the Shadow Cabinet elections. The good news for Smith was that he had achieved the best result of his career so far – second place, with 144 votes, 33 up on the previous year and 15 ahead of the next contender. First place, with 155 votes, had gone to Gordon Brown.

Previously, only a limited circle of insiders, mostly from Scotland, had heard it said that here was was a future leader of the Labour Party. Now Gordon Brown was the talk of the town. As well as being young, clever, well-read and well-liked, he and his friend Tony Blair, who had just displaced him as the youngest member of the Shadow Cabinet, had another precious advantage: Neil Kinnock trusted them more than he trusted anyone else in the Shadow Cabinet. Hence a malicious little item in the "Crossbencher" diary, in the *Sunday Express*, about Smith's impending return: " . . . how quickly the spotlight moves on. How quickly friends and colleagues forget. Almost every day of his absence, he has heard glowing reports of the brilliant way in which his deputy, Dr Gordon Brown, has stood in for him. . . . Suddenly nobody is talking about Smith any more. And everybody is talking about Brown."[26]

Later on, rivalry between Smith and Brown became one of the elements in Labour's internal politics, but not yet. For the time being, what happened was that where once the names of Smith and Gould had inevitably cropped up every time there was talk about who would be the next Labour Party leader, now Gould's name began to fade as Brown's rose. That suited John Smith. He had important political differences with Bryan Gould, but none to speak of with Gordon Brown. The younger man belonged to the right wing of the Tribune group, but in political terms that was now virtually indistinguishable from the former Solidarity group.

A much more important question was pressing itself upon John Smith: where did he stand in relation to an increasingly beleaguered Neil Kinnock?

12

Mr Kinnock and Mr Smith

The Labour Party is more merciful to its leaders than the Conservatives are to theirs. The remarkable fact about Neil Kinnock's eight and a half years as the longest-serving leader of the opposition in British political history is that there was no serious attempt to remove him from office. Harold Wilson, who saw his party through two general election victories in his first three years as leader, was in more danger from his own side than Kinnock ever was.

In the fourth year of Kinnock's leadership, Labour improved on its worst general election defeat for fifty years by achieving its second-worst general election defeat for fifty years. The government's overall majority went down from 144 to 102; the number of Labour MPs went up from 209 to 229. Yet for months afterwards, the Party lived in a warm glow of relief. They had, they believed, won the campaign whilst losing the vote. Even when the post-election euphoria wore off at the beginning of 1988, and Labour MPs came face to face with four more dreary years in opposition, despite all the discontented muttering about Neil Kinnock's performances in Parliament, his wavering on defence policy and his dictatorial temperament, none of the dozens of MPs who were frankly saying behind his back that it would be better for everyone if he quit and let John Smith take over summoned up the nerve to say so to his face. The anarchy of 1979–83 had seemingly traumatized the Party's high command so much that they could not believe they could have a leadership crisis and survive, without a tough guy to kick them into order.

There was, however, one point in those eight and a half years when there was a real possibility that Neil Kinnock's term as leader would come to a sudden end. By chance, it came in December 1988, when his putative successor was at home recovering from his heart attack. It was also, ironically, just after Kinnock had fought off a leadership challenge, winning by a majority of more than seven to one.

1988 had been a grim year for Neil Kinnock. The solid achievement which even his enemies acknowledged was that he had instilled a sense of discipline into Labour, but in March, after the warm afterglow of the previous year's election campaign had worn off, it suddenly seemed as if even that was to be undone. The start of Budget Day, a solemn event in the parliamentary calendar, was delayed by a rowdy, orchestrated interruption by left-wing MPs from the Campaign group, who demonstrated – in a way guaranteed to attract maximum publicity – that Kinnock's authority did not greatly impress them. Norman Tebbit's comment was that "it demonstrated the unfitness of this man – who combines weakness with aggression, verbosity with the inability to express clearly even simple thoughts – to carry out his duties as Leader of the Opposition, let alone any more responsible task. He is a boy trying to do a man's job. . . . "[1] In his reply to Nigel Lawson's budget speech, Kinnock made an oblique reference to the earlier disruption when he exhorted: "I, my comrades and my honourable friends should take the view: don't get mad, get even."[2] Afterwards, he returned to his suite of offices behind the Speaker's chair, shut himself away, and burst into tears.[3]

His distress was not directly caused by the frustrations of his job. He had just been told that the party agent in his Islywn constituency, an old friend who had helped him through the first big break of his career, had died suddenly – a personal loss which hit him very hard; but during the summer, there were other worrying reports that the leader was suffering moods of black depression. They surfaced in *The Independent* in June, and then on the front pages of the Tory tabloids. The grinding disappointment of the general election result and the stagnation which had overtaken Labour's electoral support whilst the Lawson boom lasted had given Kinnock good enough reasons to get mad, without offering him a chance to get even.

Twice a week, it was his task to tackle the formidable Margaret Thatcher at Prime Minister's Question Time. At one confrontation, in May 1988, he apparently hoped to trip the old warrior up by pointing out that only months earlier, when interest rates were high, she had warned that lowering them could cause inflation. Now that the government was bringing them down, as Labour had been urging, he hoped to pin a charge of inconsistency on her. So he came to the dispatch box with an immensely long, prepared question which he delivered with all the agility of someone wading through porridge. After the first eighty words or so, the barracking from the Tory benches had risen to such a tumult that no one could hear what Kinnock was trying to say, and the Speaker had to stand up and call for silence. When he finished, Margaret Thatcher rose and delivered one of those cold, cruel one-liners which made her such a dangerous opponent. "I don't think", she said, "that the Right Honourable Gentleman is entirely the master of his subject."[4] It was then her turn to have her words drowned in uproar: it was the noise of her own side laughing and jeering.

Kinnock also had to defend himself against the first open challenge to an incumbent Labour Party leader for twenty-eight years. Having Tony Benn run against him, however, was the least of his problems. In fact, though he condemned it publicly, in private, when the news was brought to him during a staff party in the House of Commons late in March 1988, he was obviously delighted. There had been a week of speculation, based on severe shortage of hard fact, that John Smith might challenge him. Even the rumours were damaging to Kinnock; an outright challenge might have succeeded. Instead, on 1 April, John Smith and Robin Cook formally announced that they would act as campaign managers for Kinnock, and for Roy Hattersley. With those two on his side, there was never going to be a serious contest. Six months later, Kinnock collected 88 per cent of the vote to Benn's 12 per cent. During those months, he could be absolutely sure that his job was safe.

On the other hand, he was forced to take John Prescott's ambition to be deputy leader seriously. Prescott had said in January that he might run against Hattersley, but was talked out of it. However, when he learnt that there would be a contest anyway, with Eric Heffer as Benn's running mate, he formally added his name to the list of candidates. By midsummer, it was a real possibility that Prescott might win, and the former Kinnock–Hattersley "dream ticket" would become the unhappy pairing of Kinnock and Prescott, two rough-house politicians who were at their best on a rostrum, speaking to a hall full of Labour Party members, and at their weakest in the Commons. It defies belief that the pair could have lasted more than twelve months without another contest. A Prescott victory might have been the event which brought Kinnock down the following year. Kinnock was certainly sure that he did not want Prescott for a deputy, and insisted on running a joint campaign with Hattersley. Thus Robin Cook, who had volunteered to be Kinnock's manager, was press-ganged into acting for Hattersley as well. It was Cook, in fact, who did most of the work, and he found Hattersley – who was, after all, fighting for political survival – an easier candidate to manage than Kinnock.

Whilst Prescott was in the running, he acted as a long stop on the Party's gradual movement to the right. Anyone who objected to a particular item of revisionism emerging from the policy review could register an effective protest by backing Prescott.

By far the most emotive political question of the day was whether the Party would end its commitment to unilateral nuclear disarmament. There was a general expectation that it would, after the part defence policy had played in the 1987 election defeat. Privately, Neil Kinnock had made up his mind that he could never again drag himself around Washington and other capitals of the world defending a policy which offended the entire NATO establishment; but to have said so during summer 1988 might have tipped the balance in the deputy leadership contest in Prescott's favour. Defence was remitted to stage two of the review process, which would begin in 1989; but that could not stop journalists from questioning Neil Kinnock about it. In fact, they scarcely asked him about anything else, and the Labour leader found himself in an exasperating position: if he gave a hint of what he really thought, he could set off a chain reaction in his own party.

In June 1988 he went in front of TV cameras for an in-depth interview with Vivian White, on the BBC's "This Week, Next Week" programme, and uttered the portentous words "There is now no need for a something-for-nothing unilateralism." He used that expression "something-for-nothing", and its counterpart, "something-for-something", several times over.[5] It could only be taken as a loud hint that he no longer believed in unilateral disarmament. That weekend the Halifax MP Alice Mahon let fly at a conference for left-wing socialists, calling Kinnock "a no-talent weak man" who was being "eaten for breakfast by Mrs Thatcher", adding: " . . . he has betrayed the whole of the movement by what he said last week, but I think actually in a sense he has done us all a favour because I think he is finished".[6] The next attack, a few days later, was a great deal more damaging because it came not from a rebel left-wing MP but from a prominent member of the Shadow Cabinet: the Shadow Secretary of State for Defence, Denzil Davies, who suddenly resigned. He announced his decision to an astonished Chris Moncrieff, political editor of the Press Association, whom he had awoken at home at one o'clock in the morning, complaining: "I am fed up with being humiliated. Kinnock never consults me about anything."

Only days later, Kinnock had lunch with the editor and senior journalists from *The Independent*, and gave them his current thinking on defence policy, for the record. To their surprise, they heard him enunciate the traditional unilateralist position[7] as if nothing had changed and all the excitement caused by his "something-for-nothing" comments, and a highly damaging resignation, had never happened. Peter Shore, who was openly in favour of removing unilateralism from Labour's programme, issued a public warning in July that Kinnock would have to achieve "moral intellectual supremacy" over Thatcher, or go.[8]

By the autumn, Kinnock was no longer a unilateralist. He backed a motion put by the GMB to the Party's October conference, which supported disarmament by whatever means were possible, be they unilateral, bilateral or multilateral agreements. It was only narrowly defeated.

Unilateralism was excised from the party programme a year later, at the 1989 conference. It had been a bumpy ride which had caused Neil Kinnock a great deal of grief, and won him very few plaudits at the end. As soon as they knew that the policy was indeed changing, the Tories opened up a new line of attack on the Labour leader, claiming that a man who would abandon a deeply held belief like unilateralism was not to be trusted.

Meanwhile, in the changed political climate, younger party members, untainted by association with the Wilson or Callaghan governments, were prepared to present an intellectual case against unilateralism. The prime example was a Fabian Society pamphlet, *Working for Common Security*, which was given a highly publicized launch in January 1989 at a special two-day conference in Oxford. It was one of the bestselling pamphlets the Society had produced for some years. The old argument that a unilateralist was a "multilateralist who meant it" – that either Britain disarmed unilaterally or nothing at all would be done to reduce the world's proliferating nuclear armoury – was, it maintained, out of date. Real disarmament talks had begun between the USSR, under Mikhail Gorbachev's leadership, and the USA; and Britain would do better to take part than to disarm without negotiating an equivalent reduction from the Soviets. But within the Labour Party, "the polarised struggle between so-called multilateral and unilateral nuclear disarmament has almost completely overwhelmed the real defence debate".[9] This argument was much more likely to convince CND members than telling them that unilateralism should be abandoned because it lost votes.

Officially, this pamphlet was a joint production by four authors, with no involvement by anyone on Labour's front bench. In reality, the Shadow Defence Secretary, Gerald Kaufman, knew all about it and approved it. And John Smith's attitude can easily be deduced from the fact that the pamphlet's main author was David Ward, who had drafted it while he was out of mainstream politics for a year, working for UNICEF. By the time it was published Ward was back in the Palace of Westminster, working as John Smith's research assistant. Smith had had to hold the line on Labour's non-nuclear defence policy on more than one occasion, which had left him with unpleasant memories. In Parliament, he had had to field questions from Tory MPs who challenged him on how many jobs in the defence industries would be lost under Labour, and what would happen, for instance, to 9,000 shipyard workers in Barrow if the order for Trident submarines was cancelled. Smith's stock reply was that there would be many more jobs in manufacturing industry generally under Labour than under the Conservatives.[10]

He had had a far more uncomfortable time during the 1987 election, when he went on a live early-morning phone-in programme. It was one of those occasions which enliven every campaign: a professional politician comes up against an amateur who happens to know the subject thoroughly. The man who tied Smith in knots identified himself on the airwaves as "Lance Corporal Ragman". The fact that he subsequently turned out to be Horace Warmington, a twenty-four-year-old supermarket assistant, hardly improved matters.[11] All in all, it was never likely that Smith was going to take action over the fact that someone in his private office was visibly campaigning against what was still nominally party policy though Labour would officially drop unilateral nuclear disarmament from its programme before the year was out.

By the end of that wretched year 1988, Neil Kinnock had run into even deeper trouble, from a direction no one had anticipated. On one of those days when she was exasperated by the Brussels bureaucracy, Margaret Thatcher decided not to reappoint Britain's two EC commissioners, but to send in someone she felt she could trust – the newly knighted Sir Leon Brittan, whose earlier career in domestic politics had ended with the Westland affair. Traditionally, the leader of the Labour Party is entitled to nominate the second British commissioner. Kinnock had not wanted to be in a position to nominate anyone: he had no complaint against the incumbent, the former Labour MP Stanley Clinton Davis. However, since he had to find someone, he sounded out John Smith, among others, for a suitable suggestion. Smith recommended the former Secretary of State for Scotland, Bruce Millan, who had helped him through some of the trickier parts of the devolution Bill. He was duly appointed.

So far, so good; but it meant a by-election in Millan's former seat, Glasgow Govan. This was not a serious problem, it appeared, since Millan's majority was 19,509; but by about October there were ominous warnings that the local Party intended to put up a candidate named Bob Gillespie, an official of one of the print unions, with a reputation that might not survive the intense scrutiny of a by-election. In the eyes of Labour MPs involved in the Govan campaign, the problem was symbolized by the words "Hong Kong" tattooed on Gillespie's knuckles, one letter per knuckle. He was also known to sympathize with the Glasgow-based Anti-Poll Tax Campaign which, contrary to the official Labour line, was encouraging people to defy the law by refusing to pay their bills. (In Scotland, the first bills were sent out in spring 1989, a year earlier than in the South.) The idea of not paying poll tax actually had popular appeal in Glasgow, and was being pursued by the Nationalists, who were putting up Jim Sillars, the strongest candidate they had. This invoked memories of a by-election in Govan in 1973, in which Labour had been sensationally defeated by the SNP candidate, Margo MacDonald, who was now married to Sillars. It was a bad time to be fielding a candidate who privately disagreed with important parts of Labour Party policy.

Warnings about the luckless Gillespie came from all directions, including the management of the *Daily Record*, whose proprietor, Robert Maxwell, remembered him as a union negotiator and was threatening to order them not to support Labour in the by-election if Gillespie ran. Uncharacteristically, Kinnock did nothing. He needed the goodwill of the two print union representatives on the NEC much more than he needed Robert Maxwell's advice on party management. He allowed the party rules to take their course, and Labour went down to its worst by-election defeat for six years. This defeat spread an atmosphere of dismay and sullen rebellion on the Labour benches in the House of Commons. It was not really Neil Kinnock's fault, but he was the man at the top; consequently, he was carrying the can. If he had decided to resign, there might not have been anyone outside his tight circle of loyal supporters who would have tried to persuade him to stay. His mood was becoming more intransigent and angry by the day, as discipline in the parliamentary Party threatened to break down. Persuading Labour MPs to vote according to the party whip suddenly became more difficult than ever. There was a public altercation over whether to abstain on the Prevention of Terrorism Act, as the whips required, or to vote against, which a significant number of Labour MPs were determined to do. One of the rebels, Clare Short, who had to step down from her post as a Shadow Employment Minister, wrote Kinnock a defiant letter complaining of "constant threats and denunciations".

Around the same time, Kinnock was visited in private by a delegation of three members of the Shadow Cabinet, to warn him of another rebellion brewing over a government order due to go before the Commons giving pensioners an annual increase, but freezing child benefit for another year. Labour's problem was that they had to vote for or against the package as a whole. The decision was to vote against, in protest at the failure to increase child benefit. The general mood of sullen rebellion was turning this into a crisis, with at least two Labour MPs publicly declaring that they would refuse to vote against an order which meant more money for pensioners. Robin Cook, whose brief then included social security, Frank Dobson, the Shadow Leader of the House, and the Chief Whip, Derek Foster, trooped into Kinnock's office to tell him that he would have to back down. Adam Ingram, the MP for East Kilbride who had just taken over as Kinnock's PPS, was also in the room. What they all heard was a tirade against MPs who refused to do as they were told, and against business managers incapable of whipping them into line. During an extraordinarily tense and emotional two-hour session, Kinnock made at least one threat to resign. According to one witness, who believed he was absolutely serious, it was repeated several times. Another of the participants, however, claims: "We just came out and said 'bollocks'. We never believed Kinnock would quit, or that he would give up without a fight."

Kinnock himself says that 1988 was the year when he came as close as he ever did to being "really deeply, chronically brassed off" – but he is adamant that he was not seriously considering giving up. There was no one else, he says, who would have seen through the policy review and the organizational changes; no one "sufficiently determined, willing to go into fine detail, expend the time and the patience on endless discussions, reassuring people, informing people, bringing them over, finding out what they thought, in order to make them part of a movement for change – and . . . who could, as the occasion required, get up and light the Labour Party's touch paper".[12]

Incidentally, since Kinnock knew as well as everyone else that if he went his place would be taken by John Smith, that answer, given in an extended television interview four months after he stood down, is as close as he has yet come to saying what he really thinks of the man who succeeded him.

Kinnock returned from the Christmas break having shaken off the depression which had afflicted him over the previous months. The story goes that the family stayed with Glenys Kinnock's parents in Anglesey, and they told him that he should start making jokes and enjoying his job, because there was no point in carrying on if he was hating it. His performance against Margaret Thatcher at Question Time improved immensely in the second half of January, and with it the morale of Labour MPs. Even so, the crisis was not over. Senior party staff were alert to the possibility that they could be working for a new boss by the winter.

In this highly tense atmosphere, John Smith, as usual, played it very straight. He was not ruling himself out as a future party leader, though just before his heart attack he had told an interviewer: "I am thankfully not a person driven by ambition either to be a leader of the Party or to be Prime Minister." He added that "some" of the speculation about him was being put about to undermine Neil Kinnock, which he regretted: "I can't do much about it. I just don't encourage it, that's all."[13] In January, he told the *Daily Mail* feature writer Lynda Lee-Potter that he would take the job "if asked". To emphasize that his health was not a problem, he repeated a remark made by Jim Callaghan, which revealed a great deal both about the former Prime Minister's temperament, and about John Smith's. Callaghan had said: "It's much easier being Prime Minister than anything else, because you're the conductor and other people are playing the instruments."[14]

On the other hand, he was scrupulously avoiding any act which could be construed as disloyal. Such plots as there were against Neil Kinnock came and went without any encouragement from John Smith. "I am a team player and I am very happy to be playing in what I think is a good team," he told the *Daily Mirror*.[15] He took the same line talking privately to his own aides, some of whom would happily have worked for him against the incumbent leader. Jenny Jeger says:

> "I got critical of Neil, and he was quite sharp about it. He was absolutely adamant; he always maintained that he would never challenge Neil, and the only time he would run for the leadership was if Neil resigned. It was never a point for discussion, even after the defeat in 1987. It was absolutely extraordinary. Undoubtedly, he must have felt he could handle some things better than Neil handled them, but he was always very loyal."[16]

John Smith would subsequently claim that even in this critical period: "I was not approached by anyone to stand, and I wouldn't have if I had been."[17] The first part of this sentence does not quite stand up to examination. Even before the 1987 election, in 1984 or 1985, one of the office-holders in the Solidarity group wrote him a long private letter, setting out the reasons why he should be available to fight a leadership contest at some unspecified date in the future.

On a trip to the USA in the later part of 1987 he crossed paths with Barry Sheerman, then Labour's spokesman on employment and a visiting lecturer at Cornell University. They met by pure chance: as Smith sat down to lunch in a restaurant in Washington called Kramer's Afterwords, he spotted Mr and Mrs Sheerman at another table, so the two parties ate together. As they were chatting, thousands of miles from home, Sheerman took it upon himself to drop a none-too-subtle hint that for the Party's sake Smith should contest the leadership at the next opportunity. The reaction startled him a little. He found Smith eyeing him with cold disapproval across the rims of his glasses. With apparently unfeigned anger, Smith demanded to know how he could be expected to be disloyal to the elected leader of the Party. Sheerman countered that there was a higher loyalty to consider. The rest of the conversation was unpleasant for everyone at the table, and when it ended the two politicians walked off in different directions. Sheerman never broached the subject again.

Moreover, while Smith was at home convalescing after his heart attack, one of his visitors was the MP for Dunfermline West, Dick Douglas. Douglas was already on the way to becoming a semi-detached Labour MP. He was so angry about the imposition of the poll tax on Scotland that he considered the party leaders should set an example by refusing to pay it, and would soon commit what Smith regarded as the unforgivable offence of defecting to the Scottish Nationalists. At this point they were still on good terms, having known each other for almost thirty years. Douglas had been one of the sixty-nine who had rebelled over Britain's membership of the Common Market. It was no secret that he respected John Smith and despised Neil Kinnock. He, too, raised the possibility of an open challenge, but got nowhere. "Smith played a long waiting game, and did the work he was picked to do. He was extremely loyal to Kinnock," Douglas said later.[18] There is also a story – which appears to be true – that it was put to John Edmonds, the GMB boss, that as Smith's main union backer he might like to be the one to go in and tell Kinnock that it was time for him to resign. Edmonds's reaction, understandably, was that even in the unlikely event that Kinnock would take his advice, to have the Labour leader step down because he was told to do so by a union baron would create the worst impression imaginable among the general public.

The Sunday Times approached 77 Labour MPs to ask who would make the best party leader; about 45 named Kinnock, 15 named Smith, and the rest would not be drawn. The probability must be that if Kinnock had not been the incumbent, or there had been a contest between the two men, Kinnock's support would have fallen appreciably. "Most Labour MPs expect that Kinnock will stand down if the party suffers its fourth consecutive defeat," the newspaper accurately predicted. "They believe that, provided Smith remains in good health, he would then re-emerge as the clear frontrunner to succeed Kinnock."[19] There were others, outside the Smith camp, making contingency plans. Bryan Gould was a little bit startled by the number of Labour MPs who approached him late in 1988 or early in 1989, urging him not to leave the field open to Smith without a challenge from the left. No doubt he was a little flattered too. In a sense, the decision to have a Smith–Gould contest was made three years ahead of the event.

To those who had backed Tony Benn the year before, a contest between Smith and Gould was not much better than a choice between a flea and a louse. But even in the isolation of the Campaign group, they knew that a leadership contest was a possibility; and they knew they could never collect enough nominations to run their own candidate. Consequently, at least one MP who had been closely associated with Tony Benn for years was touting around to see if there was a possibility of bringing another hero of the 1981 deputy leadership election back into the fray. In semi-retirement, Denis Healey was basking in a popularity of a sort he had never enjoyed during his days in Cabinet; this might have given him a serious chance of beating Smith, if age was overlooked. If you are going to have a right-wing leader anyway – the reasoning was – you may as well choose the old bastard for whom you always had a sneaking respect, rather than a younger one who might give you problems you never anticipated. The delightful idea of old Bennites collecting signatures to give Denis Healey the job most of the Party now thought he should have had in 1980 ran for a day or two, until somebody calculated that the old warhorse would be at least seventy-three years old when the next election was called.

Had John Smith taken over the leadership in 1989, it is not difficult to foresee what his first year and a bit in office would have been like. It would have been an uninterrupted march of triumph as the government's popularity sank under the weight of an economic downturn, compounded by ill-judged reforms like the poll tax, until Margaret Thatcher herself was forced from office; and everyone would have agreed that this incredible run of success could never have come to the Labour Party under Neil Kinnock. How the next phase would have panned out – with both the main parties led by cautious, unflamboyant politicians named John, who sometimes tucked their shirts into their underpants – cannot be prophesied with the same certainty, but there are some Labour MPs who are convinced that the Party would have taken such a commanding lead that the government would have been brought down. Certainly, there would have been a buoyant confidence about Labour's front bench, a feeling that they had done what they had to do to put themselves on the winning side. There are Labour MPs who firmly believe it would have provided the necessary extra ingredient to bring down the Tories in 1992. This does beg the question why, then, nobody went to Neil Kinnock to suggest to his face that he should quit. We have his own testimony to that fact: "My test always used to be when I got reports that there was restlessness, well, let's see if anybody feels restless enough to walk through that door. Nobody ever did."[20]

Sometimes, it is suggested that John Smith prevented anyone else from making a move against Kinnock by being so loyal himself, but this is simply not an adequate explanation. Denis Healey was never openly disloyal to Michael Foot, but two Labour MPs, Gerald Kaufman and Jeff Rooker, none the less went to Foot to plead with him to stand down. John Major was, if anything, more loyal to Thatcher than Smith was to Kinnock, but did not save her. At whatever moment Smith inherited the party leadership, he wanted it to be a united Party, loyal to its leader; this would have been difficult to achieve with Kinnock's blood on his hands. A truly determined group of conspirators should have been able to work out that when Smith said, over and over again, that he would stand if there was a vacancy, that was all the encouragement they could reasonably expect from him.

A much more plausible explanation is that Neil Kinnock was saved by the hugely complex and protracted system for electing a Labour leader. Unless the rules could be circumvented in some way, Smith would have had to declare himself as a candidate in July 1989, at the very latest. Then there would have been a three-month campaign before the ballot was held at the autumn conference. In practice, because of the timetable to which union branches operate, he would have needed to start his campaign in April, possibly embroiling the Party in six months of internal warfare. As it happens, when Kinnock resigned in 1992 he demonstrated that the timetable for leadership elections could be changed if it suited the party establishment, but three years earlier it was assumed that the rules would have to be followed as they were written down.

One of the key players, who was then – as now – in the Shadow Cabinet, and would have preferred to have John Smith as leader in 1989, says: "For me, the overriding thought was that a leadership contest would send Labour into a tailspin, and we would never recover. Neil would never have gone quietly. He would have fought like a tiger, and who can blame him?" Another former frontbencher who would have willingly backed a Smith campaign says: "There were no conspiracies against Kinnock. There was no point. He couldn't have been got out under the rules. Mind you, under different rules, we would have had him."

Perhaps. On the other hand, there was a residue of gratitude and respect for what Kinnock had done which might have seen him through a leadership crisis. If Smith had been reckless enough to run against him in 1988 or 1989, it would have been seen as a challenge from the right rather than the left, and Kinnock would possibly have survived. Precedent was with him. No Labour Party leader had ever been forced out of office by his own party, whereas almost every Conservative leader has. To have had Neil Kinnock damaged and undermined by a full-scale challenge to his competence as a leader, but still there as Labour's prospective Prime Minister, would have been a disaster all round, and probably the end of John Smith.

The threat to Neil Kinnock still lingered on in the first few weeks of 1989. It was being said by those in the know that he would be judged by the results of the local government elections looming in May; in a forthcoming by-election in the Vale of Glamorgan, where Labour had a chance of taking a seat from the Tories; and finally in elections to the European Parliament in June. If all three polls went badly for Labour, the pressure for a short leadership race might have been irresistible. By May, however, the government was running into trouble over its planned health service reforms, which provoked almost universal opposition from doctors and other health workers, and aroused widespread suspicion that the NHS was being privatized.

The Vale of Glamorgan by-election became almost a localized referendum on the health service. This time Labour had been careful in its choice of candidate, putting forward a local councillor named John P. Smith, who avoided controversy and fought on his record as a local man. A visit by the other, better-known John Smith caused some confusion at their joint press conference. After several questions had been answered by the wrong Mr Smith, journalists hit upon the formula of addressing one as "John" and the other as "the Right Honourable John'. Later, John P. Smith seemed to take himself rather seriously as the man who had turned the fortunes of the Labour Party around. He ran for the National Executive, and collected the votes of seventy-two constituency parties. That was pretty good for someone who had only just entered Parliament – more than twice what the other John Smith had achieved after thirteen years as an MP. There was a suspicion – which can never be proved – that many of those who voted for him mistakenly thought they were backing the Right Honourable John. Be that as it may, the Vale of Glamorgan was won by 6,023 votes, the biggest by-election swing from Tory to Labour for fifty-four years. Talk of ousting Neil Kinnock died away.

By a nice irony, it was as his personal fortunes recovered that Kinnock made a more serious and calculated threat to resign. It was an implied threat which he never needed to put into effect, but given the circumstances under which it was made, there is no doubt that it was serious. Strangely, the story has never become public knowledge, as if the thirty or forty people who were present did not quite believe what they were hearing.

The argument over Labour's unilateral defence policy was revived in 1989, as the policy review group headed by Gerald Kaufman arrived at its findings. They were unveiled at a special two-day meeting of the National Executive in May. As expected, the group recommended an end to unilateralism, and came up against the opposition of big unions like the TGWU and NUPE, and of senior members of the "soft left", including Robin Cook, Margaret Beckett, David Blunkett, Jo Richardson and Clare Short. The long debate was enlivened by an unexpected and unscripted intervention by Neil Kinnock. Part of what he said was passed on verbatim by Peter Mandelson to waiting journalists, including the words: "I have gone to the White House, the Kremlin, the Elysée, and argued the line for unilateral nuclear disarmament . . . I am not going to make that tactical argument . . . without getting anything in return. I will not do it. . . ."[21]

The way this was reported gave the impression that Kinnock was vowing to make no more journeys to foreign capitals until Labour changed its policy. In fact, he went further. He said categorically that he would not defend unilateralism at home either. He repeated that vow in public some days later, at a rally in Wales. But at the time it was party policy, and the NEC was about to vote on it again. Kinnock's staff had done a head count, and would have tipped him off that victory was almost certain; but there was always the outside chance of defeat. If the NEC had reaffirmed a policy after hearing their leader vow that he would not defend it, his own position would have been untenable. Kinnock had certainly thought this through. He was convinced that most members of the Labour Party were not now unilateralists. In the party calendar, May was not too bad a month for resigning from the leadership: it would have given him two months to collect nominations for his re-election campaign – having doubtless appointed John Smith to run it again – and three more months' campaigning, before he barnstormed back to victory. It would have called the left's bluff by demonstrating that they were prepared to defy the leader, but not to replace him; and it would have forced all those mutterers on the right to step forward and declare their loyalty to him. Quite who would have led the Labour Party in those interesting five months we can only guess. Kaufman's policy review paper was approved by seventeen votes to eight. Neil Kinnock's position was never seriously threatened again until his resignation three years later.

13
Lambasting Lawson
1989

As the economy took a turn for the worse, and pent-up tension within the Cabinet burst into the open, John Smith was given his opportunity to take revenge on Nigel Lawson.

First, though, there was a question which had to be answered urgently – not one to set people talking in the pubs of Basildon, because it was apparently so technical that only a specialist could have any opinion on it at all; yet it would have a more lasting effect on British politics than anything else involving the government of the day. Certainly, John Smith must sort it out before he could venture into the City of London to make contact with opinion-formers in the world of high finance, as he intended to do.

It may well be said in Prime Minister John Major's obituaries that the most important decision he ever made – and perhaps the worst – was to sign Britain up to the Exchange Rate Mechanism (ERM) of the European Monetary System (EMS) at a parity of three marks ninety-five pfennigs to the pound. John Smith made an equally momentous choice when he decided not to oppose the Chancellor's action. At the time this decision produced scarcely a murmur of dissent in the Labour Party, where everyone was enjoying the sight of the Cabinet tearing itself apart over Europe so much that the last thing they wanted was to reopen their own internal conflict on the subject; but it dominated British politics during Smith's first hundred days as party leader.

The European issue had moved on since the 1970s. Tony Benn, still denouncing the Treaty of Rome as a barrier to socialism, was now a voice in the wilderness; nationalization was not on Labour's agenda on a scale likely to bring the Party into conflict with the Brussels bureaucracy. Nor were Labour MPs particularly agitated by the question of British sovereignty, which exercised the right wing of the Tory Party. Opposition to European integration on the Labour side could be summarized in the form of a question: which is the greater evil – unemployment or inflation?

The European Monetary System was founded on the assumption that the enemy is inflation. Each member state has to protect the value of its currency, whatever the cost to the vitality of the domestic economy. The shock of the hike in oil prices in 1973 cast such a long shadow that most of Europe – and especially Britain – was governed throughout the 1980s on the assumption that no one can ever doubt what the first duty of government is. "I never thought I would live to see the day again when newspapers would be questioning whether it is right to get inflation down," exclaimed Chancellor Norman Lamont in his first interview after the 1992 election.[1]

But, like many other things which politicians dress up as imperatives, it is a matter of choice; and, as with any political choice, there are winners and losers either way.

The ERM would have created problems for a Labour government, just as surely as it has for the Tories – more so, it could be said. The main reason why it offends the right wing of the Tory Party is that, being patriots, they hate to see Britain's elected government being told what to do by German bankers. What happens to workers who are made redundant in parts of the country which never vote Conservative anyway is not necessarily at the forefront of their minds; but another argument often used against the ERM was that by 1992 it was prolonging the British recession. The Labour Party, by contrast, is elected to protect the victims of recession. Even in the days now talked of as the "era of full employment" – between the Second World War and the oil crisis, when jobless figures were below half a million – politicians like John Smith consistently complained that unemployment was too high. The main point of joining the Common Market, he had claimed in the early 1970s, was that it would bring jobs to parts which the British economy on its own couldn't reach – like North Lanarkshire.

That was still his refrain after he became Shadow Chancellor. In his first long philosophical speech after the 1987 election, he repeated Keynes's famous argument that it would actually be better for the economy if the government were to bury money in the ground, have rubbish tipped over it, then issue licences to private firms to dig it up, rather than to have large numbers of able-bodied people on the dole. Full employment "must be a fundamental objective of a socially just society", Smith insisted. "Leaving aside the moral question, what on earth is the economic advantage of unemployment? . . . I see in the millions of unemployed not just personal catastrophe but unused and untapped energy or talent."[2] The Labour Party had always thought that way, whether the Party was heading to the left, as in 1983, or back to the centre, as in 1987. Jim Callaghan, as Prime Minister, had balked at joining the EMS when it was first instituted in 1979 because he feared that Britain would be tied to an overvalued pound.

There was, however, a very strong counter-argument: Labour needed the ERM much more than the Tories to prevent the sterling crises which had bedevilled every Labour government since the 1960s, particularly the last. An incoming Labour administration would face what is sometimes called a "crisis of expectations", when its own natural supporters want a better life – immediately. In particular, wage earners might set off a spiral of price rises by demanding pay increases above the inflation rate, to the detriment of others to whom the Labour government is beholden, like state pensioners and the unemployed. And there were other arguments in favour of the ERM. Giles Radice, who lost his place on the front bench at the 1987 Shadow Cabinet elections, was warning that outside the ERM, Britain would be excluded from crucial decisions affecting the whole of Europe.[3] Although the British government would still have its sovereign right to devalue the pound, he doubted whether that would have the desired effect of reducing the price of British-made goods abroad, because he forecast that the unions would demand pay rises to cover the increased cost of foreign goods, and firms would then raise their prices to meet their extra wage bill, setting up a vicious circle. Hard-headed politicians like Kinnock and Smith also accepted that Britain was never truly going to be outside Europe's monetary system anyway: when German interest rates rose, Britain's invariably followed; when the Bundesbank sneezed, London caught a cold. And Kinnock, particularly, saw that while Thatcher led the Tories, there was a political advantage for Labour in presenting itself as the pro-European party.

However strong the arguments, it was a striking piece of political revisionism. To honour Britain's place in the ERM, Smith went in front of the cameras during the 1992 election and promised unequivocally to do whatever was necessary to protect the value of the pound in world money markets. There have been Labour Chancellors who have presided over a rise in unemployment under pressure from the money markets; but John Smith was breaking new ground: he was making that an implicit election promise. He hoped, of course, that talking tough before he took office would reassure the pension funds and other holders of sterling, so preventing a crisis. It is unlikely that it would have worked.

There were four key players in the decision to endorse the ERM: Neil Kinnock, his economic adviser John Eatwell, John Smith, and Gordon Brown. Smith may not have been directly involved in dropping full employment as an aim of party policy, even though it followed as a direct consequence of his policy on the ERM. It appears to be attributable to Neil Kinnock, and to Tony Blair as Shadow Employment Secretary. As soon as Smith was party leader, and Frank Dobson had taken over from Tony Blair, full employment made an instant reappearance on Labour's agenda, but with a key difference: a British Labour government would be undertaking to alter the ground rules within the EC, so that all twelve member states could expand their economies and eliminate their dole queues together.

On the government side, Margaret Thatcher had no more of a fetish about protecting the value of the pound on foreign exchanges than she had about keeping unemployment down: she had, after all, presided over a 27 per cent devaluation of sterling in the early 1980s. Nigel Lawson had then experimented by making the pound "shadow" the Deutschmark, which meant that he did what was necessary to keep the exchange rate stable, without entering into a formal treaty which obliged him to do so. Thatcher considered the experiment an irritating failure which had allowed German busybodies to dictate the pace of economic growth in Britain. She also suspected that the ERM would prove to be a step towards fixed exchange rates. In other words, it opened the prospect of the end of sterling as a distinct currency, and the arrival of a single European currency. The end of sterling as a currency, in Thatcher's eyes, would be the end of Britain as a sovereign nation. In her early days as Prime Minister she had relied on a personal adviser named Professor Sir Alan Walters, who shared her opinion that exchange rates should be left to the markets. He had been absent in the USA for five years, but it had already been announced that he would take up his former role as Margaret Thatcher's economic guru in the autumn – a development which could only undermine Nigel Lawson and make British entry to the ERM less likely.

Knowing that serious trouble was brewing in the Cabinet, John Smith naturally did all he could to make it worse. "Why has there been the continued comic farce over who runs the government's exchange rate policy?" he taunted Nigel Lawson, as early as March 1988. "Is it the Prime Minister or is it the Chancellor? Some day the Chancellor might tell us." The affair, he said, was "an idiotic Punch and Judy show . . . it seems that Judy has slaughtered Punch. She may go on beating him again, because . . . Judy always wins."[4] In June the following year, when Labour used one of its allotted "opposition days" to have an economic debate in the Commons, Smith amused his own side by quoting the lyrics of *Neighbours*, which he had had his secretary Ann Barrett solemnly take down from the TV. "Hardly a day goes by when we do not have a further indication of dissent and confusion in that border zone between No. 10 and No. 11 Downing Street," he said.[5]

On a visit to Glasgow for a by-election later in the month, he claimed that the Chancellor, once known as "Lucky Lawson" was now "Unlucky Lawson" – "She is determined to blame him. . . . He is stubbornly refusing to be the fall guy. He is fighting a fierce rearguard action against Sir Alan Walters . . . "[6] Then, to Labour's surprise, Punch suddenly beat Judy. At a European summit in Madrid, Margaret Thatcher, her Foreign Secretary Sir Geoffrey Howe, and Chancellor Nigel Lawson had jointly accepted the principle of British membership of the ERM. Attached to the agreement were three conditions – the so-called "Madrid conditions", which had to be met before Britain would join. Howe and Lawson later claimed that they forced a reluctant Margaret Thatcher to accept the Madrid conditions by threatening to resign if she refused, and that it was her bad faith over the deal which caused their resignations – and hers.

Given Kinnock's recent decision to make Labour the party of Europe, he naturally decided that if the Tories had a clear set of conditions for ERM membership, so must Labour. They would not, of course, be the same conditions. The Madrid conditions were all about free markets and inflation rates; Labour's would relate to jobs, regional policies and rates of industrial growth. All this was decided in private meetings over the summer between Smith's team and John Eatwell, who was acting for Kinnock. What was not obvious then was how they could sell a new policy to the Labour Party. The old one was still grinding its way through the official machinery, to be adopted by the party conference in October, and there was really no stopping it at such a late hour. Then fate dealt a golden opportunity, only days after the conference had concluded.

Coincidentally, John Smith and Gordon Brown were on a flight to Belgium for their first meeting with the new EC President, Jacques Delors. Reading *The Financial Times* in midflight, Gordon Brown spotted an explosive article by Sir Alan. On the eve of taking up his appointment, the professor had allowed the pink 'un to reproduce a piece he had written months earlier for an obscure US publication, in which he rubbished the EMS for being "half-baked". Coming from the Prime Minister's adviser, it was an open insult to the Chancellor. By another happy chance, the following Tuesday was one of the days set aside for the opposition to choose a subject for debate. Labour chose economic policy, and put John Smith up to open. Convention then dictated that Nigel Lawson had to reply for the government.

From the dispatch box, Smith milked the indiscretions of Sir Alan Walters for all they were worth. "These are not the antics of some eccentric outsider: they are the work of a specially appointed insider in No. 10," he scoffed.

> "When assessing this happy bond between Nos 10 and 11 Downing Street, one extracts the true flavour of the team approach and a proper understanding of why no one in his right mind will believe that a team approach to anything is

> ever possible under the present Prime Minister. Isolated in Europe, isolated in the Commonwealth, at home she is increasingly isolated by deference and lack of courage of a Cabinet who dare not challenge her overwhelming pretensions. . . . I used to feel sorry for the Chancellor of the Exchequer, but it is time that he did something for himself. It is time for enterprise and individual responsibility. It is time he told the Prime Minister that the moment has come to end the confusion and disarray. . . . I advise the Chancellor to make an early decision on the important question of whether he will jump or be pushed . . . "[7]

This was during a trial period when TV cameras were operating in the House of Commons. Viewers could see John Smith enjoying himself; they could hear MPs laughing – though they might not know how much some of the Tories were enjoying his jokes too. The cutaway shots of Nigel Lawson glumly soaking up his punishment told their own story.

If the debate started badly for the Chancellor, its ending was no better. Convention demanded he be back in place to hear Gordon Brown wind up for the opposition. The speech was a wind-up in more than one sense. "Many lonely, sad and embattled people labour under the delusion that their thoughts are being influenced by the Moonies next door," he taunted. "I assure the Right Honourable Gentleman that he is not paranoid. They really are out to get him."

"Go on – smile," Labour MPs jeered at the stony-faced Chancellor – who must, by now, have decided that he had had enough. That same week, to Thatcher's astonishment, he resigned, giving Sir Alan's appointment as his reason. The professor also resigned. Their going added to John Smith's reputation as a parliamentary performer. The following morning's *Financial Times* judged that Smith's "dogged and skilful onslaught on the Government's economic strategy and on the growing rift in Downing Street helped to bring yesterday's dramatic events to a head".[8] A month later, it brought him the accolade of Parliamentarian of the Year for the second time in four years. At the celebratory lunch in the Savoy he was placed at the same table as Nigel Lawson, who was being awarded recognition for a first-class resignation speech.

To one admiring MP, John Smith and Gordon Brown are "like the grandmasters of political strategy, capable of seeing fifteen moves ahead". As they mulled over Sir Alan's article, thousands of feet above the North Sea, they appear to have spotted a way to head off what could have been a serious dispute inside the Shadow Cabinet.

There had already been a broad hint of what was to come when the new Institute for Public Policy Research, a think-tank set up in offices near Covent Garden by John Eatwell and Kinnock's former press secretary, Patricia Hewitt, opened for business in July 1989. Its first discussion paper, published in September, was an essay by the economist Gavyn

Davies from the merchant bank Goldman Sachs, whom the Kinnocks knew well, arguing that sterling should enter the ERM without delay. This was still unofficial. It was well known that the IPPR broadly represented what Kinnock thought, but it had no formal relationship with the Party. Official policy on the EMS and ERM, as sanctified by the October 1989 party conference, was that:

> the European Monetary System, as at present constituted, suffers from too great an emphasis on deflationary measures as a means of achieving monetary targets and that it imposes obligations which are not symmetrical. . . .
>
> Substantial changes would therefore be required before the next Labour government could take sterling into the Exchange Rate Mechanism. There must be less reliance on interest rate adjustments and more on co-operation between central banks. There would have to be an EC-wide operation trade policy which contributes to balance of payments stability for individual members. There must be a co-ordinated EC-wide growth policy. The pound would have to enter at a rate and on conditions which ensured that British goods became and remained competitive.[9]

Nothing here suggests that Labour was only days away from embracing the ERM; but then what was written was not what John Smith thought. The ERM question came within the remit of the Productive and Competitive Economy review group. Although Gordon Brown was a member, he was not an assiduous attender. The group's convenor was Bryan Gould, a long-standing anti-marketeer who had been sacked from the only government job he had ever held, as Parliamentary Private Secretary to Peter Shore, for his opposition to European integration. In 1979 he had spoken from the back benches, warning Britain not to join the EMS. However, Gould had seriously weakened his position by falling out with Neil Kinnock over another matter. During a Sunday lunch-time TV interview with Brian Walden, he had suggested that a Labour government would make it harder for would-be house buyers to obtain mortgages, as a means of reducing the amount of money available for private consumption. The Treasury team had also talked of reducing the amount of easy money being loaned to consumers, but they were talking about bank loans and consumer credit available through plastic cards. They certainly did not want it implied that Labour would deny young couples their dream of home ownership. In a rare operation, a number of political journalists, who are always on the lookout for internal party quarrels, had this one pointed out for them by a Labour Party press officer, in order that Gould's remarks could be disowned almost as soon as they were uttered. In consequence, Monday morning's newspapers were full of reports that Neil Kinnock was furious with Bryan Gould.

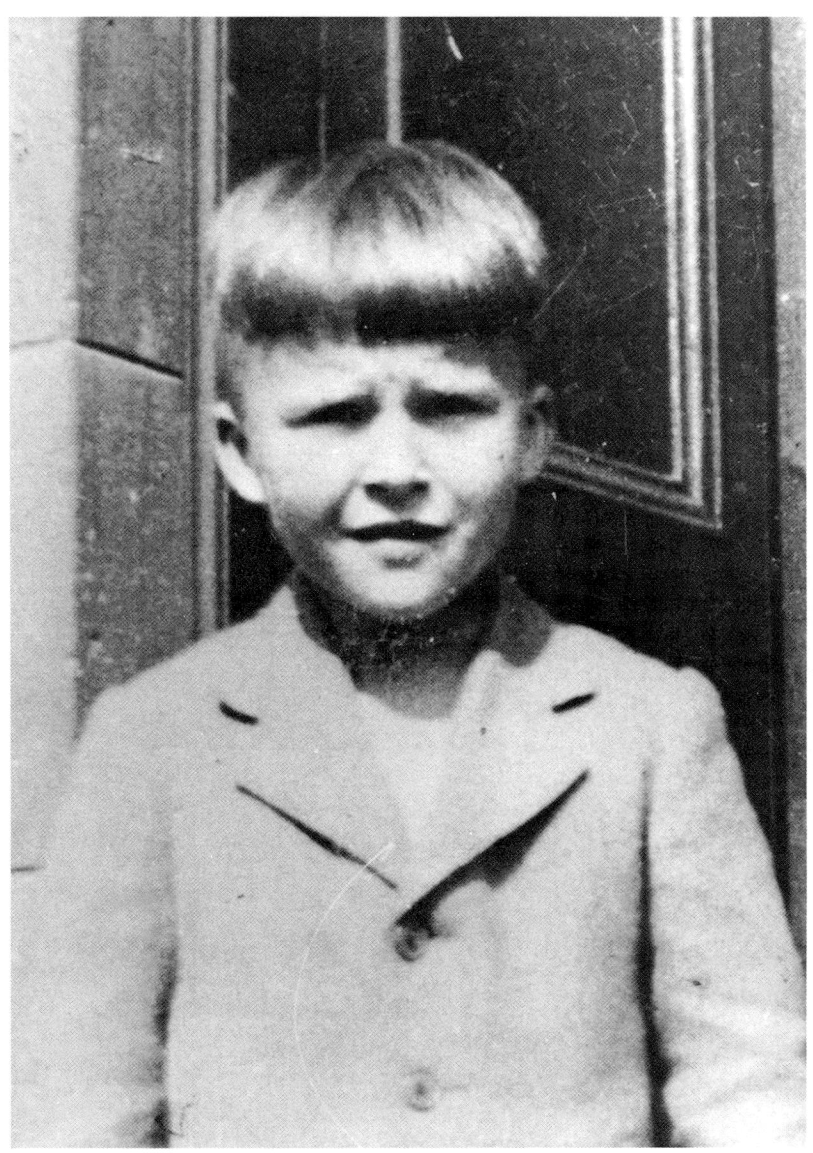

The headmaster's son, outside the family home in Ardrishaig. (*Daily Record*)

Top The final year at the 'big school' in Ardrishaig. Four of those in the photograph, including the teacher Ella Aitken, were still living in the village more than forty years later.

Bottom The class of '51, Lochgilphead. John Smith, aged 13, is seated at the centre in the front row. (Both photographs kindly loaned by Mrs Grace Clifford, of Ardrishaig.)

Top Canvassing in the East Fife by-election, 1961. (*Glasgow Herald*)

Bottom January 1976 – the Secretary of State for Energy and his deputy hold a press conference at Glasgow's Central Hotel. (*Glasgow Herald*)

October 1974: John Smith in his new office on the Monday morning after his appointment as Parliamentary Under Secretary for Energy. (Press Association)

Britain's youngest Cabinet Minister pauses at the threshold. (Press Association)

Labour's Shadow Chancellor advertises his return to politics in January 1989 after a heart attack, with a brisk walk in the hills over Edinburgh. (*Daily Mirror*)

Top The rivals: John Smith and Bryan Gould arrive at a debate organized by the Fabian Society during the party leadership election. (John Sturrock, Network)

Bottom Moment of glory: John Smith and Margaret Beckett on their election as leader and deputy leader. NEC members Diana Jeuda and Tom Burlison are behind Smith, and on the edge of the picture is Labour's long-serving Director of Organization, Joyce Gould, holding the statutory baby. (*Daily Mirror*)

Top The Smiths and daughters on the morning after his election as leader. Left to right: Sarah, aged 23, Elizabeth, John, Jane, 22, and Catherine, 19. (*Daily Mirror*)

Bottom Hallelujah: John and Elizabeth in church on Sunday morning, at the start of the 1992 Party Conference. (*Daily Mirror*)

As it happened, one of the people who did not read that day's newspapers was John Smith, because he was in Paris at the time. He was, however, scheduled to link up for a live interview about the trip on Radio 4's "Today" programme. Minutes before he was due on air, a producer mentioned in passing that he would, of course, be asked about Bryan Gould. Smith had no idea what the story was, and it had to be explained to him, second-hand, over the telephone. On air, he resorted to one of the favourite tricks of politicians who need to talk their way out of a tight corner: he claimed, without any supporting evidence, that Gould had been misquoted. His mind was made up, he said later, by what he and Gordon Brown learnt during their tour of three European capitals. The people they met included the French Prime Minister, Michel Rocard, and his Finance Minister Pierre Bérégovoy; the Bundesbank President Karl-Otto Pohl, and the German SPD's finance spokesman, Wolfgang Roth; and, most important of all, Jacques Delors. Except for Pohl, these were leading members of the left, whose thinking was close to John Smith's; they were all committed to merging the twelve European currencies into one eventually, and convinced that the process need not depress their economies or spread unemployment and deprivation in the poorer regions. It could be accompanied, they claimed, by growth in all twelve economies, and an enlightened social policy. The French were already drafting a Social Charter to guarantee certain minimal rights for vulnerable workers.

If this is what finally converted Smith, it worked quickly. As early as 18 October 1989, the day when Sir Alan Walter's article appeared, he told a meeting of socialist MEPs: "We are keen to play a full and constructive part in the debate on progress towards monetary union"[10] – which contrasted with the bald statement adopted as official party policy a fortnight earlier: "We oppose moves towards a European Monetary Union."[11] On his return to Britain, the Shadow Chancellor executed an adroit shift in Labour's policy on the ERM, which passed almost unnoticed in the excitement of Lawson's resignation. Every objection Labour had once had to joining the ERM either disappeared, or became a starting point for negotiation.

During his witty demolition of Nigel Lawson in the Commons, Smith slipped in the advice that the government should "negotiate to join the ERM under the important and prudent conditions that the Labour Party has outlined".[12] When he dropped this interesting comment he had been speaking for about twenty minutes, virtually without interruption – highly unusual in a raucous debating house like the Commons. The Tories appeared to be mesmerized by his assault on Lawson, and solidly united in their unwillingness to come to their Chancellor's rescue. After another two or three minutes, what he had said suddenly appeared to sink in. The

Tory benches came alive. There were so many Tories on their feet, demanding more details about Labour's proposals, that the Deputy Speaker had to call for order. Smith carried on, with the brass-necked aplomb of a true professional. He could rely on the two or three hundred Tory MPs across the aisle not to have read Labour's policies with any care; they would look to *The Daily Telegraph* to keep them abreast of any changes. So Smith could behave as if he had said nothing new. They must surely know about Labour's "prudent" conditions for entering the ERM, he insisted, with an air of controlled impatience with people who wasted Parliament's valuable time by asking questions to which they should already know the answers.

A few minutes further into his speech, the Commons came alive again as the Tories, who were now on the alert, detected an interesting omission. Although he plainly wanted sterling to enter the ERM, he was being circumspect about the point of entry: how many marks and pfennigs there would be to the pound. This was almost as vital to Britain's economic future as the fact of ERM membership. Labour's policy review document referred to a "competitive" rate, meaning not many pfennigs to the pound. A devalued pound would make British goods easy to sell abroad, but would make foreign goods expensive in British shops. It would be good for jobs, but bad for inflation. It was the policy upon which the Tory government stumbled in September 1992. It was also what the Tories thought John Smith was implying. "The Labour Party rests for the success of its policies on a very considerable devaluation. His statement cannot conceivably mean anything else. What size of devaluation has he in mind?" exclaimed Sir Peter Hordern, a backbench Tory. Smith retorted enigmatically that Sir Peter was "mistaken".[13]

These "prudent" conditions on which a Labour government would have signed up to the ERM were set out by John Smith in a newspaper article early in November. They were "entry at an effective rate, adequate central bank swap arrangements to tackle speculative attacks, increased support for regional policy, and agreement on a strategy for growth".[14] In his Commons speech he had listed only three, omitting regional policy; but that, presumably, was a simple slip. The complaint included in the 1989 policy document: that the EMS was not "symmetrical" – which means that it forced states with weak currencies to depress their economies but placed no obligation on those with strong currencies to stimulate growth – seemed to vanish from Labour's thinking altogether. It was next heard of two and a half years later, when Bryan Gould was challenging Smith for the party leadership. Another significant change was the appearance of the word "effective". Previously, the Labour Party had said it wanted entry at a "competitive" rate, which plainly meant that it was prepared to let the value of the pound drop until there was an assured European market for British goods. "Effective" was an ambiguous adjective. It would emerge in the months which followed that it meant "effective" for the purpose of keeping control of inflation in Britain – a quite different objective.

These changes attracted almost no comment, because the eyes of MPs and commentators were fixed on the drama within the Tory Cabinet. Besides, a general election might be only eighteen months away, and there was a general will on Labour's side to do whatever was necessary to win. It would have made no immediate tactical sense for Labour to attack the principle of ERM membership. The enemy in their sights was Margaret Thatcher, not Nigel Lawson. Accusing her of being isolated and dictatorial would have lost its edge if Labour's front bench also believed, as she did, that entry into the ERM was bad for Britain. There was no point in saying, as Smith did in a television interview, that "everyone in Europe knows once again that Mrs Thatcher has no intention to be bound by agreements in Madrid or elsewhere",[15] unless Labour was agreeing to be bound by the Madrid conditions. With his adroit timing, and by turning in a first-rate parliamentary performance when it was most needed, John Smith had persuaded the Labour Party to change trains.

14
Lunching for Labour
1989–90

The period when John Smith went lunching for Labour, touring the City of London's prawn cocktail circuit to reassure its opinion-formers that he would be a responsible Chancellor, backed by sane and sensible economics ministers, was approaching.

Labour MPs demonstrated just how much they wanted stability when, for the first time in ten years, they re-elected all fifteen incumbent members of the Shadow Cabinet in November 1989. Gordon Brown topped the poll and John Smith was runner-up, just as in the previous year. Interest focused on three new members. The rules had been changed to increase the Shadow Cabinet's size to eighteen elected members, and in a way which effectively guaranteed the extra places to women MPs. The first to benefit were Ann Clwyd, Joan Lestor and the Shadow Social Security Minister, Margaret Beckett.

Neil Kinnock's last Shadow Cabinet reshuffle followed the next day. Gordon Brown, of course, was promoted: it had been obvious for at least a year that he would have to be, and it was no great surprise that he took over responsibility for Trade and Industry, when Bryan Gould was shifted to look after Environment. That was a move which suited John Smith, despite his reported rivalry with Gordon Brown. A few days later he gave an interview in which, by implication, he promised to be the first Chancellor in recent memory to relinquish power voluntarily, by allowing the Department of Trade and Industry a substantial slice of the action when government funds were being deployed to stimulate the economy and revive depressed regions. The former Trade Secretary conceded that the separation of "trade" and "industry" by the former Labour government had been "Probably a mistake." He told *The Independent*: "We need a very strong DTI. . . . The Treasury shouldn't be running industrial policy"[1] – a point he would have been far less willing to concede if it had meant leaving Gould in command of Labour's industrial policy.

Indeed, the conflict between Smith and Gould continued unabated for another ten months, on a new battleground. Gould's main responsibility now was to work out an alternative to the much-hated poll tax, a subject in which the Treasury team took a lively interest. The proposal Gould inherited was a two-tax system, combining a revised version of the rates with an element of local income tax. Two taxes for one promised to be complicated to enact and easy to attack. It was not much appreciated by Labour MPs, which is why the previous chief environment spokesman, John Cunningham, almost lost his place in the Shadow Cabinet election in 1989, coming eighteenth out of eighteen.

The view from the Treasury team was that if Labour was to produce an alternative – although there was a school of thought that no alternative was necessary because the tax was so unpopular that merely promising to scrap it would be worth a mountain of votes – whatever Labour proposed had better be simple. The overriding imperative, in John Smith's view, was that if there was an election in April, May or June, Labour could make a campaign promise that there would be no more poll tax bills. (An October poll would necessitate some interim arrangement to cover the bills due the following March.) Jack Straw, a former local government spokesman, agreed. The simplest scheme of all, of course, would be to go straight back to the rates.

Gould insisted that he was as alert as anyone to the need to abolish the poll tax immediately; but he was impressed by arguments put forward by Shadow Poll Tax Minister David Blunkett, among others, that the rates system was deeply unfair on certain people, like pensioners living alone in homes with a high rateable value, and that a modern computer system to be installed by the Inland Revenue would soon make a form of local income tax relatively simple to implement. Gould also took the view that the "rateable value" of someone's home, as it was calculated under the old system, was meaningless, because it was based on the rent which the owner would be able to charge if the house was let to tenants, but since the private rental sector of the housing market had collapsed, notional rent could not be accurately assessed. The quick and easy solution would be to say that a house's "rateable value" would be what it was worth if it was sold to a new owner; but in some parts of the country house prices were doubling every three years, and that proposal might make homeowners think their rates bills were going to increase at the same speed. All these details threw up fierce and complex arguments behind the scenes.

In the end, most points of view were accommodated in a carefully thought-out policy announced late in July 1990, which set out a three-stage reform of local taxation. First, in year one, the rates would be reintroduced with a new rebate system to protect those worst affected; next, a new system for calculating rateable values would be introduced, based on a variety of market factors rather just one; and finally, the Inland

Revenue's computers would be brought into operation for the introduction of a new tax based on a combination of property values and ability to pay. Once it was published, this policy gave the Labour Party no further trouble; but the intervening months, when the Party had no policy for financing local government, were fraught with rumours that Bryan Gould had gone on intellectual walkabout again, devising an elaborate policy which would never leave the drawing board, whilst John Smith was having to remind him of political realities.[2]

After reading several uncomplimentary newspaper stories about himself, Gould became convinced that someone in the Labour Party was running a deliberate clandestine operation to undermine him, for the benefit of John Smith. He was so angered by one BBC report that he demanded a retraction – and was told by a BBC political correspondent that their information had come from Labour's press office. An angry Bryan Gould then presented himself in Neil Kinnock's office, where he accused the Director of Communications, Peter Mandelson, of being the source of inaccurate leaks, and demanded that he be stopped. Mandelson's deputy, Colin Byrne, Smith's researcher, David Ward, and Chris Smith MP, one of the Treasury team, were also on his list of suspects. Someone in the Gould camp then leaked a story to *The Guardian* that Neil Kinnock was furious that there should have been so many leaks, which seems to have been wishful thinking. In this, as on most economic questions, Kinnock's sympathies appeared to have lain with Smith rather than Gould.

Meanwhile, Gould was not the only dissident to be shunted to one side. Michael Meacher, the former Employment Secretary who had been in open conflict with the party leader over trade-union legislation, was moved to the social security slot, making way for Tony Blair. Into Gordon Brown's former place as Shadow Chief Secretary went a surprising new incumbent: Margaret Beckett. So the new team of Smith, Brown, Blair and Beckett was in control of economic policy. This foursome was to become so familiar as the acceptable face of the Labour Party that they were known to envious colleagues as the "favoured four". (At first the education spokesman, Jack Straw, was thrown in, making it the favoured five.) Their special status was first institutionalized in April 1991, in a party political broadcast by Hugh Hudson, director of *Chariots of Fire*, whose previous political work included the celebrated Kinnock video broadcast shown during the 1987 election campaign. Mr Hudson set out to perform the same service for John Smith, Gordon Brown, Tony Blair and Margaret Beckett, dipping into their family backgrounds to uncover the roots of their political beliefs. Over the next year, there was a sequence of party political broadcasts which featured the team around the leader, rather than simply Neil Kinnock; sometimes other Shadow Cabinet members were brought in, but none of the four was ever left out.

Margaret Beckett was certainly the most daring and most unexpected of these appointments.

There had been several phases in the life of Margaret Beckett, *née* Jackson, trained metallurgist turned Labour Party researcher. She first made the limelight as a hard-nosed left-wing anti-marketeer, who succeeded at the second attempt, in 1974, in dislodging the defector Dick Taverne from his seat in Lincoln. Once in Parliament, she was identified with the Tribunite "soft left" as parliamentary secretary to Judith Hart, the Overseas Aid Minister sacked by Harold Wilson but rehabilitated by James Callaghan. She also did a stint as a government whip. In 1976, Joan Lestor resigned as a junior education minister in protest over cuts in the schools budget. It was thought that no one from the Labour left would want to take her place. Probably, it was the party whips who tipped off Jim Callaghan that Margaret Jackson might agree. During the next three turbulent years, she was a loyal member of the Callaghan administration. Having lost her seat in the 1979 election, however, she came back as a Bennite. Her change of name resulted from her marriage to a party activist from her former Lincoln seat, Leo Beckett, who proved a selflessly devoted political husband. She stayed with the Campaign group until 1988, when she resigned in protest against Benn's decision to contest the party leadership. It was as a name on the left-wing slate that she was elected to the NEC in 1985. The right-wing unions succeeded in removing her a year later but she returned in 1987, only to be ousted by the right again in 1988.

Typically, John Smith was not bothered by details from her past. He had long since learnt the advantage of working alongside someone from the left; and more recently, he had appreciated that if Labour was to be seen to take equal opportunities seriously, women would have to be given senior economic jobs rather than be confined to "caring" specialities like social security. It was in that spirit that the talented Marjorie Mowlam became Shadow City Minister within Gordon Brown's team – a job usually given to someone seen as a future member of the Shadow Cabinet. Margaret Beckett had been on one of the policy review committees chaired by John Smith, and had thoroughly impressed him by her capacity for hard work and her grasp of practical detail. He might have guessed that a challenging job would make her as loyal to him as she was to Callaghan after her previous unexpected promotion. When he went to Kinnock to nominate her as his deputy, he says, the leader had already marked her down for the job anyway.

For the next two years, she played the dual role of rebel on non-economic issues, particularly defence, and pillar of orthodoxy on matters of direct interest to the Treasury team. During a tense NEC meeting at the opening of the 1990 party conference, she was one of half a dozen Shadow Cabinet members who voted against Neil Kinnock's line on defence spending. The rebels were upholding the position voted on by the previous year's conference, which called for specific and drastic cuts in defence spending under a Labour government, whereas Kinnock wanted to keep the commitment vague. Like Robin Cook, Margaret Beckett was able to take this stand without paying the penalty in the Shadow Cabinet elections later in the month, although the other four offenders – Ann Clwyd, Bryan Gould, Joan Lestor and John Prescott – all saw their support fall drastically.

She also managed to be an occasional member of the celebrated "Supper Club", which was the focus of opposition to the Gulf War in 1991, without spoiling her reputation as a staunch upholder of Labour's new realism. That was because on the issues which mattered most to John Smith she was undeviatingly loyal, even behind closed doors. For example, during one of the Shadow Cabinet's "awayday" sessions in Edinburgh, at the end of August 1991, an entire Friday was spent discussing the economy. The sessions – predictably – included an argument about European monetary union in which, with Bryan Gould away on holiday, Robin Cook, Michael Meacher and John Prescott acted as the opposition. Margaret Beckett did not join them.

The Tories even invented the half-mocking, half-admiring "Beckett's Law" as a tag for Labour's tight control of its public spending plans. Beckett's Law laid down that the proposed increases in child benefit and the state pension were the only firm promises in Labour's programme which would be a drain on the public purse, and that they would be paid for, with money to spare, by the planned increase in the top rate of income tax and the changes to National Insurance. The national minimum wage remained a solid commitment, but that was taken as being principally a cost to private sector employers; its cost to NHS wages would be met by abolishing tax relief on private health care for the elderly. Any other proposal to spend public money which might turn up in a party document or a speech by a Shadow minister was not a promise but an aspiration, to be paid for – in another expression which became famous at the time – "as resources allow".

This could equally have been called Smith's Law, or even Brown's Law, since it was a direct outcome of the 1989 policy review. However, it was during Margaret Beckett's tenure as Shadow Chief Secretary, when Labour was soaring ahead in the opinion polls, that the Tories became aware of the discipline being imposed on Labour's spending programme. It caused them endless frustration. The clever formulation "as resources allow" gave shadow ministers freedom to carry on as an opposition: one week the health team could berate the government for starving the NHS of funds; another week the education team would step forward to expose the underfunding of Britain's schools, or the overseas aid team might be pointing out how the proportion of Britain's wealth donated to the starving in the Third World had fallen since 1979 – a spending cut which Smith himself had denounced as an "insult to the generosity of the British people";[3] but was anyone saying that a Labour government would spend more on these good causes? The answer was – only if resources allowed.

The Tory Party chairman, Kenneth Baker, was left in the exasperating position that the government was under constant attack for being parsimonious, but he could not retaliate in the manner which had worked so well in 1987: by totalling the cost of Labour's spending promises and saying how much extra tax would be needed to cover them. In the end, the Tories did not allow themselves to be disadvantaged by a shortage of information: what they lacked, they invented. None the less, Beckett's Law was an enormous factor in giving Labour an unthreatening respectability among middle-class voters.

How not to frighten prosperous professionals was the theme of one of the Shadow Cabinet's all-day sessions, at a London hotel on 16 November 1989. The idea that the state could stimulate the economy, either by expanding nationalized industries or through local councils, was out, Smith told them. The government was not going to raise enough through taxes or borrowing to be in a position to make any significant impact on unemployment because, other considerations aside, the rules of the ERM prevented it. Consequently, growth would have to come through private investment. That would mean holding fast to Beckett's Law, and meeting industrial and financial leaders to establish trust before election day. "We can leave dogmatism to the Tories," he said.[4] So began the "prawn cocktail" offensive, in which Smith and others ventured into the City for lunch-time meetings with merchant bankers, stockbrokers, market analysts and others not known for being biased in Labour's favour. This played havoc with the Shadow Chancellor's diet, but helped to reduce the risk of a run on the pound and panic in the stock markets in the event of a Labour victory. Smith himself vows that it was never a planned exercise: they had a few invitations, which they accepted, and the incongruous sight of Labour spokesmen venturing into the citadel of capitalism took off of its own accord as a newspaper story. This is quite likely, but once it was running, no one in the Labour Party showed any inclination to deny the story.

International currency dealers were promised there would be no attempt to bring back exchange controls. "That genie is out of the bottle," Smith declared.[5] In February 1990 he won an ovation from the Cornhill Club, whose membership is made up of bankers under the age of forty, after promising there would be no nationalization of the banks. In the same month he spoke to two hundred clients of the investment bankers Shearson Lehman Hutton, assuring them that Labour supported the EMS and would keep public finances under tight control. "I think he made a very favourable impression and people were pleasantly surprised," Shearson economist Peter Spencer said.[6]

In April Smith told senior members of the German SPD, during a bipartisan meeting in London: "We are ready to negotiate entry of the pound into the ERM."[7] Two weeks later, on a trip to the USA, he told the America–European Community Association that Labour was now a "significantly European" party, "eager" to be in the ERM and with a much-revised attitude to capitalism. "We welcome and endorse the dynamism, efficiency and realism which markets can provide," he assured the association.[8] In the same month, a survey of 77 eminent economists, by *The Economist* magazine, revealed that 34 thought Smith would be a better Chancellor than John Major, while 20 preferred the incumbent, and the remainder were noncommittal.

Another reason why Beckett's Law impinged on political life more in 1990 than it had the year before was that the longer it carried on, the more difficult it was for the Labour Party to stick to it. It was acceptable to everyone in the early stages of the policy review that there would be a few unbreakable promises which would be written into party policy, and no one minded that it was pensioners and children first. Promises of more investment in jobs, schools, hospitals and homes were expected to follow, as the review took its course; but as the months passed, it became increasingly clear that this was not happening. Resources were not allowing it: the economy was slowing down, and Labour's commitment to the ERM would deny the new government the opportunity of a sudden expansion in output.

As early as October 1989, on the opening day of the party conference, John Smith had warned: "There are no quick fixes, and I will not be indulging in a quick fix. A quick fix quickly becomes unfixed."[9] The warnings became more urgent, at the very time when the government was sinking into an economic quagmire and the opposition's morale was rising. By March 1990: "The situation is now much worse than it was three or four months ago, and joining the EMS will impose a new discipline. It will show up in the fight against unemployment and everything else we want to do."[10]

Labour's policies to date were summarized in a document called *Looking to the Future*, which was given a set-piece launch by the entire Shadow Cabinet in May 1990. This was the document from which a commitment to full employment was conspicuously absent. It also specified that if a Labour government negotiated Britain's entry, "the rate at which sterling enters the ERM will, of course, be judged at the time, on the basis not only of avoiding competitive disadvantage for our industry, but also of maintaining an anti-inflationary stance".[11] By this point, then, the idea of entering at a "competitive" rate to maximize British exports was out. "Devaluation will not really be an option," John Smith said in a newspaper interview around this time. "If companies make mistakes and they are beaten in the competition of the single market, I can't do very much about it." From there, he went on to warn that a Labour government would not have the freedom to accommodate trade unions who submitted inflationary wage demands. "They can cause unemployment. They must judge that," he said.[12] He emphasized the point in a lecture to the Fabian Society the following month, telling them that the ERM would give "exchange rate stability and an anti-inflationary anchor" which would be "more conducive to long term investment. The art of economic management is to a large extent about avoiding unnecessary shocks. . . . That, of course, is the real attraction of the ERM," he added.[13] There were, of course, other views besides John Smith's. Only four days before Britain actually entered, John Edmonds warned that "we should go into the ERM, but we should go in at a sustainable rate, not a suicide rate"[14] – but warning voices like that were muted.

The point about the document which excited the Tories, however, was the application of Beckett's Law. There were just not enough spending pledges to discredit Smith's tax plans. "We are going to be utterly realistic and utterly honest," Smith warned Labour MPs at a meeting called especially to discuss *Looking to the Future*.[15] It was at this point that the Tories applied some lateral thinking by converting every clause or sentence that contained any promise of government action as an expense on the public purse, and demanding that it be costed. Kenneth Baker sent an open letter to Smith, listing eighty-one spending pledges he claimed to have uncovered in the one document. If the government had actually believed the opposition was making spending pledges, and had genuinely wanted them costed, there was a simple answer, of course: the civil service could do it; but the Heiser memorandum had reminded them that civil servants were not going to make bogus costings on pledges which did not exist. And Baker's list was threadbare. There was, for example, a clause in the document covering one of John Smith's favourite themes: the estimated £5 billion a year lost to the Exchequer through tax evasion and avoidance. "Labour will ensure that the Inland Revenue and National Insurance Inspectorate have sufficient staff and resources to make sure that taxes due are actually paid," it said, thereby providing Kenneth Baker with No. 80 on his list of "spending pledges".

Labour had enjoyed eighteen months of unprecedented success, which peaked in May 1990, after the effect of the first set of poll tax bills in England and Wales had begun to fade. On one heady Sunday, four opinion polls put the opposition at least 19 per cent ahead of the government. In one, Labour registered 57 per cent support, the highest for any party since opinion polling began. The Mid-Staffordshire by-election, in March, produced the biggest swing to Labour at any by-election since the First World War: a 14,654 Tory majority became a 9,449 Labour majority. By May, though, the Tories were showing greater presentational skills. At the council elections they lost three hundred seats, their worst result in ten years, but they made it look rather good by hinting before the event that they expected to lose six hundred, and by persuading commentators to concentrate on London boroughs like Westminster and Wandsworth, where the poll tax was low and they did quite well. Later in the month, government sources hinted darkly that inflation was about to go above 10 per cent, so that when the actual figure turned out to be 9.4 per cent – a jump from 8.1 per cent, ministers could claim to be relieved. Inevitably, Labour's huge and unsustainable opinion poll lead shrank towards a more realistic 10 per cent.

As it do so, Neil Kinnock made one of those slips of the tongue which caused a minor sensation in the little world of Westminster, though it probably had no impact on opinion outside. During an extensive "Panorama" interview, he was asked to specify how many taxpayers would be worse off under Labour's published plans, and replied: "I can tell you, the people who are currently paying the 25 per cent standard rate, plus 9 per cent National Insurance – fourteen out of fifteen taxpayers in this country – will not have to pay more."[16]

The next day, on BBC radio, John Smith was questioned on the same subject and gave a different version of Labour's policy. It was fourteen out of fifteen employees who now paid the basic 25 per cent income tax rate, excluding those on the higher rate, who would be no worse off under Labour's plans. He conceded that as many as 11 per cent of all taxpayers would be paying more National Insurance.[17] Behind the scenes, Labour's spin-doctors flatly denied any difference between the leader and the Shadow Chancellor, but plainly the two statements contradicted one another, and anyone who checked Labour's published documents could see that it was Neil Kinnock who got it wrong.

This provided an excuse for another round of rubbishing of the Labour leader. For example, John Smith appeared on BBC TV's "Question Time" with his former adversary, Nigel Lawson, who said that one reason why the Tories would win the next election was that "it is not John Smith but Neil Kinnock leading the Labour Party".[18] It was all actually quite mild compared with what was thrown at Kinnock during other periods in his leadership, but it ended the long run when his position had been unchallengeable, throwing a question mark over his future again. At the same time, Smith's relations with the leader had taken a turn for the worse, because of an argument which never became public knowledge. The previous autumn, they had been in complete agreement over the ERM. Once that advance on old party policy was accomplished, Neil Kinnock wanted to push on further, making sure that Labour was ahead of the Tories as the European party. He wanted it to commit itself in principle to the disappearance of sterling and the implementation of a single European currency early in the next century. Smith felt he was rushing too fast, and that there were enormous problems yet to be resolved caused by the gap between the wealthy, prosperous nations in the centre and those on the periphery, like Ireland, Spain, Portugal, Greece and Britain. It was too early to be talking about a single currency, he thought. And having risked his career when he was young to help secure Britain's entry into the Common Market, he did not feel the need to prove his credentials to a leader who, having been an anti-marketeer, was now more Catholic than the Pope.

If Kinnock was in any doubt about what his Shadow Chancellor thought, it was brought home to him just before the Commons rose for its summer break at the end of July. A member of the Shadow Cabinet, whom we must call X, visited him in the leader's office to warn him of a potentially serious threat to his position. X had been alarmed by a brief conversation he had had with John Smith, when they were sitting together on the front bench in the debating chamber. Smith had made a mildly derogatory comment about Kinnock's leadership, but the pointed way in which it was phrased, and the manner of its delivery had made X think he was being sounded out; he suspected that an attempt was in the offing to assemble a delegation, representing several shades of opinion in the Shadow Cabinet, who would confront Neil Kinnock and tell him that he must resign immediately, allowing a new leader to be elected before Parliament reassembled. "Neil took this very seriously," he says.

This is one of those stories which cannot be satisfactorily checked, because it is impossible to ask John Smith for his version of the conversation without breaking a confidence. It could all have been a misunderstanding. Perhaps Smith was being jocular, and far too much was read into a single remark. "I am not driven, as some politicians seem to be, by the notion that if you are not leader of a party, you are somehow a failure," he had told the *Daily Express* three months earlier – though he added that if the post was vacant and was offered to him, "naturally I would accept the responsibility".[19] On the other hand, there is no reason to doubt that X believed the story he was telling Kinnock. If it was true that a firing squad was being assembled, there would be no point in restricting it to former members of the Solidarity group; there had to be one or two people in it whom Kinnock would not have expected to see there, to convince him that he was finished, and the summer of 1990 would have been their last chance, because of the possibility of an election the following May. Whatever the truth of it, no attempt was made on Kinnock's political life, and by the autumn politics had become a whole new ball game.

15
The £35 Billion Price Tag
1990

During 1990, John Smith had to take a stand on a woman's right to end a pregnancy by abortion. It was not by any means the first time he had voted on the issue and, as ever, he displayed the virtue of consistency. It is, of course, a highly emotive question, with little room for compromise. In other Western democracies, it can sway the outcome of general elections. In Britain, where it has been successfully kept out of party politics, public opinion generally tolerates abortion on demand; within the Labour Party, especially among its women members, opinion is overwhelmingly and passionately behind this. For fifteen years, John Smith consistently opposed the majority view in his own party.

He has been so undeviating that it has to be assumed that, given the chance, he would have voted to prevent abortion from being legalized at all. However, this happened three years before Smith entered Parliament, through a Private Member's Bill sponsored by the young Liberal MP David Steel. In the 1970s and 1980s there were four attempts, via Private Members' Bills, to make the legislation introduced by David Steel more restrictive. Most were aimed at lowering the time limit for an abortion, which the Abortion Act had set at twenty-eight weeks after gestation, since there was a medical argument, which gained credibility as techniques improved, that a foetus was capable of surviving outside the mother's womb before twenty-eight weeks, and that it was consequently a viable, living human being at, say, twenty-four weeks. Each attempt provoked bitter opposition inside and outside Parliament, principally from women's groups who believed that each attempt at rewriting the Abortion Act was simply a step towards the real aim of the anti-abortion lobby: to make the ending of unwanted pregnancies illegal under virtually any circumstances. Every time, Smith either abstained or supported the anti-abortion lobby.

The first attempt to amend the law was made in February 1975 by a Glaswegian Labour MP named James White, whom Smith had known for many years. He had been one of the names on the shortlist for the Woodside by-election. He proposed to set a time limit of twenty weeks, and to put legal curbs on private clinics and on laboratory experiments involving foetuses. Smith voted for the Bill twice.[1] Having won a second reading, and having had a Commons committee set up to produce detailed legislation, the Bill then became ensnared in procedure. A year later the committee's deliberations were incomplete, and a fierce controversy raged over whether the Select Committee should be re-established, or the whole project dropped and the Abortion Act left intact. Smith voted with the majority to reconstitute the committee[2] – in vain, as it happened.

The next Private Member's Bill on this question, a slightly more detailed version of the White Bill, was presented by the Tory MP William Benyon on 25 February 1977. There were three votes. Smith supported Benyon on the first two, but abstained on the third, a procedural question about whether the Bill should be dealt with by a committee or by the whole House of Commons.[3] Without government backing, the Bill never reached the Statute Book.

In July 1979 another Tory MP, John Corrie, introduced a Bill which, again, would have reduced the time limit to twenty weeks. Some of his own potential supporters accused him of bad faith, because the British Medical Association thought he had agreed to include a clause which would have permitted abortion after twenty weeks where the mother's life was in danger. This time Smith was either not there to vote, or abstained.[4] Voting on Private Members' Bills takes place on a Friday, when MPs with constituencies a long way from London are likely to be absent. On every other occasion, however, Smith took the trouble to stay in town and cast his vote. He says he has forgotten why he did not vote for the Corrie Bill.

In February 1985 Enoch Powell sponsored the Protection of Unborn Children Bill, which would have banned research or experiments on embryos. Smith voted in favour.[5] The following May the Labour MP Leo Abse tried to amend Powell's Bill, adding the word "knowingly" to protect scientists or medical staff who might become involved in an embryo experiment unwittingly. Smith voted against the amendment.[6]

Finally, on 22 January 1988, the Liberal MP David Alton put forward a Bill to reduce the upper abortion limit to eighteen weeks. This was a free vote, like all the previous votes on this issue. However, although the Parliamentary Labour Party had no official line, Labour MPs were sent a letter by the General Secretary, Larry Whitty, reminding them that the Party outside had a policy, and if they wanted to observe it they should vote against the Alton Bill. Of the twenty-two MPs who were members of the Shadow Cabinet in summer 1992, nineteen voted against, including two of the Scots – Gordon Brown and Robin Cook. The exceptions were all from Scotland. Donald Dewar abstained. The two who supported Alton were Tom Clark and John Smith.[7]

In 1990, for the first time in many years, the government produced legislation which allowed MPs another vote on abortion. The Human Fertilisation and Embryology Bill provoked less controversy than the Private Members' Bills, but it was the most significant development in this field for twenty-five years because, being a government Bill, it went on to the Statute Book instead of disappearing into the labyrinth of Commons procedure. Although the question of the time limit for abortions was incidental to the main point of the Bill, it was an opportunity for a series of propositions to be put before the Commons. On each, MPs were allowed a free vote. They were ordered so that MPs began the evening by voting on extreme positions to lower the time limit to eighteen weeks, or to leave it where it was, at twenty-eight weeks. When both were defeated, they worked their way towards a compromise. Smith voted in favour of a reduction to twenty-two weeks. Consequently, he voted against amendments to keep it at twenty-eight weeks, or lower it to twenty-six weeks; on the proposals to set an even lower limit – eighteen or twenty weeks – he abstained. When all the amendments were defeated, a new time limit was set: twenty-four weeks, which Smith accepted as a reasonable compromise.

There was also an amendment to the Bill, carried by a very large majority, designed to clear up a legal anomaly under which a doctor who carried out an abortion which was legal under the new Act could be prosecuted under the 1922 Infant Life (Preservation) Act. To those who proposed it it seemed a straightforward, almost technical matter. However, Smith abstained.[8] Finally, MPs voted on whether the amended clause should be included in the Human Fertilisation and Embryology Bill. "Only at this stage", said a statement by the Women's Action Committee, "did Mr Smith support Labour Party policy on abortion."[9]

On other sensitive social issues, like hanging or divorce, John Smith has usually taken the line most people would expect from a liberally inclined lawyer. It is only on this one issue that he is so sharply out of line with most of the Labour Party. We can dismiss the idea put about by well-intentioned champions of the Smith cause during the leadership election: that he cast his votes under pressure from his Roman Catholic constituents.[10] This is based upon a geographical error. Of the two towns in Monklands, Coatbridge is Roman Catholic and Airdrie is Protestant. There are, of course, individual families living across the denominational border; but it is well known locally that the majority of Catholics are west of the line which divides the two Monklands constituencies. The former political editor of *The Guardian*, Ian Aitken, a native of the area, claimed: "You need sensitive theological nerve ends to spot when you move from one to the t'other. But those of us who were born there can tell the difference with our eyes shut."[11] Smith's neighbour, Tom Clarke, is himself a Roman Catholic representing a predominantly Catholic seat, and has been a platform speaker at a meeting of the Society for the Protection of Unborn Children. Whatever Smith's reasons are for his opposition to the Abortion Act, the line from the Roman Catholic Church is not one of them. It is also not very flattering to the man to suggest that for more than fifteen years he voted against his own conscience on an important social issue out of political opportunism. There need be no doubt that he was motivated by personal conviction. He is, though, very reluctant to give his reasons. He seems slightly irritated even to be asked about something which he regards as a matter of private conscience. "No, my reasons are not religious, though I am a Christian. I just thought the Abortion Act needed amending. I think the law as it now stands is right," he says.[12]

Had John Smith been leader of the Labour Party early in 1988, when morale was low and the Alton Bill was provoking fierce debate, it is easy to imagine that his leadership would have faced a direct challenge on this single issue, with a woman MP running against him. However, luck may now stay with him. Despite the efforts of SPUC, there is no evidence that the abortion issue has had a measurable effect on British elections, and anyway the Embryology Act has taken some of the controversy out of it. In particular, John Smith now feels that he can support his own party's policy with a clear conscience. As long as other things go well for Smith, this question will probably lie dormant. Voting on the abortion issue was like an interlude in the endless dispute over economic policy.

By autumn 1990, the Lawson boom had ended in tears. Interest rates had doubled to 15 per cent. House prices were tumbling, leaving a million unfortunate people who had bought at the height of the boom having to pay mortgages greater than the value of their properties. Thousands gave up trying: more than 75,000 homes were repossessed by building societies or other finance companies in 1991 alone. Unemployment was rising again. During a confrontation in the Commons in November, Smith taunted the Chancellor of the Exchequer, John Major, with being "unable to utter the word 'recession'", but a recession was surely on the way. According to the government's own prediction, which sounded grim at the time but proved grossly optimistic, it would last until the second half of 1991.

Everyone agreed that Nigel Lawson was responsible, because he had pumped too much ready cash into the economy. It was John Major who awarded his former boss the blame, on behalf of the Cabinet. Government and opposition diverged, though, on precisely what Lawson had done wrong. John Major accused him of overreacting to the Stock Exchange crash by lowering interest rates too quickly to avert the risk of recession, giving mortgage-holders too much extra spending money. This analysis conveniently incriminated John Smith, because Labour had wanted even lower interest rates. Smith maintained that reducing the cost of borrowing was the one thing Lawson had done right. His fault was to let loose too much easy money with a credit free-for-all and "irresponsible" tax cuts.[13]

The Chancellor and Shadow Chancellor also agreed that sterling ought to be in Europe's Exchange Rate Mechanism to protect it from attack by currency speculators. Smith guessed that Major might succeed where Lawson had failed, and persuade a reluctant Margaret Thatcher to acquiesce. He described the government's strategy, satirically, as the STES, or "short-term election strategy", adding: "The plan is to maintain high interest rates – as indeed the government must – until Britain joins the ERM and then, in the period of lower interest rates which may occur following entry, to encourage a boomlet to coincide with the election . . . "[14] All the signs were that after the boomlet, the economy would take another turn for the worse.

The announcement that sterling had joined the ERM came late in the afternoon of Friday 5 October, as political journalists were taking the train south from Blackpool at the end of the Labour Party conference. With ERM membership came a long-awaited one per cent cut in interest rates. John Smith at once attacked the way it had been done: "The timing is cynical – all about politics, not economics."[15] It had been timed, obviously, to upstage the end of Labour's conference, and create the right atmosphere for the Tory conference the following week. In the House of Commons later in the month, Smith claimed that Thatcher had been forced into a "humiliating U-turn". Since the Madrid summit in June the previous year, she had insisted that Britain could enter only when its inflation rate was falling, but the Retail Price Index had actually risen in that period from 8.3 per cent a year to 10.9 per cent.[16] "All the other conditions had to be fulfilled by other people, and they were. Only one had to be fulfilled by the Right Honourable Lady, but it was not," he added.[17]

What, however, of Labour's "prudent" conditions for ERM membership, with which John Smith had surprised the House of Commons the previous year? Or the tougher conditions agreed by the 1989 Labour Party conference? From Labour's back benches Peter Shore raised this unwelcome topic, pointing out that none of the conditions which Labour had set in *Meet the Challenge, Make the Change* a year earlier had been met. Those, of course, were Bryan Gould's conditions, not Smith's; but his had not been met either. Europe had not made any serious progress in bringing the economies of its backward regions any closer to German levels. The best Labour could claim was that the European Parliament had been passing resolutions which broadly supported Labour's line of argument.

There was an even more pressing question: had John Major made the right decision by taking sterling in at a parity of 2.95 Deutschmarks to the pound? Two years later, of course, the government's economic strategy would come crashing down when the money markets proved that the pound had been overvalued, and nothing the government could do would keep it at that level. After the election, but before the dramatic collapse of Britain's ERM experiment, Roy Hattersley claimed that "everyone knew" at the time that 2.95 Deutschmarks was too high – not necessarily because of what the money markets would accept, but because an overvalued pound makes British goods harder to sell abroad, and simultaneously obliges the government to keep interest rates high to maintain confidence in sterling, hitting firms manufacturing for export in two ways at once.

Although that was what Labour's leaders thought, they decided not to say it. For eighteen months they kept silent, even giving the impression that they were thoroughly satisfied with the exchange rate and would maintain it when they were in office. They felt they had no choice, because to do anything else would invite a massive run on the pound whenever a Labour election victory was imminent. Hattersley said: "There was a general belief that John Smith would soon be chancellor. To imply that the new government might devalue would have had a disastrous effect on international confidence in the pound."[18] Over a year later when, in the privacy of a Shadow Cabinet meeting, Michael Meacher raised the possibility that the pound might have to be devalued, he caught a blast of Neil Kinnock's famous temper just for raising the question.

A fascinating conundrum is what John Smith actually would have done had he become Chancellor of the Exchequer in April 1992: would he really have struggled on, raising interest rates to crippling heights and depleting the Bank of England's foreign currency reserves as Norman Lamont did, until the policy collapsed; or would he have faced reality earlier, and struck a deal with the Bundesbank before the money markets forced him to devalue? We shall never know.

Far from wanting to unravel the ideal which had taken Britain into the ERM, Labour was wanting to move on to the next big step towards European integration: when the pound, franc, Deutschmark and other currencies would disappear in a European Monetary Union. Neil Kinnock wanted Labour to be ahead of the Tories in Europe. He was due to take part in a Summit of European Social Democratic parties in December, and wanted to go there able to say that Labour had accepted EMU as a principle, and was working out a realistic scheme to bring it about. A document issued in November came very close to tying Labour to the policy. There was an escape clause to the effect that closer integration of Europe's currencies "does not automatically require the creation of a single currency"; but it was also claimed that most of the EC's member states wanted monetary union, that everyone's interests would be served if ERM rules were gradually tightened, and that Britain had better not leave itself on the sidelines. In order to avoid putting the Bundesbank in control of the whole of Western Europe's monetary policy Labour called for a European Central Bank, controlled by elected politicians and located in London.[19]

This statement had originated from the Shadow Cabinet's economic subcommittee. Kinnock and Smith therefore shared responsibility for it; but they reacted with varying degrees of enthusiasm to different parts of it. In Madrid, Kinnock was anxious to promote Labour as the party that was all but committed to monetary union. In the Commons, Smith hedged much more, insisting that there was "no inevitability" about it, and emphasizing that each of the EC's national economies must first be capable of growing steadily without mounting up huge government borrowing. Without "convergence", "monetary union . . . would create unbearable strains within the Community, threatening fragmentation rather than integration," he warned.[20]

No one in Labour's economic team was much impressed by another John Major idea which came and went. In June 1990 the Chancellor proposed that instead of twelve currencies the Community should have thirteen, the new one being a 'hard ECU" which would be legal tender anywhere in the Community. The purpose of the proposal was to find a way out of the irreconcilable differences inside the Tory Party over monetary union, whose chief opponent was, of course, Margaret Thatcher. The hard ECU offered a "market" solution, acceptable to all wings of the Tory Party. If the markets liked hard ECUs, other, weaker currencies would gradually go out of circulation and monetary union would be achieved from below. "Whatever else could be said about the hard ECU . . . it had its political uses for the Conservative Party," John Smith said. "It enabled the then Prime Minister to claim it could not develop into a single currency. It enabled the then Chancellor to say . . . it could." In no time, the idea had withered away, and Smith was able to mock: "Did it die? When did it die? Who killed it? Where is it buried? I hope that the Chancellor can give us a full report on the sad demise of the hard ECU."[21]

Labour's efforts to agree on whether Europe should have one currency or twelve were hardly noticed at the time, because they were drowned out by massive and dramatic events. The tension in the Tory Party over this issue came to a head, and Margaret Thatcher was brought down. Less than two months later, the crisis in the Gulf had erupted in war. Events on that scale obviously reverberated in the internal politics of the Labour Party. It came dangerously close to splitting over the Gulf War. Six Shadow Cabinet members were in more or less open opposition to the hard line taken by Neil Kinnock and Gerald Kaufman. Even Roy Hattersley was in and out of Kaufman's office, voicing reservations. Their differences were thrashed out in a day-long session of the Shadow Cabinet in January 1991. Labour held together, but only just.

A problem over which they had no control was a sudden surge in the popularity of the Conservative Party. For as long as Margaret Thatcher was in Downing Street, Labour's hopes of victory had been rising by the day. They had a thirteen-point lead, on average, in the opinion polls in October 1990. That disappeared as Thatcher was driven away into enforced retirement. John Major began on a wave of public relief, which was sustained by the successful prosecution of a short war with only a few British casualties. The Tories were consistently ahead in opinion polls until the middle of March, when the picture began to blur. There was no doubt, though, that Labour's three best political weapons – Margaret Thatcher's grating personality, her anti-Europeanism, and the poll tax – had gone.

Once again, there was a murmur of speculation about whether Labour could do better with a different leader. This time, Tory MPs were deliberately stoking the rumour that Kinnock had to be the next party leader to go. In December, *The Independent on Sunday* published a poll suggesting that if Smith were leader, Labour's support would leap from 40 per cent to 48 per cent. On the day it appeared, Hattersley dismissed it as "preposterous".[22] Smith himself was equally emphatic: "The question does not arise. I supported Neil Kinnock for the leadership and continue to support him. It's all part of the relentless campaign against Neil Kinnock by the right wing press. It has surfaced before and the best thing to do is give it no credence or currency."[23]

Neil Kinnock's standing in the Party and the polls dipped uncomfortably from time to time during the following year. The first occasion was around December 1990 and January 1991, when opinion polls appeared to show that John Major was the most popular Prime Minister since Winston Churchill. Then the following August, Kinnock had the bad luck to be on holiday in Italy when President Gorbachev was toppled by a Kremlin coup. Paddy Ashdown had a good coup, giving interviews round the clock. So did Robert Maxwell, Margaret Thatcher and, after an uncertain start, John Major. Neil Kinnock's contribution was made over a crackly international phone line. He had a bad coup. Numerous people thought this was important, especially when the first opinion poll in September showed Labour's support down to 35 per cent – 4.5 per cent behind the Tories. The rumours about Kinnock's future were audible enough for the leader to allow himself to be drawn by a TV journalist who tossed questions at him. "I have been, and am, a very good captain of the team," he replied. "You certainly do not drop winning captains."[24]

Two months later there was a set-piece debate on Europe and the forthcoming Maastricht Summit, in which Kinnock was thought to have performed badly. The part which everyone remembered afterwards was an off-the-cuff reply to a Tory backbencher, Robert Adley, who reminded Kinnock that he had once opposed British membership of the Common Market, and challenged him to say whether there was any subject on which he had not changed his mind. The answer came back: "Immediately the Honourable Gentleman and I entered the House, on the same day, I formed the view that he was a jerk, and I still hold that view."[25] In everyday conversation that would have sounded like a very effective put-down, and on the quiet there are Tories who would not dissent from the view that Mr Adley is a "jerk"; but it was the wrong word to use in the gentlemen's club that is the House of Commons debating chamber, and seemed to reinforce the opinion that Kinnock did not know how to sound like someone who was only months away from becoming Prime Minister.

Finally, there was an incident involving a dinner with journalists at Luigi's restaurant, Covent Garden. Each event set off another round of murmuring that changing their leader had worked well for the Tories, and might be equally felicitous for the Labour Party. There was even a low-level conspiracy against Neil Kinnock, which amounted to very little. There are several MPs, mostly connected with the whips' office, who are adamant that Dennis Skinner was goading MPs sympathetic to Smith to make a move. There is even a story of an open letter calling on Kinnock to resign, which was scrapped because of a shortage of signatories. But this does not ring true. However much Skinner opposed Kinnock, he was never cut out to be a conspirator. Nothing he does is secret. Moreover, he is not an admirer of John Smith, and did not vote for him in the leadership election. A more likely story is that one of the junior whips had an idea that a letter calling for Kinnock's resignation should be put around, to test the response and see whether he could be forced out. Rather than do it himself, he wanted Skinner to do the deed. That way, if the secret got out, it would look like just another round in the struggle between Kinnock and the left. Skinner himself says he did not want to waste his time on a project with no real hope of success, for the supposed benefit of John Smith.

By now, the Labour Party rule book ensured that no one was going to run against Neil Kinnock, even if the parliamentary Party had been in a state of open rebellion, because leadership elections necessarily take at least three months, while general elections can be over and done with in less than four weeks. In other words, once the Labour Party had committed itself to a leadership election in October, John Major could announce that the general election would be in September. So, despite rumours which have sometimes made their way into print, there was no serious conspiracy to remove Kinnock from office at this point in the parliamentary session. It was at around the beginning of 1991, however, that the choice of John Smith as the next leader, after a general election defeat, was effectively settled.

That was not the outcome of conspiracy in the usual meaning of the word, in that no group of people met secretly to plot a common course of action to secure the job for Smith. However, when scores of politicians are milling about in the same tea rooms, dining rooms and bars, reacting to the same events, the effect is often just like a giant conspiracy. It was widely expected that John Major would call a quick election as soon as the troops returned from the Gulf, and according to the opinion polls he could hardly lose, although the government majority would probably be reduced. A lot of Labour MPs looked into the future, saw the possibility that by the summer they could be back in opposition again, and thought to themselves that there was no way Neil Kinnock could carry on.

For the right, there was no doubt at all about what they would do next. Smith had been their prospective candidate for several years. *The Sunday Times* turned up one example: of a routine business meeting of the right-wing pressure group Labour First, in February 1992, at which someone asked the hypothetical question what would happen if Labour lost the impending election, and everyone in the room agreed that they would back John Smith as Neil Kinnock's successor.[26] For most right-wing Labour MPs, that was such an obvious conclusion that it was thought to be hardly worth discussing. The difference in 1991–92 is that Smith's support expanded into the "soft left", taking in people who, two years earlier, would have been more likely to support Bryan Gould or another Tribunite. Since then, the policy review had effectively broken down the old distinctions between left and right. There was no fundamental political issue which divided Smith from the majority of the Tribune group. It was around this time, therefore, that former left-wingers like Robin Cook and Margaret Beckett quietly made up their minds that if it came to the worst, and Labour had to face five more years in opposition, they would back Smith for party leader.

In January 1991, Smith was again asked whether he had an ambition to be leader of the Party, this time by the *Daily Record*. He replied: "Of course, if for one reason or another there arose a vacancy for leader of the party, then I've no doubt I would be considered for it. And if they elected me, then I would undertake the responsibility."[27] He had said it before, particularly during the interviews he gave after he had recovered from his heart attack; but this time, his remarks had an edge. There was no need for him to say so much. His comments contributed to the resentful suspicion within Kinnock's entourage that there was a conspiracy afoot. And as if to remind anyone who might have forgotten that he was still one of the best parliamentary performers around, John Smith seized an opportunity thrown his way to display his quick wits and sharp humour. The new Chief Secretary to the Treasury, David Mellor, thought he could make his reputation by taking Smith on in the House of Commons, so he challenged him unexpectedly in the middle of a debate to find a "pain-free alternative" to high interest rates, as a means of keeping consumer spending under control. It was a foolish move. Back came the answer, heavily ladled in irony:

> "I do not think I have ever heard a question such as that from any minister since I came to the House of Commons. I accept that the Chief Secretary appeared to have a genuinely inquiring tone. He knows the government's policies are not working, so he asks in despair, 'Is there something better?' I give him one. If he were to rid his mind of some of his prejudices, he would carefully consider the use of credit controls . . . "[28]

Curiously, the person who seemed to be more hurt than anyone else by the new buzz around John Smith was Gordon Brown. He had had a year of being talked up as a potential party leader. It was assumed – probably rightly – that Neil Kinnock wanted Brown to succeed him eventually, when he departed from Downing Street after serving for many years as Prime Minister. This talk had found its way into the newspapers. If Smith was now to be talked up as the next Labour leader, it followed almost automatically that Brown would be talked down. That certainly happened. A number of MPs who thought Brown was overrated – some of whom were doubtless motivated by jealousy – put it about that his Trade and Industry team of half a dozen was too large, that he was good at attacking the government but not at forming original policies, and that he was fond of repeating himself. Brown is said to have found this depressing – the more so when he suspected that some of Neil Kinnock's personal staff were joining in. In the long term, though, it seems to have done him no damage. He topped the poll in the Shadow Cabinet elections again in November 1991, and then for a fourth time the following July.

Instead of an election in 1991, which is what they expected, Labour was given a foretaste of what the Tory campaign would be like. It began with the tabloids, and then the politicians moved in. Increasingly, John Smith found he could not go on radio or TV without generating headlines in the next day's Tory newspapers, even when he had said very little. His comment, in a radio interview, that there would be no cuts in income tax under Labour – "My duty will be to remind people of the economic realities of the need to create wealth before you can spend it"[29] – produced the *Sun* headline "Five Years of Misery if Neil Gets In". But that was nothing compared to the reaction to a TV interview in which he spelt out that anyone on an income over £20,300 would be affected by Labour's planned changes to National Insurance.[30] The *Daily Telegraph, Daily Mail* and *Daily Express* all treated it as the biggest story of the day. Joe Haines of the *Daily Mirror* commented: "If the last three days are anything to go by, the next general election will be as mucky as any in living memory."[31]

David Mellor had been given the job of rubbishing Labour's programme on lines which had worked very well for the Tories in previous elections: by totalling the cost and warning voters what it would do to their tax bills. The last time this had been attempted – a year earlier, using the civil service – it had come to nothing because Labour's programme had been too carefully screened for expensive promises. Since then, Beckett's Law had been vigorously applied, so the Tories knew perfectly well that there were only two solid promises on Labour's agenda: to raise pensions and child benefit. The rest had to wait until "resources allowed".

That was obviously not a good enough story to put before the electors, so Tory researchers went through every policy document and speech they could lay their hands on, looking for any other suggestions from the Labour front bench as to how they might spend public money. Neil Kinnock and Jack Straw had complained more than once that the Tories had cut the education budget by an equivalent of £2,600 million a year since 1979: fine, that was a pledge to spend £2,600 million a year more on education. Bryan Gould had once told a magazine that he would like to provide £8,000 million for council house repairs and construction: okay, subtract the £5,000 million which was already being spent every year, and call it a pledge to spend £3,000 more. Robin Cook had promised that Labour would "start to tackle" what the Party regarded as a £3,000 million shortfall in spending on the NHS, and Neil Kinnock had warned that "nobody would promise that with a flick of the switch, overnight, we would provide the £3 billion" – proof enough that Labour would add £3,000 million to the health budget. In every case, it was assumed that all the extra money was to be found within five years. The total came to £35 billion – £25 billion more than would be raised from Labour's published tax plans. Divide that by 25 million taxpayers, and it would be an extra £1,000 a year from everyone. Another way of looking at it was that it would be an extra 15p in the £ on income tax. An entire Tory Party political broadcast was constructed around this £1,000 a year figure, while John Smith had the unusual and dubious honour of having a broadcast made all about him. It featured eight other ordinary people named John Smith, all of whom would have their future shattered by the extra 15p in the £ tax or some other aspect of Labour policy, as interpreted by the Tories. The broadcasts coincided with a new poster campaign warning: "Labour's Going for Broke Again".

It was rubbish, of course. John Smith was not going to allow a Labour Cabinet to add £35 billion to public expenditure, and even if he had, he would not have spread the bill so evenly. The Tory campaign suffered, in fact, from being too overstated to be believable. There was no visible effect on the electorate. On the contrary, the opinion polls, which had been contradicting each other in June, all showed Labour ahead in July, allowing Smith to remark in the Commons that "the Conservative party's expensive summer campaign, although it has been conducted all over the country, does not seem to have had a very dramatic effect".[32]

Perhaps it would have been better for Labour if it had. They might have been better prepared for the next Tory assault on their tax plans.

16

A Night at Luigi's, January 1992

There had once been a time when Neil Kinnock liked journalists, but that was before he was leader of the Labour Party. He could not bring himself to forgive eight years of destructive attacks. He was not placated by the argument that they were aimed not at him but at his position; he took it personally. His relations with the political press corps had broken down. Some of his advisers, though, knew that it was a bad idea not to be on speaking terms with the representatives of the mass media, that some journalists were not as bad as others, and that there ought to be a way for the Labour leader to meet them on his own turf and on his own terms. Hence the occasional evenings out at a restaurant of the Kinnocks' choice, to which half a dozen journalists would be invited to share a meal, in relaxed surroundings, with Neil, Glenys, and a couple of his aides. At one of these soirées, at an Italian restaurant called Luigi's, in Covent Garden, Neil Kinnock committed a tactical error which angered John Smith more than anything the leader had done in all the years they had worked together.

The Tories had hit the ground running when they returned from their Christmas break, with a sustained and well-planned assault on Labour's spending plans and tax policies. They held a press conference virtually every day, with never fewer than two Cabinet ministers wheeled out to warn of the dreadful impoverishment which would face the nation under a tax-hungry Labour government. The campaign was based on the same calculations as before, with a few revisions and extra details which produced a total of £37 billion. On 6 January 1992 the Chancellor of the Exchequer, Norman Lamont, personally unveiled a new poster, displayed on billboards around the country, with a picture of a missile and the caption "Labour's tax bombshell", again using the £1,000 a year figure. "Anyone who believes otherwise is living in cloud Kinnock land," Lamont told that morning's press conference.[1]

The evidence to support the Tories' case was no better than before. This was brought home late in the day by a succinct comment from Brendan Bruce, who had been Conservative Central Office's Director of

Communications for two years until the fall of Thatcher: "No one sensible in the Tory Party actually believes the Labour Party would put up public spending by £37 billion."[2] John Smith's reaction was: "We have not committed ourselves to a £35 billion spending programme. So I believe that what they are engaged in is the Big Lie. Say it often enough – it doesn't matter whether it's true or not – and hope some people will believe it."[3]

However, the election was now obviously very close, and this time the Tories' loyal backers among the tabloid newspapers decided not to be fussy. On the morning of Lamont's press conference, its whole contents were trailed in the *Daily Mail*, complete with an easy-to-read tax table showing readers how much extra they would pay if Labour were to raise public spending by £37 billion and spread the cost among ordinary taxpayers. Two days later, the *Daily Express* claimed to have documentary evidence substantiating the Tories' original figure of £35 billion. It came in the form of a private memorandum written two years earlier by Chris Smith, for private circulation among fellow members of Labour's Treasury team. There, in black and white, was the very same figure of £35 billion – independent confirmation of the Tories' calculation, according to the *Daily Express*. Chris Smith was able to explain that coincidence straight away. He was referring to the campaign the Tories had run in 1987, when they had put a price tag on Labour's promises and arrived at exactly the same total. The real mystery is how a note which was never shown to the rest of the Treasury team, or to anyone else outside Chris Smith's own office, suddenly resurfaced after so long. The favourite explanation was that it had been left in a photocopier at the time when it was written, and whoever found it had kept quiet about it for two years – which suggests that the finder was not a journalist but someone in the Conservative Party. The party chairman, Chris Patten, flatly denied that the leak had come from him.

Although the "tax bombshell" stunt looked at first as if it might misfire, it actually worked in a way which the Labour Party had not foreseen.

Leaving the Tory tabloids to serve up Norman Lamont's claims as if they were true, the heavyweight newspapers turned their attention to what was actually in Labour's published policy documents. They did not like what they found, especially the heavy tax increases due to be imposed on people like themselves. As a group they had, of course, watched the development of Labour Party policy and knew in a general sense about the proposed increase for top-rate taxpayers; but up to now, the election had seemed far enough away, and the possibility of a Labour victory sufficiently remote, for it to be no more than an interesting subject. Suddenly, commentators became like reporters at the scene of battle who discover that the guns have been turned on them. It was as if it had hit them that within three months John Smith's tax plans could be *their* tax deductions. For every pound they earned above an as yet unspecified figure – around £35,000 a year – they would have to part with an extra 19p. Unlike the freezing of child benefit, or a rise in unemployment, this was not a bombshell which would explode in some faraway place where people at the bottom of the pile lived. For well-paid political commentators, a rise in the top rate of income tax was something direct, personal, and painful.

Some confronted the situation with their sense of humour intact. For instance, when Channel 4's political editor, Elinor Goodman, was asked by her friend Maurice Saatchi – of Saatchi and Saatchi – how she would cope under Labour's tax regime, she replied that she would probably have to shoot one of the horses. She then had an awful vision that another Tory advertising slogan had been born: "They Shoot Horses, Don't They?" Others failed to see the funny side of it at all. Hamish McRae, City commentator for *The Independent*, published a table demonstrating that someone whose gross annual pay was £100,000 would actually be more than £1,000 a month worse off, as a Labour government reduced their disposable income from £65,666 right down to £52,635. "These people may not attract much sympathy," he wrote,

> but that is not the issue. The issue is the impact on the economy. . . . Rightly or wrongly, many people responded to the 1988 tax cuts and the rising house market by spending more and borrowing big. Many took on long term commitments, particularly large mortgages. For them the readjustment will be extraordinarily painful. . . . Labour's plan would be an economic experiment at the wrong time. At worst, it would lead to a sharp rise in personal bankruptcies. Further, by tipping house prices into a new decline, it would hit consumption and make economic recovery more difficult. . . . The changes projected now . . . would mean those affected would be facing the sharpest ever peacetime tax increases.[4]

This piece was an instant hit, especially his phrase "the sharpest ever peacetime tax increase", which was quoted in the Commons the following week by no less a person than the Prime Minister. Even the *Sun* momentarily forgot its contempt for *The Independent*, and reproduced the whole article a couple of days later – not as political comment, but as a hard news item, which described McRae as "one of Labour's most influential supporters" and his employers as "the left wing *Independent*", to the vast amusement of other journalists.

The McRae piece was at least based on solid fact, and provided anyone who read it with the information to make up their own minds about what they thought of Labour's planned assault on the living standards of the highly paid. But when the *Sun* reproduced it for a much larger and less prosperous audience, it appeared alongside the claims made by Norman Lamont, and photographs of a miner, with the caption "£28 a week worse off", a nurse – "£18 a week worse off" – and a car worker – "£21 a week worse off".[5] In other words, it was used to give some "left-wing" supporting evidence to Tory Party claims which *The Independent*, like other newspapers, had refused to believe. Yet despite its undeniable success, McRae's article did not quite have the passion and eloquence later achieved by Charles Moore, the thirty-five-year-old deputy editor of *The Daily Telegraph*, as he brooded on what John Smith's tax regime might mean to him:

> One reason that I feel so angry is that I shall be forced to work more, not less, and it is this element of compulsion which I so resent. This situation arises because I am well paid, but not rich. . . . As for the people who say they are happy to pay the extra in order to ensure that we live in a more civilised society, I am afraid I want to punch them on the nose. The contrast is so vast between the tangible good I can do for the people I love (including myself) with the annual £10,000, or whatever it is, that Labour would take from me, and the extremely tenuous benefit that it will give to people in general among whom it is distributed. I could put carpets in the bedrooms and on the stairs so that the children would not get splinters in their feet. I could take them abroad for a holiday. I could save some money for their education. I could buy some curtains for our drawing room. We could have another child. Last week, the Conservative candidate for Hampstead and Highgate came to dine with us, and we drank the last bottle of good wine which I possessed, Château Talbot 1979, matured over 13 happy years. *Ils sont passés, ces beaux jours*. . . . No doubt most readers will dismiss all this as the ravings of a man who has had it too good for too long; some may enjoy my discomfiture. But I suspect my feelings are common to most of humanity.[6]

The impact on Labour's support in the opinion polls was immediate. In the last poll of the old year, the opposition party was six points ahead, with 44 per cent support compared with 38 per cent for the Tories.[7] By 15 January, an ICM poll in *The Guardian* put the Conservatives back in the lead, for the first time for several months, with 42 per cent to Labour's 41 per cent. "It's not surprising, considering they have thrown everything they've got at us, including the kitchen sink," one senior party member claimed. Even so, it was unpleasant and unnerving to be losing their lead so close to an election.

John Smith's view was that Labour should stay calm and say nothing that was not already public knowledge. There were options still open to them. The extra revenue from the higher top rate of income tax and the extension of National Insurance would be more than enough to pay for the promised increase in child benefit and state pensions, so there was leeway for more public spending commitments, or last-minute tax concessions; but the Shadow Chancellor saw no point in making announcements in January, when the government was going to have a budget in March. They did not know what surprises would be contained in Norman Lamont's budget, but they could be sure that it would be designed with the sole purpose of securing the re-election of the Conservative Party. There was everything to be said for waiting and seeing. That was the tactic adopted when the party leader and Shadow Chancellor appeared side by side at their first press conference of the year, on 8 January. Predictably, they were asked about Labour's tax plans, but they said nothing that was not already known. There was no hint that they would give an inch.

Similarly, John Smith went through a Sunday morning interview with TV-am's David Frost. Frost, too, ignored Lamont's outpourings; grilled Smith over the fact that Labour had so few expensive promises that the revenue from the proposed tax and National Insurance increases would more than pay for them, and invited him to say that he had the scope to adjust the tax plans downwards. Smith replied that he was reserving his position, because in addition to the increased state benefits there was the health service to be paid for.

Behind the scenes, though, there was one figure worrying Neil Kinnock more than any other: £20,280. Anyone whose annual salary was at that figure or below already paid 9 per cent of the income as National Insurance, and would be unhurt by Labour's proposals. When the ceiling on National Insurance contributions was scrapped, those above it would lose 9p out of each extra £. In vast numbers of cases, the difference would be so small it would hardly be noticed. Someone on £21,000, for example, would lose little more than a £1 a year, while someone on £30,000 would lose around £750. However, the 1987 campaign had taught Neil Kinnock that it was not the amounts themselves which mattered, but the symbolism. To quote Bryan Gould's expression in the leadership election a few months later, Labour's plan appeared to set a "cap on aspirations". Find a job worth £21,000 a year – it seemed to say – and you go from being the sort of person Labour is there to help to being someone they intend to tax. An income like that could be earned by a train driver on the London Underground, if he did enough overtime. There were millions more with salaries above about £16,000 a year who might aspire to reach £21,000 in the near future, all of them potential Labour voters.

Kinnock's advisers were impressed by a letter in *The Independent* from Ken Judge, director of the King's Fund Institute, which studies health policy, who declared that much as he hated paying an extra £4,000 a year in tax, he would vote Labour anyway because of the importance of tackling poverty. But he warned that the "real issue" was how quickly the tax changes were brought in: "Tax objectives phased in over, say, a period of three years would enable many individual families to adjust their personal circumstances in a more realistic way than if very sudden changes are introduced within a few months."[8] That idea was in line with the Party's published policies. For instance, *Looking to the Future*, issued in 1990, had pledged that "at all stages in reforming the tax and social insurance systems, we will ensure that changes are carefully phased in so as to cushion the impact on personal incomes".

Kinnock asked his economic adviser, John Eatwell, to go through the whole business one more time, to ensure that as the Treasury team pored over their calculations, checking that their tax and spending plans added up, they were not forgetting those essential political touches which could make the difference between victory and defeat. Eatwell fixed up a meeting with John Smith and his advisers, to take place on the Wednesday morning. On the Tuesday, Neil Kinnock raised the matter directly with John Smith. The Shadow Chancellor was not highly impressed with the idea of phasing in tax changes, because in the long run it made no difference to those on the receiving end, and in the meantime Labour would be implicitly conceding that these changes were too onerous to be introduced in one go, and promising instead a tax increase every year for three years or so. None the less, he promised to keep an open mind, and include phasing in among the options up for discussion. That night, the leader went to dinner at Luigi's.

The company included journalists from the BBC, ITN, and four newspapers which, on the whole, were prepared to give Labour fair treatment: the *Daily Mirror*, *Financial Times*, *Guardian* and *Times* – not their political editors, but middle-rank lobby correspondents.[9] Neil Kinnock's PPS, Adam Ingram, his press secretary, Julie Hall, and Glenys Kinnock made up the rest of the party. The hacks arrived expecting to find the Labour leader down in the dumps, because he had come off second best in a parliamentary exchange with John Major that afternoon, and the following day's *Guardian* poll was already public knowledge. Their first surprise was that he was confident, ebullient and expansive. During the course of a long answer to a question on tax policy, Kinnock slipped in the possibility that the National Insurance changes could be introduced in phases. It was one of those occasions when journalists hear something and are, at first, not sure if it is significant or not. Kinnock himself behaved as if it was a minor detail, which could be found anyway in Labour's published documents. Julie Hall backed up her employer, and said it was the Party's own fault that this aspect of their policy was not better known. One of the guests, who was deep in conversation with Adam Ingram at the far end of the table, left the restaurant later, unaware of what had been said. The others dispersed after midnight, unsure whether they had been let into a secret or reminded of something they should already have known. So began twenty-four hours of spectacular muddle.

John Smith's meeting with his advisers began on time the following morning, in his office at 1 Parliament Street. With John Eatwell there as Neil Kinnock's representative, they ran through all the different options, summarizing pros and cons and agreeing that a final decision could wait until March. No one mentioned the possibility that the leader might have closed their options off with his comments the previous night, because none of them knew.

Next, Smith went on to lunch with the French ambassador. His meal was disturbed by a call from the Commons, warning him of strange goings-on. BBC TV had reported on its lunch-time bulletin that Labour was on the verge of a change in tax policy, which, coming so soon after a dip in the opinion polls, looked like a retreat under fire. Moreover, Margaret Beckett had been approached with precisely the same story by a lobby journalist who seemed unusually surprised to be given a flat denial. He was then told that one of his staff had had a call early that morning from Julie Hall, who was checking on party policy about phasing in the changes to National Insurance. It seemed an innocent inquiry at the time, but that was now the very story which was running in the gallery. Late in the afternoon the Shadow Cabinet held its weekly meeting, without discussing taxation. As they emerged, Bryan Gould was approached by a journalist from the Press Association, who asked whether any change to tax policy was being contemplated. Gould not only denied it, but implied that anyone who was putting about such a story was being mischievous – unaware that it came from the party leader.

When they saw the following morning's newspapers, all concerned could have been forgiven if they heaved a sigh of relief. Cryptic reports on the front of *The Financial Times* and *The Times*, and a paragraph buried well down a story on a different subject on the back page of *The Guardian*, were all that dinner at Luigi's had produced. Even the BBC had dropped the story from its early-evening bulletins onwards, because its political editor, John Cole, took the view that it proved nothing except that a lot of journalists had not read Labour's policy documents properly. And there the matter would doubtless have ended, had not a general election been due so soon.

The Tory Party had recently taken on a new parliamentary press officer named Tim Collins, whose job was to skulk around the parts of the building where journalists worked, picking up whatever scraps of information he could, and report back. No one could accuse him of failing to do what he was paid for. On this occasion he knew all about what was going on on the afternoon before the first newspaper story appeared – and he knew much more than was printed. He was even to be seen in the Commons press bar raising a glass in celebration of a story which the public would be able to read the following morning. From breakfast onwards, television stations were bombarded with telephone calls from Tory spin-doctors tipping them off that this was a much bigger story than it appeared. Chris Patten, commenting on something which still had not appeared in print, claimed: "All their solemn statements on tax and all the policy documents they have published are now apparently to be junked in one moment of blind panic. It proves what we've been saying all along. You just can't trust Labour." At his Thursday morning press conference Patten made an oblique and convoluted answer to one journalist's question, linking the names of Neil Kinnock and Margaret Beckett in a way which made it plain that he knew more than was in that day's newspapers.

In case anyone missed the point, John Major rammed it home at Prime Minister's Question Time on Thursday afternoon, by calling Neil Kinnock "a tax dodger".[10] It was an obscure insult, but an awful lot of people understood what he was driving at by now. The story was told in full in Friday's newspapers, and again on Sunday. The *Daily Mail* had a photograph of the interior of Luigi's, and reproduced its menu. They calculated that the bill, paid by the Kinnocks, had come to £400.

What angered John Smith about all this was that it seemed so cack-handed and unnecessary. He did not agree with Kinnock over phasing in, but if the leader had insisted on having his way, he would have deferred to him on the old-fashioned grounds that it was up to the man in charge to make the final decision. There was no need to go behind his back, bringing journalists into the argument, he felt. To do it, and then not tell him, compounded the injury in his opinion. When he finally spoke to Kinnock privately, however, he was quite disarmed by the younger man's demeanour. Whatever he expected before he stepped into the leader's office, it was not an unqualified apology, yet that is roughly what he got. Neil Kinnock admitted that he had miscalculated the effect of his own words, and accepted full responsibility.

After that incident, it might be thought that Labour politicians would have learnt that it was hazardous to dine with journalists, even friendly journalists, so close to an election. Less than a fortnight later, however, the very same Tim Collins was to be seen shuffling from office to office in the press gallery late one evening, handing out a Conservative Central Office press release about a story due to appear in the following day's *Daily Mail* and *Sun*. "Labour Split on Tax Plans" ran the next day's *Daily Mail* headline, over a front-page splash which claimed that John Smith and Roy

Hattersley had had a blazing row, in private, over whether or not National Insurance increases should be phased in.[11] This story also turned out to be the product of a meal in a restaurant. A mixed group of lobby correspondents had taken the Party's deputy leader out to lunch.

"I think now that I lunched with four people, though the newspaper reports said three. I can never remember who the fourth one was," says Roy Hattersley.

> "But anyway, the lunch was organized by Colin Brown [of *The Independent*]. On reflection, had I known who the other people were, I wouldn't have gone. I shouldn't have gone. The actual words used during that conversation I cannot recall, but it wasn't possible that I said anything that suggested that Smith and I were in conflict, because Smith and I were in agreement. I visited his room to try and persuade John to go with me to see Neil to argue the case for not staging in. I have always been the high-tax proponent in the Labour Party, not the let's-pussyfoot proponent. And John said: 'We can't undermine the leader. Right or wrong, the leader has said that it might be staged in and it might do our electoral prospects damage if newspapers said that I insisted and overruled him.' But John and I were absolutely on the same side over this, with the exception of the point that I wanted to put his case more strongly to Neil than in the end he did. So there was no question of me ever having given the slightest suggestion that I was a stager-in and Smith was not.
>
> "Somebody tells me – I can't remember who – that the story was invented by two of them in a taxi on the way back. In any case, Colin Brown phoned David Hill [Labour's Director of Communications] the day after and said nothing happened at the lunch which could possibly justify the story. Before the newspapers were in the lobby, Conservative Central Office was sending out handouts saying Roy Hattersley and Smith and Kinnock are all at loggerheads. I think this is the great example of the organized conspiracy."[12]

"My leader right or wrong" was certainly the line John Smith took in public. On BBC Radio he insisted that Labour would indeed abolish the ceiling on National Insurance contributions – "but we might judge", he added, "that we might not want to do it immediately".[13] He repeated this line on television, though it was said by some who knew him that he had the look of a man talking through gritted teeth. Or, as David Mellor put it when he was taunting Smith in the Commons: "He looked like a man who had just found that his tax returns had been filled in by Ken Dodd's accountant, or that Kitty Kelley was going to write his biography."[14]

The Luigi's incident took place at a time when Neil Kinnock's poll rating was 20 per cent below John Major's, while Smith's was well above Norman Lamont's. All the controversy it attracted at the time was posited on it being another Kinnock blunder which his long-suffering Shadow Chancellor had had to clear up for him. Only later, after Kinnock ceased to be a worthwhile target and John Smith was about to take his place, was the story rewritten around the premiss that it was Smith who had blundered.

What is now the authorized Conservative version of the story was written by the new Chief Secretary to the Treasury, Michael Portillo, and issued from Tory Central Office when Smith was elected party leader. It runs:

> Mr Kinnock, recognising the unpopularity of the proposal to abolish the upper earnings limit on employees' National Insurance contributions, briefed journalists, at a now notorious dinner at Luigi's restaurant in January, that the changes would be phased in. Mr Smith would not have it. He made clear that the changes would be brought in at once. Mr Kinnock had dined in vain. The clever Mr Smith had committed a blunder which the less intellectual Mr Kinnock had striven valiantly to avoid.[15]

Mr Portillo's pamphlet makes two assumptions: that Labour's proposals for National Insurance were a blunder, and that it was Smith's blunder, not Kinnock's.

The first point has been implicitly conceded in parts of the Labour Party. Something was plainly wrong with the menu the Party placed before the electorate, and a proposal to increase the taxes of people earning about £21,000 a year was the most obviously suspect item. The second point, perhaps, is academic, except that it reflects in a small way on Smith's political judgement. It is universally assumed that the phasing in of National Insurance increases was kept out of Labour's election manifesto because Smith overruled Kinnock and refused to put it in. The testimony of witnesses, albeit those friendly to Smith, is that this is not true.

The rubbishing of Neil Kinnock which followed the Luigi's incident produced a reaction in the Party. For some of the loyalists in the Kinnock circle, there had been altogether too much talk about Smith as the next party leader. The whispering campaign against Gordon Brown had also left a residue of bad feeling. Then Smith's popularity on the left took a downturn after an incident which began when Labour's housing spokesman, Clive Soley, was speaking at a seminar. Some alert journalists heard him say that Treasury rules might have to be amended by Labour to speed up the construction of council houses. It is a long-standing grievance among Labour councillors and housing specialists that most of the billions received from selling council houses have gone towards paying off public-sector debt, instead of being used to tackle council waiting lists. Labour's policy was that there should be a "phased release" of the money. Under the rules, however, if the money were spent, it would add to the Public Sector

Borrowing Requirement, and ERM rules set a limit on the size of the PSBR. Consequently what was spent on building council houses would have to be saved somewhere else.

Soley suggested that the rules governing the PSBR would be altered to circumvent that problem: an idea which could only appal orthodox opinion in and around the Treasury, where the PSBR is taken very seriously indeed. He claimed: "I've already talked about this to Neil Kinnock and John Smith. . . . Both Neil Kinnock and John Smith have said that we would change the PSBR rules to bring them into line with the conventional accountancy used in the European Community. . . . "[16] Smith or Kinnock evidently did not agree. The unfortunate Soley was forced to eat humble pie. "There is no plan to revise the PSBR," he told *The Times*. "I was wrong, I withdraw it."[17] The Environment Secretary, Michael Heseltine, remarked later, with cruel accuracy: "We have witnessed the phased release of the opposition spokesman on housing."[18] Although Soley had been forced to back down, he privately believed he was right, and there was a lot of sympathy among Labour council leaders. This explains why, despite Smith's overwhelming victory in the leadership election a few months later, there was a marked bias in favour of his rival, Bryan Gould, among MPs who considered housing to be their specialist subject.

During February 1992, with that special recklessness which seems to descend on the Labour Party as an election draws near, some person – or persons – decided that it was time Smith was given a little of what had been dished out to Kinnock, Brown, and others.

At the end of the month Labour moved into the attack by floating a claim that the Tories were likely to increase VAT again. The backcloth to John Smith's press conference was a huge poster, featuring a masked Norman Lamont as "Vatman". His own side liked it, but wondered why the counterattack had been so long in coming. "Mr Smith's reluctance to chase every allegation thrown by Central Office has contributed to the impression that Labour has failed to regain the initiative . . . " warned the next day's *Guardian*. A more damaging piece appeared in *The Guardian* three weeks later: a "whispering campaign has started that Mr Smith is not only less clever than he thinks, but less busy than he should be."[19] This attack appeared to come from the left, because it made a particular point of criticizing Smith for tying Labour into the ERM straitjacket. Whatever its source, it spoilt Smith's day. "Labour's Knives Out for Smith" ran the headline on the front page of the London *Evening Standard*. In the week when he was accused of laziness, incidentally, he delivered two lectures at the Manchester Business School and a speech in Scotland, gave a Radio 1 interview, held talks with Bundesbank officials, and led off for the opposition in a parliamentary debate on the economy.

That debate was an uncomfortable one for him, because it came on the same day as the piece in *The Guardian*, which was gleefully thrown at him by Tory MPs. Moreover, Michael Heseltine made some good jokes at the expense of Smith's legendary prawn cocktail offensive, after Michael Meacher had injudiciously remarked that, despite it, the City was "almost 100 per cent" against Labour's spending plans. Said Heseltine: "Think of the tragedy! All those prawn cocktails for nothing. Never have so many crustaceans died in vain. With all the authority I can command . . . let me say . . . 'Save the prawns'."[20]

It was, however, a difficult period for everyone. Labour had been ready to fight a general election almost a year before it happened. "The problem", one frontbencher was quoted as saying, "is that everything is so fraught that nobody is doing any work at Westminster. There is an awful lot of backchat going on."[21]

17

The 1992 Election

It was the election which confounded the pundits. No party for centuries had ever won four general elections in a row, or ruled without interruption or coalition for more than thirteen years. No Prime Minister had ever called an election when his party was behind in the opinion polls, and gone on to win. It had not happened in recent memory that the Labour Party had opened an election campaign by successfully challenging the Tories on whether they were competent to manage a capitalist economy. All these things happened in 1992, yet Labour was trounced again.

In the immediate aftermath, serious commentators like Robert Harris in *The Sunday Times* suspected that the British political system had been changed for ever. It seemed that the body politic would settle into a system like Japan's, in which the only political struggles which mattered were the factional manoeuvrings inside one right-wing party which was in government for generation after generation. Others concluded that there was now only one certain rule about modern elections: that no party which threatens to increase taxes will ever win. Either conclusion held out no future for the Labour Party except a lingering death. If it could not even secure something as basic as improved social benefits, paid for by taxing the wealthy, then it was questionable whether there was any point in having a Labour Party. The nation which invented two-party politics had apparently become the first to give it up without bloodshed.

And there could be no falling back on the stock excuse that the policies were good, but they were badly presented. No one could have put the case for raising taxes more skilfully, or in blander, more reassuring tones, than John Smith.

An enduring memory of the 1992 election campaign was the strange goings-on on the government front bench as Chancellor Norman Lamont delivered his Budget speech on Tuesday 9 March. Although this event was called a Budget, and was accompanied by the usual rigmarole of the photocall with the red box and the rest, it was actually a manifesto for the impending election. Observers became aware that something at the end of the speech had excited the government Chief Whip. Periodically he would turn round and hold up his printed copy of the Chancellor's text for the MPs behind him. They seemed to agree that it was very clever. Eventually, the rest of the Chancellor's audience were let in on the joke: he was creating a new tax band which was sure to be a winner among the crucial C1 and C2 class voters. Income tax on the first £2,000 of everyone's income would be 20p in the £, instead of the standard rate of 25p: equivalent to a flat-rate reduction of a little less than £2 a week from everyone's tax bill. Since it was a fixed amount, obviously it was of the greatest benefit, proportionately, to the lowest-paid. The reason for their glee was that the Tories knew it was not what Labour had been expecting, and they could anticipate the problem Neil Kinnock would have when his turn came to speak directly after the Chancellor had finished.

The ploy succeeded in inflicting ninety minutes of indecision and a day's frantic policy revision on the Labour Party. Neil Kinnock had to deliver his reply to the Budget speech without even mentioning the new tax band, because he needed time before he could commit Labour either to keeping it or scrapping it. When he and Smith conferred afterwards, they agreed that they must stick to the line they had been hammering out for several weeks, as they anticipated tax cuts for the better-off. "The government are borrowing money that they do not have to buy votes that they do not deserve," John Smith told a noisy Commons the following afternoon.[1]

That, however, did not answer the real problem suddenly thrown at them. Lamont was offering the low-paid an unexpectedly generous tax cut. Smith's team had more or less completed a "Shadow Budget" for him to unveil the following week, which included the idea Kinnock had floated to journalists in Luigi's: to phase in the increases in National Insurance. It had been drafted in the expectation that Lamont would announce a cut of 1p off the basic rate of income tax: from 25p to 24p. Smith planned to counter this with 1p off National Insurance contributions, which would have had the same effect as a 1p tax cut for anyone whose income was below £21,000 a year.

Now, as his advisers redid their calculations, a ghastly hole opened up in their well-laid plans. A tranche of people on very low wages were actually going to pay less tax under Lamont's Budget than under Labour. It was early Wednesday evening, more than twenty-four hours after the Budget, before Smith and Kinnock could meet to decide what to do. In the meantime, the election had been announced, both leaders had been caught up in a whirlwind of studio interviews, and Smith had delivered the opening speech of the debate which traditionally followed a Budget. Kinnock's answer to the problem was short and to the point: Labour existed as the defender of the low-paid, no one on low wages must face a bigger tax bill under Labour than under the Conservatives, and the Shadow Budget must be changed accordingly.

There was an answer ready: to alter the system of allowances. Every taxpayer is allowed to earn a certain minimal amount every year tax free, a system which saves the Inland Revenue from having to collect tiny amounts from very low-paid workers. If £330 was added to everyone's personal allowance, Smith's advisers calculated, that, combined with other tax reforms, would be enough to make everyone on a low wage better off under Labour, and an extra 740,000 taxpayers would be exempted from paying tax altogether. The snag was that it would cost more than a billion pounds a year. There was not enough to raise allowances, fulfil Neil Kinnock's promise that National Insurance increases would be phased in, and carry out manifesto promises unless Labour was to commit the offence they had laid against the Tories: borrowing money to reduce taxes.

Smith therefore told Kinnock that he had a simple choice: either a small number of low-paid workers would be worse off under Labour, or the idea of phasing in National Insurance, which he had so famously raised, must be dropped. Victory came surprisingly easily. The Labour leader was still irritated with himself for saying too much to journalists, and gave in without a quibble. The principle that Labour was there to protect people at the bottom of the social pile overrode everything which had been said on the night out at Luigi's. With that detail settled, Labour pushed ahead with the bold idea of spending the first week of the campaign fighting a political battle over the economy. It had always been assumed that this was territory on which the Tories could not lose. As expected, they went straight into the attack on Labour's tax plans. To Michael Heseltine went the honour of the first big speech of the campaign, in which he likened Labour to the Light Brigade: "Taxes to the left of them, taxes to the right of them – into the valley of taxes rode the Labour Party." The *Daily Mail* hailed it as an "electrifying curtain raiser".[2]

Meanwhile, John Smith, Margaret Beckett, and the rest of the Treasury team were hidden from view, working on Labour's Shadow Budget. This was a deliberate piece of theatre, mimicking the way real Treasury ministers are required to disappear from the public eye from New Year's Day until Budget Day. The show was maintained on the morning the Shadow Budget was unveiled, which began with a photocall featuring Smith and his team on the steps of the Treasury. At the press conference which followed, Smith claimed to be making history by setting out the opposition's tax plans in such detail before an election. "The chaps in the Treasury have got this in front of them. They can start working today," he said.

Almost everyone would have paid less tax under the plans published by Smith than under the Tories. Not much less, it has to be said: those on incomes between £7,000 and £20,000 were to be just 10p a month better off. Right at the bottom, the gains would be big enough to make a difference. This was achieved, of course, by taking large amounts from the higher-paid. A married man on £50,000 a year stood to lose almost £284 a month. One small surprise, which went down well in the City, was that a proposal to tax investment income from people's savings was dropped. Smith had been persuaded that this could be very hard on workers who had been made redundant, and lived on the income from their severance pay. Having been attacked by the Tories for even considering the idea, he was now, of course, sniped at by the Tory press for not sticking to it. "A modest earner on £40,000 a year would pay more extra tax to a Labour government than a millionaire," the *Daily Express* pointed out; while the same day's *Daily Mail* ran a headline: "Smith to hand 'idle rich' a cash bonus".[3]

The extra tax income was £3.5 billion a year more than a Labour government would need to honour the promises on state pensions and child benefit. Out of the extra would come a £1.1 billion package to revive the economy. It was not a vast sum of money by government standards. Labour had, in fact, committed itself to spending twice as much on improving state pensions as on reversing Britain's industrial decline. Even so, forty business leaders, headed by Lord Hollick, managing director of the advertising firm MAI, were prepared to put their names to a letter in *The Times* on 18 March backing Labour's plans for getting Britain out of recession. They were not, it is true, such big names in the business world as forty industrialists – including Alan Sugar, the head of Amstrad – who signed a different letter to *The Times* backing the Tories; but the fact that there was any support for Labour from business, considering the tax increases facing senior executives, was something.

The Shadow Budget ritual had not been agreed without the image-makers responsible for planning the election falling out behind the scenes. The person in the centre was David Hill, the Party's communications director. Because he had worked for many years as Roy Hattersley's aide, it was suspected that where there was friction between Neil Kinnock and John Smith, his natural bias would be towards the Shadow Chancellor. Later on, staff in the leader's office objected to having Smith take the leading role in what was to be one of the main events of Labour's campaign. It might look as if the leader was being slighted. Hill took the matter directly to Kinnock, who agreed that since the Budget was presented by the Chancellor, the Shadow Budget should be the Shadow

Chancellor's preserve. In that way, Labour tried to give the impression that their Budget was equal in status to the Tories'. Indeed, according to that day's opinion polls, it had the better chance of becoming law. Smith also wanted to kill speculation that he had secret plans for extra tax increases to be introduced once he was in government. Everything was there, set out in detail, he vowed. There would be no other tax increases.

It seemed to work. That evening, the BBC newscaster Martyn Lewis, in a momentary slip, described John Smith as "the Chancellor of the Exchequer". Later in the evening, there was a confrontation with Norman Lamont on "Panorama" which even Tory MPs conceded was a victory for Smith. During the rest of the week, he was aided by the fact that the economy was in such a bad state. The Tories unwisely launched their main attack on Labour's tax plans on Thursday morning, with a set-piece press conference featuring John Major and a bevy of Cabinet ministers, only hours before it was announced that unemployment was up more than 40,000.

At the end of the week, Labour could say that they had attacked the Tories on their home ground. Even *The Sunday Times* ran an editorial signed by its editor, Andrew Neil, headed "Round one to Labour", warning that Labour had been boosted by glum economic news, and that "it was also helped by John Smith's skilful budget presentation which, at a stroke, sidelined Norman Lamont's feeble effort of the week before. . . ."[4]

Smith's frankness carried risks. The well-off readers of upmarket newspapers were told in great detail how a Labour government would hit them, and given a strong incentive to do something to prevent it. It emerged later that there had been a huge operation by employers to help managerial staff avoid the new taxes by giving them large one-off payments in lieu of the next year's pay rise. The scale of tax evasion in managerial circles generally was such that average earnings, as measured by Incomes Data Services, leapt a whole percentage point in the month of March.[5] But, the number of people affected was only a small proportion of the population – one in ten, by Labour's calculations.

The *Sun* devoted a whole page to just one of the victims. The industrialist Alan Sugar had been so provoked by Gordon Brown's comment that he and other tycoons publicly backing the Tories had done well out of the recession that he decided to set out the facts. "I do not know who Gordon Brown is," he wrote.

> Excuse my ignorance, but I don't. Whoever he is, he has not done his homework. . . . How he has the audacity to say that Amstrad, or Alan Sugar, has flourished in the recession is a complete mystery to me. . . . The value of my shares collapsed from £500 million to £100 million more or less overnight. The

> salary I have been taking in the company is pretty meagre – about £170,000. . . . So this talk that I have prospered in the midst of the recession is total nonsense.[6]

But his plight appears to have left *Sun* readers unmoved. Generally, whilst the Shadow Budget was attacked for what was actually in it – and particularly for its threat to tax the very wealthy – there was no sign of a shift in public opinion away from the Labour Party. That began when the Tories' fantastic claim that Labour would increase the average tax bill by £1,000 a year took hold in the public mind.

But there was the ever-present danger that some prominent spokesman would spoil Smith's carefully built-up impression of openness, by saying something out of line. Roy Hattersley, for all his reputation as a leader of the Labour right, believed in high taxes more than most. On TV-am he was cross-examined by David Frost over whether he could guarantee that the 50p top rate of income tax would remain unchanged throughout the lifetime of a Labour government, and replied: "We have not said that. John Smith has not said that. Nobody would say that."[7] Before the day was out, John Smith was on TV saying the very thing Hattersley claimed that nobody would say: "It's very kind of Roy to seek to get flexibility for me, but the position is quite clear."[8]

After a week of fighting over the economy, Labour's plan was to switch to the health service and education, their home ground where they believed they were bound to win, just as the Tories were sure they could not fail to win an argument over tax. After he had presided over a Tuesday morning press conference, Smith was sent travelling in the provinces while correspondents were given a preview of Labour's latest party political broadcast, a dramatized story about a little girl forced to wait a year for ear treatment. The case dominated the newspapers for days, after the girl on whom it was based was traced and it emerged that while her father supported Labour, her mother and grandfather were committed Conservatives. Making the NHS the talking point of the election turned into a mixed blessing for Labour.

Smith, meanwhile, was racing about the country, accompanied by Helen Liddell, sometimes by Elizabeth Smith, and for a time by Andrew Graham, an economic adviser. The Smith office also maintained a base camp run by David Ward, in the building next to Labour's Walworth Road headquarters. Much of the travelling was done by helicopter, with Liddell constantly on the verge of travel sickness. She was there to handle the press and, where necessary, the public. She also had detailed instructions from Elizabeth Smith about John's diet. Something Mrs Smith never found out was how much her orders were being flouted. There were too many early mornings in breakfast television studios, followed by sneak visits to a greasy spoon café near Waterloo Station.

"Everywhere we went, the warmth of response to John was terrific," Liddell says. "It was overwhelming. Never once was there any negative response. There were people who said they would definitely have been voting Labour if John had been leader, but his response to that was always absolutely correct. He would say we have got a leader whom we must support. Never, even in private conversation, would he run Neil down."

First stop was the Midlands, which had just been visited by Norman Lamont. "Mr Smith proved more adept at getting his message across than did the Chancellor," *The Financial Times* reported.[9] Later in the week he was in Ipswich, just as a poll of forty-five economists from City banks had shown that over half thought Smith would make a better Chancellor than Lamont. It was back to Scotland at the weekend, then on Monday to Hampstead, where he was photographed with the Labour candidate, Glenda Jackson, playing bowls at a pensioners' centre. That evening it was a helicopter journey to Lichfield to support Sylvia Heal, winner of the sensational Mid-Staffordshire by-election. It was a foul day, and John and Elizabeth had to brave the weather to go out and meet the voters. There was a long interview to be done with Irish television. In the evening, a rally. Afterwards, when the Smiths were upstairs, socializing with other people who had been on the platform, Helen Liddell spotted a very elegantly dressed white-haired man waiting outside, hoping to speak to Smith. It was not unknown for dapper, middle-aged voters to come forward to offer their respects to the Shadow Chancellor, but this one did not look the type. He was, in fact, Lou Kirby, former editor of the *Evening Standard*, now a political consultant with the *Daily Mail*, who said he had a document he wanted to discuss with Smith.

The country learnt what it was all about over their cornflakes the following morning. Two discussion papers drafted for a brainstorming meeting between Smith and his economic advisers in January 1990 had been passed to the *Daily Mail*. Both had been penned by the Oxford don Andrew Graham, who postulated in one that the way to close the gap between private- and public-sector wage levels was to give public-sector workers an annual pay rise 1 per cent above the rate of inflation; and warned in the other that a Labour government might be forced to choose between increasing taxes or cutting public expenditure. These papers represented neither the policy nor the official thinking of the Labour Party; they were one set of ideas among many put forward by an adviser with no formal status in the Party; and they were two years old. In the opinion of *The Financial Times*, "It is not the smoking gun of this election campaign."[10] None of that was going to deter the *Mail*, of course;

especially since they had located Graham earlier in the day at Walworth Road, which demonstrated that he was involved in the election campaign. The story was splashed in Tuesday's paper under the heading "Plan to Pay Unions More".

The decision to be made immediately was whether it was worth talking to Lou Kirby at all. Helen Liddell telephoned Joe Haines, at the *Daily Mirror*, for instant advice. He told her succinctly that Kirby was the "Rottweiler who trained Rottweilers", and advised her and everyone else to stay away from him. The Smiths were whisked out to their car, and started back to London. A call on their car phone from a Labour press officer, Anna Healy, warned them that they were being followed. The Smiths' driver, by chance, was an ex-policeman with some experience of high-speed chases, so with a scream of tyre against Tarmac, they hurtled off into the night. A Keystone Cops-style car chase ensued, with the newspaperman in the car behind trying to keep up, his progress being monitored by Anna Healy in a third car, in constant contact with the one in front. Typically, John Smith refused to let the excitement get to him: he slept for most of the journey. Somewhere between Lichfield and London, their pursuer gave up.

On Tuesday, it was a visit to a factory in north London; on Wednesday, Sheffield, to take part in the rally which has featured since in every discussion of why Labour lost the election. It was an exercise in "triumphalism", based on the premiss that if you want people to vote for you, you must look as if you expect to win. It was modelled on a huge election rally staged by the French Socialist Party, in which François Mitterrand and his Cabinet walked slowly down a central aisle under a sweeping spotlight, surrounded by exultant supporters. "I had forbidden the idea of us walking down the hall because I thought it would be arrogant, it would be imperial," Kinnock said later. "And I got into the Sheffield Rally, came out of the light into the dark and walked along a short path, shaking hands and so on, and to my horror realized that the Shadow Cabinet were assembled all in one place at the back of the hall. The great walk would take place. There was nothing that could be done about it. . . . "

Nothing – except mess it up. A voice over the loudspeakers called out the names of the Shadow Cabinet, one by one. The audience was supposed to applaud each name, but they themselves were meant to wait until all the names had been called, and proceed down the aisle together. But when Smith heard his name booming over the loudspeakers, he thought it was his cue to move. So, in an accident rich in symbolism, John Smith marched ahead, with Margaret Beckett at his heels and the rest of the team following behind.

Those who were present at the rally seem to have been very moved by the sheer excitement of 10,000 cheering party supporters. Even hard-bitten political journalists confessed to being almost in tears. The real significance of the night, however, was that it drove home to several million television viewers, who were not present to share the atmosphere, that in just over a week Neil Kinnock could be their Prime Minister. By coincidence, that morning's opinion polls had been the best yet for the Labour Party, apparently showing that they had at last made the break-through they needed for a conclusive victory.

From the podium, John Smith, as part of the warm-up act, exuded reassuring *gravitas* of a kind which could only dampen the excitement. Neil Kinnock was caught up by the euphoria of the moment, and opened his act with a cry of "We're all right! We're all right!". The crowd, of course, answered with a roar; viewers, perhaps, with a groan. When the NEC held its inquest on the campaign, Dennis Skinner accused Kinnock of having "destroyed in ten seconds" the previous eight years' effort to build him up as a statesman.[11] He himself later said: "I will for ever curse myself for bouncing on to the stage. . . . I got on to the stage, turned round and it hit you like a furnace door opening. And there was an ecstatic feeling in the hall and I guess I responded. . . . It was a departure from the steady, confident approach that I and my colleagues had sought to take . . . a moment of indiscipline."[12]

The following day on the prompting of two of his senior advisers, Philip Gould and Patricia Hewitt, who read the entrails of opinion polls, Neil Kinnock used his morning press conference to mark "Democracy Day". This particular item on the calendar was the creation of Charter 88, a pressure group which had been campaigning for four years to have the Commons elected by proportional representation. The Labour leader read out a short statement, offering the Liberal Democrats a place on the Royal Commission which an incoming Labour government would set up to examine electoral reform. By doing so, he guaranteed that the next day's headlines would be dominated by the interrelated questions of the Constitution, the apparent alliance between Labour, the Liberal Democrats and the nationalist parties, and the very real prospect that the election would result in a hung Parliament and a coalition government. John Major, who was outwardly very calm as his government seemed to hurtle towards defeat, and displayed a shrewd grasp of tactics, seized the chance to stand on his soapbox and declare that he would defend the British Constitution against all comers.

The problem was compounded by the fact that Kinnock himself had no stated position on proportional representation. For almost all his political life he had been instinctively opposed to it, but had decided not to take a fixed view while the Party was discussing the matter, so that the debate was not obscured by calls for loyalty to the leader. Roy Hattersley had a profound intellectual objection to PR. Patricia Hewitt tried vainly to persuade both of them to make personal statements backing electoral reform on Democracy Day, but was turned down. On the Monday evening Neil Kinnock went into a live TV programme, with a studio audience, and was asked to give a "yes or no" answer to the question of whether he supported PR. He refused, despite being pressed by Sue Lawley, who was chairing the programme, and barracked by his audience. It gave a very bad impression of a politician wriggling when he was asked a straight question.

In Scotland that weekend, John Smith was certainly not making overtures to the Scottish Nationalists, who had gained ground in opinion polls at Labour's expense. "Why make a protest vote when you can make a difference?" he told a press conference in Glasgow.[13] Until that final weekend, all the polls pointed to the Tory government being brought down, with Labour probably emerging as the largest party in a hung Parliament. As late as Monday evening Sir Terry Burns, Chief Economic Adviser to the Treasury, held a private meeting with Smith and his staff to exchange telephone numbers and discuss the possibility that there could be a run on sterling in the Tokyo markets on Thursday night if the early results showed Labour winning. Smith had already had to act once during the campaign to quieten down the money markets, after Saudi Arabia had reportedly dumped hundreds of millions of pounds' worth of sterling, forcing its value to drop by three-quarters of a German pfennig. He repeated what he had said before: that as Chancellor he would do whatever was necessary to protect the pound's position within the ERM. Sir Terry warned that another statement, with a veiled warning of an interest rate rise, might be needed before all the votes had been counted on Thursday night.

Even on Tuesday morning the polls were showing that support for the Tories had fallen, and there was a look of defeat and exhaustion around Conservative Central Office. But the Tory tabloid newspapers, which hitherto had not served the party cause as well as they might have, were perking up. In the last few days they ran an inspired campaign to reproduce all the old stories about the horrors of life under Labour, put together with flair and urgency at the very time when wavering voters were making up their minds. The *Sun*, for example, ran a memorable feature which ran for page after page, under the heading "Nightmare on Kinnock Street". On polling day, the same newspaper ran a headline which took up almost the whole front page: "If Kinnock wins today, will the last person to leave Britain please turn out the lights".

In the final days the polls showed a last-minute swing to the Tory Party, but even after the polling booths had closed the pollsters forecast a hung Parliament, which would almost inevitably have meant the end of the Conservative government. For the Labour Party, the scale of their defeat, measured against earlier expectations, was numbing: three and a half million votes fewer than the Conservatives, a lower percentage of the total poll than they gained in 1979, and a large enough Tory majority to last five years.

18

The Leadership Election

What came after the general election scarcely deserves to be called a leadership contest. Still numb from the shock of defeat, the Labour Party heard it announced on weekend television by the heads of the big trade unions that John Smith would be their next leader. No one seriously doubted that they were right. The problem was not whether he could win. He could even dispense with the custom by which the job of deputy leader is awarded to the runner-up, the leader's main political rival. In effect, John Smith picked the deputy he wanted from three or four possible runners. The question was whether the election could be carried off without looking as if it was fixed.

On the Monday after polling day, lobby journalists assembled in the Shadow Cabinet room to hear Neil Kinnock read a terse sixteen-paragraph statement, announcing the end of his term as Britain's longest-serving opposition leader. That part was what everyone was expecting; but the statement also had its surprises: he accused the Tory tabloids of having "enabled the Tory Party to win again when the Conservative Party could not have secured victory for itself on the basis of its record, its programme or its character . . . "; he announced that he would run for a place on the National Executive in the autumn; but meanwhile, he was not going to serve his term by waiting until the party conference, as Michael Foot had in 1983. He added – and Roy Hattersley's office later confirmed – that when he went, his deputy would go too. "I will be proposing to the National Executive Committee that the elections be held as quickly as proper organization allows. The elections will, therefore, take place in the second half of June," he declared. With this one sentence, he proved, in passing, that the Labour Party does not have to take six months to elect a new leader. If the old leader refuses to carry on, and his deputy refuses to stand in for him, two months will do.

Even before the Kinnock resignation, TV viewers had been treated to the thoughts of several heads of Britain's trade unions, who forecast that he would go, and announced that they were backing John Smith to succeed him. John Edmonds, General Secretary of Smith's own union, the

GMB, seemed to be hinting that he should run even if Kinnock decided to hang on. In Labour's electoral college, the opinion of the general secretary of one big union – assuming that he could whip his union delegates into line – had an equivalent weight to the votes of about fifty thousand ordinary party members. Something like 10 per cent of the electoral college vote was pledged to John Smith before the Party even knew there was to be a contest. The Sunday newspapers announced the name of his campaign manager in the forthcoming contest: John Cunningham.

The fact that the election was to be over so quickly simply aggravated the problem. Since the completion of the policy review, the Labour Party had been through more than two years of self-denial, in which those who differed from the party line had on the whole kept their mouths buttoned up to avoid giving comfort to the enemy. Considering how addicted large portions of the Party are to arguing, it had been a difficult self-discipline. Now the need for it was over, and a leadership election seemed a good opportunity to air the issues and think again on what the Party was all about. But instead of an open season of debate and discussion stretching into the autumn, party activists were told by their outgoing leader that they must settle for a rushed contest whose outcome was a near-certainty.

Smith himself has said that he would have preferred Kinnock to stay on – which was the right thing to say to avoid antagonizing the Party, though it is difficult to believe that he spoke from the heart. Kinnock explained at the time that he wanted to go early to allow a new leader, deputy leader and Shadow Cabinet to be appointed before the summer recess, giving its members all summer to study the subjects on which they were to speak. That must have made perfect sense to John Smith, but he had to consider the sensibilities of someone like Clare Short, who complained:

> Before we had time to mourn and analyse Labour's election defeat we were told the results of the next leadership election. People throughout the party felt stunned and angry . . . the instigator of the plan to elect a new leader with indecent haste was Neil Kinnock. He appeared to be acting alone. Many of us suspected that he just could not bear it any more and wanted to go quickly . . . he does not trust the party to have a civilised election.[1]

The cries of "fix" were not coming only from people who blamed it on Neil Kinnock. On the Monday after the election, *The Guardian* carried a letter from Colin Byrne, a former party official, complaining: "we wake up to read that the party leadership has been handed over without anyone asking us, the members. . . . " He went on: "Last autumn, after three years as head of Labour's press office, I quit my job at Walworth Road. Until now I have not publicly commented on why. The truth is simple: I refused to be part of what I believed to be a conspiracy which for over a year had been manoeuvring John Smith into position to walk into the leadership should Labour lose. . . . " The next day, the Welsh MP Kim Howells pitched in:

> Our defeat in last week's general election felt like the death of a loved one. We wandered like sleepwalkers through last weekend only to be woken on Monday by the realisation that apparently there was to be no funeral. . . . We were being informed by journalists that [Neil Kinnock's]successor was bound to be John Smith. . . . Labour Party members, including MPs, began ringing me to express anger. . . . Why the rush?[2]

The NEC was sufficiently disturbed by these rumblings to risk humiliating Neil Kinnock at its first meeting after his resignation by voting 15:10 to delay the election for three weeks, until 18 July. They would have voted for a poll at the end of September if Kinnock could have been persuaded to stay.

The leading figures in the Smith campaign, like Robin Cook, naturally dismiss the talk of a conspiracy. They say that if they had really spent twelve months planning how to stitch up a leadership election, they would have been more democratic. They would not, for instance, have allowed trade-union bosses to be the first people out in front of the cameras, endorsing John Smith. The rumour that Cunningham was running Smith's campaign would not have appeared in print were it not for the fact that no one was running it. The politicians were waiting for John Smith to make his first move, but he had decided there was no hurry. First, Neil Kinnock must be allowed to resign, at the time of his choosing, without any hint that he was being rushed. Besides, after three weeks on the campaign trail, Smith decided – with his customary unflappability, and his sometimes exasperating fondness for doing one thing at a time – that he was going back to Edinburgh for a quiet weekend with his family.

On the Monday, after it was confirmed that Kinnock would resign, Smith asked Robin Cook to be his campaign manager. It made more sense than having John Cunningham – partly because Cook had more experience, having managed both of Kinnock's leadership campaigns, but more because Cook's past association with the left made it an immediate signal to anyone who might be in doubt that Smith's support was not confined to the former Solidarity group but transcended all the old Party factions. The down side was that Cook had just twenty-four hours to organize the press launch of the Smith campaign, which was predictably chaotic. "The normally unflappable Scots lawyer had an uncomfortable time," *The Sunday Times* recorded. "For once he appeared badly briefed and was reluctant to give a clear statement of his views on issues such as the unions' block votes and proportional representation. His lacklustre performance was even more apparent when Gould launched his campaign in the same room five hours later. . . . "[3] That night's *Evening Standard* dubbed John Smith and his rival "Mr Cautious and Mr Radical".

None the less, Smith's bandwagon set off at such a speed that he had to be more concerned by whose sensibilities might be injured as it hurtled along than by the result. Although he had been associated with the right of the Party for more than twenty years, it was at once clear that he was not just the candidate of the right. An astonishingly diverse crowd of MPs lined up to have their names on his nomination papers. Every shade of party opinion was there – from John Spellar, former political fixer for the EETPU, on the right, to members of the Campaign group, like Denis Canavan, on the left. Some of those who signed, of course, had an eye on their own chances of promotion under the new leader, but there were dozens who cannot seriously have seen a future for themselves in John Smith's frontbench team, and simply wanted the Party to be led by the person best qualified to do it. It was eloquent testimony both to Smith's personal pre-eminence and to the way the old left and right factions had lost their cohesion.

In those first few days, there was a strong feeling at the top end of the Party that it would be better if Smith was given a walkover. The argument ran that what the Party needed most after defeat was a display of unity. There was just one person standing in the way. The party rule book effectively prevented a candidate from the outside left, like Ken Livingstone, from getting his name on the ballot paper. The only person who was inclined to challenge Smith, and capable of collecting the necessary signatures on his ballot paper, was his old rival Bryan Gould. Some of those who saw themselves as Gould's friends thought he would do himself no favours by engaging in a match which he was bound to lose. With the Party in a state of shock, he was not going to be able to open a serious dialogue on Britain's future in Europe, the issue closest to his heart. Smith himself was receptive to the idea that the problem could be settled through a time-honoured political fix: as a reward for not challenging Smith, and saying nothing that could be construed as disloyal to the leader elect, Gould could run for the deputy leadership with the unofficial blessing of the new boss. Under those circumstances, he could probably have won.

Gould, however, was not to be persuaded. In fact, he rapidly made it obvious that it was not going to be worth anyone's while even making the approach. On television, on the same day as he and Smith launched their campaigns, he revealed that he intended to fight on economic policy. This was the chance he had been awaiting to air his profound opposition to Britain's membership of the ERM. He was convinced that the pound was overvalued, placing a severe handicap on British exports; the government could not stimulate growth by borrowing money to invest in public works, because ERM rules forbade it; nor could the Chancellor cut interest rates dramatically to encourage firms to invest, because he was obliged to uphold the value of the pound on the foreign exchanges; any government attempt to restrict the amount of capital which could be shifted abroad was also bound to fail, assuming that it was not already banned under one European directive or another. Altogether, a government which wanted to create jobs had no room to move. By agreeing to be bound by ERM rules, the Labour Party had given up being the party which promised full employment. It had, Gould believed, abandoned the unemployed.

"I've loyally not opened up on any of these issues over the past three years because we've placed a premium on self-discipline and party unity in order to win the general election," he said. "What I'm not prepared to do is to say that as we've just lost a general election we ought to go back into purdah on this kind of issue," he declared a few days later.[4] He also believed that John Smith understood only the Labour heartland in Scotland, and had a weak grasp of what was needed to win the floating voter in the South. "The leadership of our Party must have some experience of what it means to fight and win in those areas outside our heartlands," he claimed during a live debate between the two leadership candidates, organized by the Fabian Society – one of the campaign's livelier evenings.[5]

It was bad luck and bad judgement on Gould's part that he picked on this issue when he did. It was like asking someone who had just lost their job to take an interest in the technical problems of office management. The Party had just discovered that it was to spend four or five more years out of power, and was in introspective mood, more interested in questions like the trade-union block vote and the selection of parliamentary candidates, over which it had control, than in strategic economic questions. Also, attacking John Smith's tax proposals might have appealed to the wider electorate, and to party members in marginal seats in the South, but not, on the whole, to a party which has always believed in taking from the well-off and redistributing to the poor. During their confrontation at the Fabian Society, Smith scored with the audience by running through the list of Labour's public spending commitments, and turning to Gould to say: "Which one would you cut, and how would you present it to the electorate?"

After the events of "Black Wednesday" – 16 September, when Britain was forced out of the ERM – the mood changed radically. The question of whether the pound had been overvalued within the ERM – or, indeed, whether Britain should have been in the ERM at all – was no longer purely academic: it was of vital concern to everyone who was interested in politics. If the Party's leadership election had followed the timetable set down in the rule book, the final votes would have been cast just eleven days later, on Sunday 27 September. The last few days of the contest might have shown some life. In the event, Gould's first achievement was to irritate Smith and other members of the frontbench economics team. Before the election, they had all meticulously avoided saying anything which might trigger a run on sterling in the international money markets. They had no choice, in their view. The past record of Labour governments, which had devalued the pound in moments of crisis, had compelled them to promise to defend the pound's value against speculative attack. Now Gould was implying either that Smith was wrong on a central tenet of economic policy, or – worse – that he was concealing the truth: that Labour would have devalued. In May, this was treading on dangerous ground. In the Smith camp, it was taken as a signal that Gould did not want a friendly fight, in which case there was no question of helping him into the deputy leadership.

The second thing which helped Smith was that Gould and his advisers were not very good tacticians. He was the only candidate in the race who decided to run for both vacancies. They seemed to take it for granted that this would work for Gould as it had worked for Hattersley in 1983. The difference was that Hattersley had behind him a solid group whose support Kinnock badly needed. Kinnock let it be known that he was ready and willing to have his rival as his deputy, but Gould was not in a position to make bargains. Smith flatly refused to pay him the compliment of offering to serve as his deputy, and when they appeared on joint platforms he mercilessly emphasized that he was interested only in being leader. Gould was left looking as if he was running for one job which he wanted but did not expect to get, and another which he did not actually want but hoped to pick up as a consolation prize.

At one point, it even looked as if he would suffer the ultimate humiliation of not being able to get his name on the ballot paper as a candidate for the deputy leadership. A rule introduced in 1988, to prevent a repeat of the Benn–Heffer campaign, required any candidate to be nominated by at least a fifth of the Parliamentary Labour Party. Five MPs had put their names forward, making it impossible that they could all be properly nominated. Margaret Beckett was so far ahead that all the others had to work hard just to stay in the race. John Prescott was the first to be confident that he could collect the fifty-five names he needed. Four days before the closing date for nominations, 28 April, Gould had fifty signatures. It appeared that he could reach fifty-five only if his team was allowed to approach MPs who had already nominated Ann Clwyd or

Bernie Grant, who were both clearly going to be eliminated, and persuade them to switch to Gould as their second preference. No one was certain whether that was allowed under the rules, and the Party's General Secretary and Director of Organization were asked to give a ruling. The fact that it was done at all was used to good effect by John Prescott supporters, to establish that their man was the real challenger in the deputy leadership contest.

By June, Gould was having to drop the hint to potential supporters that he had lost the leadership, and all efforts must go into the deputy leadership campaign. He announced at a press conference: "While I am not in the business of withdrawing from the leadership race, it is clear that the contest for the deputy is the closer of the two."[6] Here, though, he was running against a reluctance on the part of left-wing unions or constituency parties to nominate him for both jobs. Frequently, they went for the combination of Gould and Prescott, only raising Gould's chance of being trounced in both races.

Gould could take some satisfaction, however, in the fact that he made headway along the difficult path he had chosen. The party really did begin talking about Britain's membership of the ERM – especially as the strains it caused on the British economy became more visible, and the Tory government was pushed into a position in which it seemed to have no other policy but to keep the pound strong, whatever the cost in company bankruptcies and rising unemployment. In the last week of the leadership election campaign, Neil Kinnock unexpectedly broke his silence with a letter to *The Financial Times*. "This morning I can write without having my words treated as formal Labour Party policy," he said – which was stretching a point, because he was still the party leader for another two days. "I do so to urge that the government takes a real lead amongst the ERM countries in pressing for an immediate revaluation of the D-mark. . . . "[7]

It is a moot point whether Kinnock was proposing that the mark should "revalue" or that the other eleven EC currencies should simultaneously devalue. Obviously, he did not want Britain to take disruptive unilateral action; but even if European finance ministers had agreed a realignment of currencies, official wisdom was that the French would have insisted on the franc retaining its parity with the mark. Germany's small neighbours, like the Benelux countries, might also have revalued. Once the currency markets had done their work, the "realignment" would almost certainly have turned out, in the real world, to be a devaluation of sterling and of the EC's other weaker currencies. The Tories would have no part of it. The word handed down from John Major was unequivocal: if the Germans revalued the mark, Britain would revalue sterling. Major even confided to senior *Sunday Times* executives his fantasy that sterling would supplant the mark as the strongest currency in Europe.

The first reaction to Kinnock's letter from political journalists was to see it as a split between Smith and his predecessor. Even members of his own circle were a little surprised by it, remembering how strictly Kinnock had banned any talk of devaluation in the past. It seemed to bear out a report which had appeared in *The Sunday Times* three months earlier, predicting that Kinnock would vote for Gould, rather than Margaret Beckett, in the deputy leadership election, as a "calculated snub" to Smith.[8] (In the event, Kinnock abstained in both elections.) It was actually a demonstration of good political timing. By July, there were not many Labour MPs who wanted to get into an argument in defence of the pound's value against the Deutschmark. Smith certainly was not going to get involved in any controversy with Neil Kinnock.

The word from the Smith camp was that, had anyone but noticed, Smith had already hinted at the very thing which Kinnock had now set out baldly in print. Where had he said it? bemused observers might ask. Their attention was drawn to the speech he had given to the European Parliamentary Labour Party in Strasbourg, on 9 June, in which he had described the ERM as "a fixed but adjustable system", membership of which "does not preclude the possibility of a general realignment. I believe such a realignment is indeed likely"[9] – a point he had made again in the Commons early in July:

> "It should be remembered that the exchange rate mechanism is a fixed but also an adjustable system and that a long time has passed since the last realignment in 1987. It is worth considering whether highly unusual circumstances . . . do not justify a concerted strategy to achieve lower interest rates which could involve some realignment of the currencies. . . . "[10]

A "Final Report to Supporters" put out by the Gould camp, as they headed towards overwhelming defeat, complained: "At the start of the campaign it was whispered that Bryan's insistence that an overvalued exchange rate was a key obstacle to economic recovery disqualified him from a place in the leadership team. Just three months later it is the top economic question, and everyone supports a realignment." There was truth in that. It was bad luck for Bryan Gould that government policy collapsed in shambles after the leadership ballot rather than before, but it could hardly have made any difference. When the votes were counted, under the complicated electoral college system, Smith turned out to have won by a bigger margin than Kinnock's victory over Tony Benn in 1988. He had 90.9 per cent of the vote, to 9.1 per cent for Bryan Gould.

Among MPs and MEPs Smith collected 229 votes out of 297 who voted, compared with 68 for Gould – a majority of more than four to one. Smith's supporters included 17 out of 22 MPs who were members of the Shadow Cabinet at the time. The exceptions were Neil Kinnock and John Prescott, who abstained, and Bryan Gould, Michael Meacher and Jo Richardson, who voted for Gould. By November, the figure was 18 out of 22, the exceptions being Prescott, Meacher, Gould's former campaign manager David Blunkett, and the PLP chairman Doug Hoyle. Smith collected the support of 38 of the 49 trade unions and other affiliates, while four abstained. But the only sizeable union to back Gould was UCATT, the construction workers' union, with a block vote of 160,000. Consequently, Smith won the union section by 4,822,000 votes to 187,000, a majority of more than twenty-five to one. The block vote system, of course, distorts the result. Where unions conducted individual ballots, Smith's majorities were not of that order. He won the GMB, for instance, by 110,177 votes to Gould's 30,267; and the shopworkers' union, USDAW, by over 76,000 to a little under 10,000, in each case collecting the whole of the union's block vote. Even so, he had an undeniable claim to be the favoured choice of affiliated trade-union members, by a margin of a good four to one.

The truly decisive result, though, was among constituency Labour Parties, which had been the stronghold of the left in the early 1980s. Now, however, with the advent of one member one vote, it was the section in which the greatest number took part. Smith collected 597 constituency votes to Gould's 12, a majority of almost fifty to one. Again, Labour's arcane electoral college system made the gap between the two look wider than it really was. What is often not appreciated is that CLPs also operate a block vote. It goes unnoticed because it is so small: 1,000 votes per constituency, or 2,000 each for the dozen or so largest parties, compared with more than a million for the TGWU. When constituency parties balloted their members, however, all their votes went to the winner, however narrow the result. If they had been allocated proportionately, Smith's margin of victory might have been nearer two to one. Even so, it would have been convincing.

Where the deputy leadership election was concerned, there has been almost as much interest in those who decided *not* to run as in those who did. It is a very common assumption that when Smith vacates the Labour Party leadership, his successor will be either Gordon Brown or Tony Blair. It was very widely assumed that one of these two would run, so that the Party could have a king and a crown prince in place. Either of those two, or Margaret Beckett, had the additional advantage of being TGWU-sponsored, like Neil Kinnock. For that reason, TGWU General Secretary

Bill Morris was keen to have her stand. Yet she took several days before announcing that she would enter the race, because she was reluctant to run against either of those two, and was waiting to be sure they were not taking part. Neither did, and no one who knows the answer has ever said why not.

However, certain facts can be established. Since they shared an office as new MPs, Brown and Blair have been very close, and have always operated in tandem. The *Evening Standard* once ran a perceptive piece comparing them with Roy Jenkins and Tony Crosland, who started out as inseparable chums and ended up as rivals. It predicted that the same must happen eventually to Blair and Brown.[11] Perhaps when the Party has to choose one or other as its next leader, it will. In the days which followed the general election defeat, however, they were in constant contact, and their past friendship held together – so much so that party staff nicknamed them the "Push Me, Pull You" candidate.

Gordon Brown had always been seen as the senior member of the team. He is slightly older; he was the first to get on to the Shadow Cabinet; he topped the poll in the 1992 Shadow Cabinet elections; while Blair came second. Brown was awarded what is usually considered the most important job in the Party after the leader's, as Shadow Chancellor, while Blair was allocated one of the other "great offices of state". When both men achieved the feat of being elected to the NEC at the first attempt later in the year, it was Brown who took third place, behind Neil Kinnock and David Blunkett. Blair just got in, in seventh place. In the past, the general assumption had been that, if Neil Kinnock reached Downing Street, he would eventually be succeeded as Labour leader by Gordon Brown, with Tony Blair as his effective second in command. With one Scot on the verge of becoming party leader, however, there was a general prejudice against another Scot becoming his deputy. Smith might not have attached much importance to this, Brown may not have thought it was sufficient reason to disqualify him, but it was a problem. Suddenly, overnight, the order of precedence was reversed. All the talk was of Blair becoming John Smith's deputy and eventual successor. In a TV interview soon after the election, John Cunningham was mischievously asked by David Frost whether he believed the next Labour Prime Minister would be John Smith or Tony Blair.[12] Soon, the talk was that Labour had got it wrong again: they were choosing the leader they should have had at the last election, instead of the leader they needed to win the next. On the morning after Smith's election, *The Sunday Times* colour magazine had five pages devoted not to the new leader, but to "Labour's leader in waiting" – Tony Blair.

Blair himself, on being asked why he did not run for the deputy leadership, has mentioned his young family in Sedgefield, which can be taken as a partial explanation from someone who does not really want to discuss the subject. Probably, there was a combination of reasons: his family, his friendship with Brown, a lukewarm response from Smith, and a calculation that with the deputy's job he would be the target of endless speculation about the future leadership which could damage both Smith and himself, whereas without it he could look forward to a worthwhile job as a leading figure in the Shadow Cabinet, with an unspoilt chance of becoming party leader one day. He spoke to John Smith over the phone whilst he was making up his mind. Smith, no doubt, was courteous and tactful, but not encouraging. He was aware that another north-eastern MP, John Cunningham, was also wondering whether to run for the deputy leadership. There was no advantage, from Smith's point of view, in having a free-for-all between ambitious rivals, each claiming to be his natural running mate. It is unlikely that he leant heavily on Blair to stop him from running, but it appears that he did not encourage him either.

When Margaret Beckett contacted John Smith, what she heard left her in no doubt that he would be pleased to have her as his deputy. He was used to working with her; she was someone he could trust absolutely to be his deputy, not his rival; and she had the political advantages that she came from the left of the Party, and her election would make her the first woman to be the Party's deputy leader.

Women's issues were not Smith's strong suit. So much had changed in the Labour Party in the late 1980s that his previous ideological incorrectness on Europe, defence, nationalization and other matters had turned to his advantage. But feminism had not been struck off during the policy review. The argument over positive discrimination for women and related social issues had generally been won by women. Smith's worst moment during the leadership campaign was brought to him by the Labour Women's Action Committee, who decided to send a letter to every woman MP, and all trade-union and CLP women's officers, about his voting record on abortion. Signed by the committee's chair, Pam Tatlow – a lecturer who had taken on the near-hopeless task of trying to hold the Labour vote together in Cheltenham in 1992 – it warned: "A leader whose election will undoubtedly give encouragement to the anti-abortion lobby will lead Labour into a public and political confrontation with women." The committee followed this up with a press conference involving four women MPs – Jo Richardson, Diane Abbott and Alice Mahon from the left, and Gwyneth Dunwoody from the right.

While Smith won overwhelmingly in almost every section or subsection of the electoral college, there was one group among whom the result was almost a draw. Labour's 37 women MPs divided 18 for Smith, 16 for Gould, with three abstentions. Those who voted for Smith, curiously, included Diane Abbott and Alice Mahon, who had appeared on a platform to attack his voting record on abortion. Clare Short and Jo Richardson, who had been more publicly identified with the women's movement than anyone else, voted for Gould on both ballots. "Bryan is the equal opportunities candidate in these elections," Jo Richardson claimed.

Having Margaret Beckett as an unofficial running mate obviously helped Smith to defuse the issue. When she was asked whether Gould was the "equal opportunities candidate", she could – and once did – produce the incontrovertible reply: "I am a woman and Bryan isn't. There's nothing he can do about that." That apart, she also had a credible track record on "caring" issues, especially social security, in which Smith had never been closely involved; and as a former head office researcher, she understood the party machine in a way which Smith could not.

However, the issue of the deputy leadership campaign – and, indeed, of the whole campaign – turned out, unexpectedly, to be the trade-union block vote. This question had scarcely arisen during the general election, but afterwards it arrived on the agenda so dramatically that some aggrieved trade-union leaders scented a conspiracy. One wrote that it was "puzzling at first, but reading the articles that were written, the speeches that were made, and talking to journalists about briefings that were taking place, I now understand that there were influential people in the Party who were preparing, in the event of a defeat, for a concerted attack on the union link".[13] These were not the words, incidentally, of a minor union functionary: they were written by Tom Sawyer, deputy general secretary of NUPE, who, as chairman of the NEC Home Policy Committee, had more influence on party affairs than any other full-time union official. Sawyer was one of the leading figures in a defensive campaign to make sure that in the rush to modernization, the Labour Party did not try to cut its institutionalized union links altogether. At his union's annual conference, he uttered the ominous slogan "No say, no pay", to remind anyone who might have forgotten that at least three-quarters of the Party's income is from trade-union subscriptions. Bill Morris of the TGWU also emphasized that the unions must retain an influence over party policy, come what may.

Of all the candidates in the leadership contests, the one closest to the trade-union position was John Prescott. He scored a triumph at what was billed as the first beauty contest of the campaign, when all four candidates appeared on the same platform, one after another, at the annual conference of the white-collar union MSF. "It is a sad reflection of the political climate in Britain today that it is necessary for me to say that I am proud to be a trade unionist," he announced.[14] On that note he carried the meeting, and later collected the union's block vote. However, he was not denying that the links with the unions required reform; he was objecting to the political atmosphere in which the issue was being approached. Prescott came a respectable second in the deputy leadership ballot, with 28 per cent of the electoral college vote to Margaret Beckett's 57 per cent.

The speed with which Smith was endorsed by big names in the union movement left him in danger of being cast as the candidate of the block vote. This might have helped him, if he had been relying on the block vote. However, he was well aware that he could win with or without a couple of the big unions. It was more important to him to be seen to be promising continuity of the Kinnock party reforms. Consequently, after some initial hesitation, he arrived at a formula which was vintage Smith, in that it organized the political furniture so that there was one extreme on one side, with the label "No change", another on the other side, marked "Radical change"; and, in the middle, sensible John Smith. He pledged: "We will have one member one vote for all our key decisions, but we have to find a way in which omov [one member one vote] is consistent with organizations being in the Party. . . . If radical change involves the Labour Party subverting its principles and aborting its mission, then I'm conservative in that very narrow sense – I don't want to abort our mission."[15] It was the right formula for the time. Whether it will see John Smith through four or five years as party boss is another question.

19
The Party Boss

No Labour Party leader ever began from a stronger position than John Smith. His support ranged right across the Party. The right wing was solidly behind him; part of the "soft left" positively enthused about his candidature, pulling most of the centre of the Party in behind him; even members of the so-called "hard left", like Tony Benn, cast their votes for him. The great range of political support he attracted was partly a tribute to his personal standing; even more it reflected the mood of the Labour Party: docile, respectful, and anxious to win.

To party members at large, Smith is a reassuring, trustworthy, living link with the days when Labour governed. He is almost without enemies. In one of the largest surveys ever conducted into grass-roots opinion in the Labour Party, in which five thousand party members were asked by the academics Patrick Seyd and Paul Whiteley how they rated each of the dozen or so best-known Labour MPs, John Smith emerged as the one with the fewest enemies. On a scale of 1 to 100, only 12 per cent of the sample gave him a mark below 50. He also had more enthusiastic fans than anyone except Neil Kinnock, in that 29 per cent of respondents awarded him a mark of 80 or more. However, considering that this was a sample of paid-up party members, there was a rather large 16 per cent who had felt unable to express any opinion of John Smith at all. For good or ill, more party members felt able to give an opinion about Neil Kinnock, Robin Cook, John Prescott, Dennis Skinner, Bryan Gould, Roy Hattersley, Tony Benn or Ken Livingstone than about the man who would soon be overwhelmingly elected as their leader.[1]

Yet despite having been around for about as long as most active party members can remember, John Smith was an unknown quantity, and uniquely inexperienced. He has never involved himself in the running of the Labour Party. It was the first time in more than sixty years that the Labour Party had a leader who had never been a member of its National Executive Committee. Nor has he had any other experience of the inner workings of the Party – as an election agent, or a constituency activist, or a shop steward, or a city councillor, for example – to make up for this gap;

his experience of politics has come to him in just two ways: as a student debater, and as an MP. Yet his leadership campaign was run on a promise that he would personally take charge of the party machine, about which he knew next to nothing, and shake it into shape for the coming century. There were more solid promises to change and modernize the internal workings of the Labour Party in John Smith's leadership manifesto, *New Paths to Victory* – a page and a half of a ten-page document – than Neil Kinnock ever made in 1983.

And some sort of modernization or revival of the party machine was desperately needed. Not for the first time, the Party was heading for serious financial trouble. The causes of its chronic money problems were political: the links with the traditional source of cash, the trade unions, were being weakened, but the campaign to build a solid base of a million individually paid-up members was floundering badly. In December 1992, a working party on finance warned the NEC that individual membership could fall below 200,000, and trade-union membership could drop by a million to 3.6 million, unless action was taken to halt the decline. It was costing £500,000 a year just to service the Party's huge overdraft, and another round of redundancies and sackings for full-time staff was in the offing.[2] The new leader was committing himself to learning a great deal very quickly.

One of Smith's great advantages is that there is no clique of personal supporters who expect to be paid off for helping him to get where he is. Obviously, he is to some extent beholden to old allies from the Solidarity group, like John Cunningham and Donald Dewar, but no more so than to supporters more recently won over from the "soft left", like Margaret Beckett and Robin Cook. Even if he was using the former Solidarity group as his political base, it would be much more firmly established and cohesive than the precarious "soft left" faction which sustained Neil Kinnock in 1983. When Smith appointed his first frontbench team, however, there was only one area of policy which he appeared to want to shore up with a solid bank of right-wing spokesmen: John Cunningham became Shadow Foreign Secretary, with the devotedly pro-EC George Robertson remaining as his deputy; and David Clark, who had been sacked as a defence spokesman under Michael Foot for opposing party policy from the right, made a comeback as Shadow Defence Secretary. Otherwise, there was no obvious sign that old Solidarity members were being rewarded for their loyalty.

There was also grumbling from English and Welsh MPs that a "Mac-Mafia" of Scots was taking over the Party. It is true that the Scots are over-represented at the top, though this is not Smith's doing. It was by a free vote of MPs that two Scots, Gordon Brown and Robin Cook, were placed in the top three in the Shadow Cabinet elections, alongside Tony Blair, who was educated in Scotland, with two more Scots – Donald Dewar and Tom Clarke – further down the list. Also, among party employees, being a Scot or a Munro-bagger, or both, is a good path to promotion. Murray Elder, the new head of Smith's private chancellery, and Mike Elrick, a newly appointed press officer, qualified on both counts. Smith's new foreign policy adviser, Meta Ramsey, was a contemporary at Glasgow University. The new secretary of the Parliamentary Labour Party, Alan Howarth, had served loyally in a lesser job throughout the Kinnock years and before, without great reward; but the job had allowed him sufficient free time to scale 177 Munros over the years, with 100 still to go – whereas his leader had bagged 100, and had 177 left.

There is nothing remarkable in this: all party leaders surround themselves with aides and advisers they know and trust. Smith also promoted Hilary Coffman, one of the last remaining members of Michael Foot's personal staff, who had served right through the Kinnock years as deputy to the leader's successive press and broadcasting secretaries, and now, belatedly, was awarded the job herself. There was also an enhanced role for David Hill, her husband, who had been Roy Hattersley's personal assistant for almost twenty years before becoming the Party's Director of Communications. In Smith's book, loyalty and long service are virtues to be rewarded.

The appointment which sparked off talk that the Jocks were taking over came later than others, as an indirect result of Bryan Gould's resignation from the Shadow Cabinet. This led to a mini-reshuffle, in which the job of Shadow Minister for Agriculture became vacant, and went to a Scot, Gavin Strang. His appointment was a surprise. Strang had queered his pitch in the early 1980s by resigning from the front bench in opposition to the Falklands War, and by publicly accusing Jim Callaghan of sabotaging the 1983 election campaign. He was out of favour throughout the Kinnock years, languishing in the Campaign group, running for office on a left-wing ticket without a chance of success. On the other hand, he was uniquely qualified for the job: a farmer's son and a former agrarian research scientist and Agriculture Minister. Smith remembered him as the young high-flier in the Wilson government who had been his own predecessor in his government job as Energy Minister in 1974. Some time after 1976, when Strang's career went into decline under Callaghan, Smith had probably made a mental note that here was someone who was being underused and ought to be promoted. And a decade and a half later, he promoted him.

In general, the surprises John Smith sprang with his first appointments were evidence of his willingness to forget and forgive. Clare Short and

Tony Banks, who had both resigned from the front bench in opposition to party policy on the Gulf War, were both brought back. Although Bryan Gould and some of his supporters were passed over, his former campaign manager, David Blunkett, landed the prestigious job of Shadow Health Secretary, and was allowed to appoint as his deputy Dawn Primarolo, who had been a central figure in the bitter factional warfare involving Tony Benn and the former Chief Whip, Michael Cocks, in Bristol.

Times had changed for those who were on the receiving end of Neil Kinnock's rages. The former leader rarely took the time to be courteous to his opponents on the left. Circumstances compelled him to be seen with Tony Benn during the Chesterfield by-election in 1984, but the next time their paths crossed they passed each other by coldly without a greeting, and they never exchanged another friendly word in eight years. The story is told that the last time Kinnock had a friendly conversation with Dave Nellist was in 1981, during a train journey. He had to deal with Ken Livingstone while he was leader of the GLC, but after its abolition, again, not a word of greeting passed between them.

But Smith is of that school which says that you must treat your opponents with respect, no matter who they are. He remained on friendly terms with Benn and members of his family, and dealt with Dave Nellist over problems with the car industry as if he were any other Labour MP with a constituency problem. During the 1987 election campaign, against the advice of party officials, he accepted an invitation to officiate at the formal opening of new party rooms in Sunderland, where the two Labour candidates were Bob Clay, secretary of the Campaign group, and Chris Mullin. There were two occasions when he was billed to appear before a TV studio audience on a panel which included Ken Livingstone, for example – the first in 1984, the second late in 1987, after Livingstone had been elected to the NEC. The whole point of having them both on one programme, from the producer's point of view, was to get them to argue in public. That did not suit John Smith. On both occasions, he contacted Livingstone privately; they had a meal together and went through the issues, setting out their separate positions to see how a collision could be avoided. Livingstone forecast, a few days before Smith's election as leader: "It will be like the liberation of Europe having a personally secure man in charge. I am sure I shall go on disagreeing with him. I shall keep banging on about defence cuts. But it will be a whole different atmosphere."[3]

It was not only the Bennite left who looked forward to better days under a more tolerant party leader. The "soft left" – who thought of themselves as genuine friends of Neil Kinnock, and therefore entitled to criticize him from time to time – had discovered one by one that criticism was not as well taken as they hoped, and that the old leader's temper was quicker than they would have liked. One prominent frontbench Member complains: "I voted for Neil Kinnock, and I had an absolutely miserable time for eight years. I didn't vote for John Smith, yet I expect I shall have a much better time. Why haven't I learnt to vote in my own self-interest?"

In the early days of Smith's leadership, when a review group had been assembled by the NEC to look at the Party's links with trade unions, and various other committees were in the offing, participants soon noticed a change in the way difficult issues were being handled. It was expressed in the look of confusion on the faces of some of the less bright committee members, the little-known functionaries sent along by their trade unions, who were not accustomed to having to make up their own minds on questions outside their immediate sphere of competence. For years, they had got by on telephone calls from Charles Clarke or Neil Stewart, in Neil Kinnock's office, which would tell them beforehand what the contentious questions were, and how they were expected to vote. This relentless – and sometimes quite heavy-handed – vote-fixing derived from the early days of Kinnock's leadership, when he was frequently outvoted and every battle had to be fought ferociously. Having been bequeathed a huge majority on the NEC, with only Tony Benn as the last leftover of the former Bennite left, Smith had no need for such a tight operation. The loyal troops would turn up and be confronted with difficult decisions, without having been told in advance what they were supposed to think. Observers said it could be quite comical to watch their faces light up in expectation when Margaret Beckett, or Robin Cook, or someone else who might be taken as John Smith's representative, spoke, only to see them dimmed when it transpired that they were expressing only their own opinions, whilst the leader was allowing different views to have an airing before he pronounced. This "chairman of the board" style of leadership appealed to some, but not to everyone. The Party's own professional staff, on the whole, preferred the old leader to the new. All of Neil Kinnock's own staff, except Hilary Coffman, lost their jobs with the changeover. There were numerous other advisers or researchers who regretted the change of face at the top. These were people who had entered politics to make a career of it, often beginning in the National Union of Students or National Organization of Labour Students; fast risers who liked working to a clear chain of command, with a strong leader at the top as a source of quick decision-making. Now they found themselves working to committees, in an atmosphere in which being bright, tough and disciplined did not necessarily count for so much as long, loyal service. The first complaints about the Smith leadership came from the Party's professional staff.

The first and most unbridled attack on Smith so far from someone loyal to the old leader was Colin Byrne's letter to *The Guardian*, written in the bitterness of an election defeat. Byrne had been deputy to Peter Mandelson, Labour's Director of Communications, and part of a political set who would sometimes gather for dinner out at a restaurant near the Oval cricket ground. Other diners were ambitious, youngish MPs from Scotland and the North-East of England, including Gordon Brown and Tony Blair. When Mandelson resigned in 1990, he – and Neil Kinnock – wanted Byrne to succeed him; but the NEC voted heavily in favour of John Underwood, an outside candidate with television experience and no previous involvement in internal party politics. Within a year Underwood left, after he had tried – but failed – to get Kinnock to agree to the sacking or transfer of Colin Byrne. The rift generated an amazing amount of publicity, most of it centred on the mews house in north London which Byrne shared with his fiancée Julie Hall, who was Kinnock's press and broadcasting secretary, and with Peter Mandelson. It has never been suggested that Byrne was put up to writing an attack on John Smith. When Kinnock read it, he probably felt a little as Henry II did when he learnt that his knights had murdered Thomas à Becket; but the letter must have been influenced by the small talk in the old leader's office, and for that reason it is worth quoting at length:

> If there was any justice in this world Neil Kinnock would now be Prime Minister . . . because of what he has achieved through eight years of radical reform of a party that was all but dead and buried. Now, as we wake up to read that the party leadership has all but been handed over without anyone asking us, the membership, it is that record of reform that is under threat.
>
> John Smith may be a very nice man. His smile may not frighten the voters (though his insistence on playing tax changes his way during the campaign, brushing aside his Leader's view and three years of policy that talked of tax changes being phased in and on the £22,000 figure itself cost the Party dear). But what is his record, or that of a handful of centrally-placed right-wing Shadow Cabinet members and trade union leaders who are about to emerge as his campaign managers and backers on the radical reforms Labour . . . must go on making if it is not to tread water, sink and die?
>
> What did the Right ever do about Militant during the bitter years up to Neil Kinnock taking over? What did they do about reforming the Party's relationship with the trades unions and its industrial relations policies? What did they do about Europe? The answer, as I saw myself . . . was usually to sit on their hands and let the Kinnocks and the Blairs take the flak.
>
> In the argument about support for the principle of a single currency, John Smith effectively opted out . . .
>
> During the Gulf war, the Shadow Cabinet held an all-day strategy meeting. It was an issue that, without Kinnock's tough leadership, could have split the

> Party. The only member not to put forward a view in the long and heated discussion was John Smith. Hattersley, a pacifist, at least made his view evident – he walked out.
>
> What is Smith's view on trade union reform? What is his view on electoral reform? After years of intense debate in the Party, ask yourself why we don't know these things.
>
> Last autumn, after three years as head of Labour's press office, I quit. . . . Until now I have not publicly commented on why. The truth is simple: I refused to be part of what I believed to be a conspiracy which for over a year had been manoeuvring John Smith into position to walk into the leadership should Labour lose and had orchestrated the ruthless undermining and behind-the-hand rubbishing of perceived rivals in a future contest. Another feature of their campaign was the – ultimately frustrated – attempt to downgrade Neil Kinnock's own role in Labour's economic campaigning and even off the record attacks on Kinnock's economic competence as recently as the aftermath of the Luigi's dinner earlier this year. I have seen the way these people operate and abuse their position and then call it politics. In short, it stinks.[4]

There are two small points here of interest to anyone who follows the Kreminology of the Labour Party. One is the unexplained appearance of the name "Blair", without a mention of "Brown". The other is the way the terms "left" and "right" are deployed. There is no political issue on which Neil Kinnock can sensibly be said to be to the "left" of John Smith. The words hark back to where individuals stood ten years earlier; but Colin Byrne is not by any means the only Kinnock loyalist to use them in that way. In this context, the "left" are those who believe that internal party reforms must push ahead apace; the "right" are the defenders of an old conservative order which sits heavily on the Labour movement.

The mention of Militant also revives an issue which many people regard as dead. The Militant Tendency no longer has any significant influence within the Labour Party, though in Glasgow, at least, it survives as a left-wing opposition outside the party. Who played what role in ousting the Tendency is history. Questions of history, however, can cause bitter political arguments. Militant is one example of a more generalized disagreement about recent party history. The Kinnock version of history says that the party organization was scandalously neglected or very badly led for a long period, particularly by Hugh Gaitskell and Harold Wilson, until Kinnock himself and a small group who came from the left took it in hand. The implication is that unless the Kinnock reforms continue, the Party will slip back into its old habits, and the destructive civil war of 1979–81 could happen again. Members of the old Solidarity group do not go along with that version of events. They admire Gaitskell and Callaghan, though not necessarily Harold Wilson, and think that the Party's problem began when the Bennite rebellion gathered pace in the 1970s. Whilst they have unqualified admiration for the way Neil Kinnock halted and shattered the Bennite left, they would criticize him for being part of the problem before he stepped forward to offer a solution. Byrne's letter provoked several replies from old Solidarity stalwarts claiming that in the early 1980s their wing of the Party had led the fight against Militant while the "soft left" prevaricated. The correspondents included Mike Connelly, a Solidarity member who lived in John Smith's North Lanarkshire seat in the early 1980s. Even he, however, could not produce an instance of Smith personally appearing in the front line of the anti-Militant campaign.

There seems, in fact, to be only one recorded instance of Smith becoming directly involved, and that was when the Party was in sore need of good legal advice. When Michael Foot set out to deal with Militant by creating a register of affiliated organizations, with the intention of declaring Militant ineligible to affiliate and its leaders, consequently, liable for expulsion, the Tendency took party head office by surprise by seeking legal advice and warning that the action could be a breach both of the Party's own rule book, and of natural justice. Jim Mortimer, the Party's General Secretary at the time, was not inclined to take them seriously. John Smith thought they might have a case, and called on his old university friend Alexander Irvine, now one of England's leading barristers, for an opinion. That also brought in a much younger barrister working in Irvine's chambers – Tony Blair. Much to Mortimer's surprise, Irvine advised that Militant was on strong legal ground. The threat of litigation was one reason why the Foot leadership contented itself with expelling the five editors of the newspaper *Militant*, leaving the rest of the organization alone.

Apart from that, Smith had, of course, made speeches in support of the anti-Militant campaign. In May 1986, for instance, he forecast, somewhat optimistically, that it was "only a matter of weeks or months that the pestilence called the Militant Tendency is firmly put in its place". Since his audience was the annual conference of the right-wing EETPU, he could assume that they were on his side. But he was not directly involved because he did not like internal feuds, and because he was not in the right place. The battle was fought within the NEC, and on Merseyside; consequently "soft left" NEC members like David Blunkett or Clare Short, who backed Bryan Gould in the deputy leadership campaign, took a much more direct part in the final defeat of Militant than anyone who had been in Solidarity.

Margaret Beckett, though, was also an NEC member, so she, too, was forced to take sides on Militant. She was part of the original inquiry team of five male trade-union officials and three women MPs who were sent to

Liverpool to investigate late in 1985. Six of the team – including the future Speaker of the House of Commons, Betty Boothroyd – brought back a report alleging organized infiltration of the Liverpool City Labour Party by Militant, who were thus able to exercise control of the city council. It was this report, endorsed by the NEC in February 1986, which led to the expulsions of Derek Hatton, Tony Mulhearn and five others. Two members of the team, Margaret Beckett and Audrey Wise, dissented. In the light of the fact that it is Beckett to whom Smith will devolve much of the management of party affairs, their minority report makes interesting reading.

It consists of eleven pages and more than seventy paragraphs of carefully argued analysis of what had been happening since a left-wing Labour administration gained control of Liverpool in 1983. It is not by any means a whitewash of the Liverpool left. Its two authors acknowledged that the atmosphere at some of the Liverpool district party meetings had degenerated to a point where some of those present believed they were being intimidated; and that large numbers of people who were not delegates – and some who may not even have lived in Liverpool – had crowded into "aggregate" meetings, where they outnumbered and outvoted the accredited delegates; while other Liverpool party members had complained that they were not even told when meetings were taking place. (A local tradition, predating Militant, laid down that decisions taken in district party meetings were binding on the city's Labour councillors.) The two women also expressed "anxiety" that Liverpool's uniformed "Static Security Force" had been acting as "over-officious stewards". In a separate section, they also noted that there were council departments in which it was impossible to get a job except by being nominated by the appropriate branch of the GMBATU, but suggested that this was a matter for the unions to sort out themselves.

Other members of the investigating team – including NUPE Deputy General Secretary Tom Sawyer – put these facts together and concluded that Militant was using its control of the key GMBATU branch to run the Static Security Force, pack district party meetings, and maintain an intimidating hold on the Labour council; but not Beckett or Wise. They covered Militant in the concluding five paragraphs, under the heading "A Final Note of Dissent". Among their comments were:

> We have always set our faces as individuals against expulsions from the party on political grounds. . . . We are very conscious of the terrible dangers involved if action is taken on the basis of assertions which cannot easily be proved without question. . . . If expulsions are contemplated where doubt exists as to the quality of the evidence on which they are proposed, we are on a very slippery slope where such proposals may be made on more and more tenuous

> evidence and thus in reality on the grounds not even of real convictions, though that would be dangerous enough, but even of personal likes and dislikes. Because of our anxiety in this respect, we must disassociate ourselves from any suggestion that expulsion of members of the Liverpool District Labour Party should be recommended.[5]

Beckett was not then directly involved in the NEC hearings which resulted in the expulsion of Derek Hatton, Tony Mulhearn and others, because a judge ruled that NEC members who had conducted the inquiry could not take part in the hearing which adjudicated on its findings. The NEC was bitterly divided on the principle of whether Militant supporters should be expelled: seven were opposed, fourteen were in favour. Old Bennites like David Blunkett and Michael Meacher supported the majority. If Beckett had been able to vote, the logic of her position was that she would have lined up with those who thought that Derek Hatton should retain his party card. Later – when it came to expelling the Militant MPs Terry Fields and Dave Nellist, for instance – Beckett was with the majority; but her early record is one of those details from the past which have not been completely forgotten. Although she did well in the deputy leadership contest in almost every other region of Great Britain, she collected support from only two of the twelve Merseyside Labour MPs. Those who had been in the thick of the campaign against Militant and the Merseyside left – John Evans, Frank Field, George Howarth, Jane Kennedy, Peter Kilfoyle – voted for other candidates.

John Smith, by contrast, has been on the right wing of the party for so long that he has seen wave after wave of former left-wing radicals returning to the fold, and his attitude has always been to welcome them all. When, in effect, he chose Beckett as his deputy, he clearly demonstrated that he was not interested in who did what when Derek Hatton came to Walworth Road. By 1992, Militant was a dead issue within the Labour Party anyway. Even so, Smith's attitude is not likely to appeal to the hard-nosed political professionals who cut their teeth in the battle with Militant in student Labour clubs, and it has implications for the next political battle within the Labour Party: between the so-called "modernizers" and the traditionalists. The Smith–Beckett team might find that they have unintentionally put themselves on the side of the old against the new.

20
Masterly Inactivity

Convention allows new party leaders a honeymoon of about six months – until their novelty value wears off and they run into trouble. John Smith was unlucky; his was over by November 1992, when he had been in post for only four months; but then, the leadership election had been such a formality that it seemed as if he had been there longer. By the end of the year virtually every national newspaper was offering its analysis of the crisis in the Labour leadership, and there seemed to be no one who wanted to step forward to say that Smith and Beckett were doing well.

Still, the criticism was mild compared with the crises which had engulfed Labour in the past. There had been no spectacular setback, like a lost by-election, to indicate that voters were deserting the Party. Far from trailing in the polls, as it was over a year after the 1987 general election, Labour was already so far ahead that it was beating the records set at the height of the poll tax controversy. No scandal had touched John Smith. No one could accuse him of a serious political blunder. He was insulated from any risk whatsoever that anyone would try to remove him from the leadership. His problem was that nothing much seemed to be happening.

This says a great deal about the nature of the man the Labour Party had chosen as its leader, and about the hidden pressures which ensured that other possible candidates would never enter the race. After the by-election disaster at Govan in December 1988, a procedure nicknamed the "*Sun* test" was introduced to vet future Labour by-election candidates. Nominees are interviewed by a panel of NEC members, to see if their private lives and political histories are clean enough to see them through the intense publicity generated during by-elections – whether, in other words, they could withstand being investigated by the *Sun*. No one is better qualified to pass the *Sun* test than John Smith. The point is not a trivial one: when a member of the Shadow Cabinet moves up to be leader of the Party, it is as if they have been shoved up a cliff face. Members can be homosexual, or have a mistress, or drink too much, or execute an about-turn on policy, without it being common knowledge, but not the leader.

Everything about the leader of the Labour Party becomes the stuff of pub talk.

What the public will gradually learn about Labour's new leader is that he is a deeply moralistic family man, with a strong sense of public duty, rooted in religion. While he was running for the leadership, he told Radio 4's "Sunday" programme: "I am an active and professing member of the Church of Scotland. . . . It gives meaning to my political activities, because you have this sense of obligation to others." In another interview just before he won the leadership election he said:

> "Just as the Christian stands by the fundamental tenets of Christianity, so the socialist should stand by the tenets of socialism. For me, socialism is largely Christian ethical values. . . . Politics is a moral activity. Values should shine through at all times. You could either call it evangelism or salesmanship. I want the spirit of the evangel but the success of the good salesman."[1]

The public will also discover a man who adopted certain beliefs when he was young, and has held to them undeviatingly through long, difficult years. This protects him from the some of the taunts of inconsistency which were aimed with deadly effect at Neil Kinnock. When Smith took over, there was a wave of relief that the Party now had someone in place whose character could not be destroyed in the same way. "Because John Smith is widely perceived as trustworthy and dependable, and because he is free of embarrassing policy baggage from the past, he is in a strong position to ride out such attacks," claimed Nick Raynsford, newly elected MP for Greenwich.[2]

There was only one attempt to embroil John Smith in scandal, which failed for lack of evidence. His elevation to the party leadership provoked a sudden interest in the affairs of Monklands District Council, where there was a feud between Airdrie and Coatbridge councillors. At first there were hints that religious sectarianism had broken out, because of the traditional religious divide between Catholic Coatbridge and Protestant Airdrie. What spoilt that story was that all seventeen Labour councillors in Monklands – be they from Coatbridge, Airdrie, or the surrounding countryside – were Catholics. The dispute was a common enough parish pump row between councillors from rival communities, shoved together in a boundary reform of questionable wisdom. When Monklands council was established in 1974, Coatbridge was allocated ten councillors, Airdrie seven, and the outlying villages three. Three of the Airdrie seats were later taken by the Scottish Nationalists. The Labour group was therefore, naturally, dominated by Coatbridge councillors, and there were allegations that Coatbridge was taking more than its share of council-funded investment projects, although by 1992 its population had fallen to 45,000, while Airdrie's had risen to 40,000.

Class differences were also involved. Airdrie's four Labour councillors were all university graduates who were or had been in the teaching profession. Coatbridge had thrown up self-made working men like Tom Clarke, who was Provost of Monklands for the first eight years of the council's existence, until he went into Parliament. The Airdrie councillors complained that despite their qualifications, none of them was allowed to rise above the level of vice-convenor of a council committee. All the committee chairmanships went to Coatbridge councillors. They also appear to have resented the rapid rise of Tom Clarke's brother, a taxi driver who was elected vice-convenor of the Planning and Development Committee after only six months on the council.

Public opinion was never likely to be roused over the question of who received which committee vice-chairmanship, but in August the local *Airdrie and Coatbridge Advertiser* began delving into the more interesting question of how vacancies on the council workforce were filled. There were the standard application forms, which were pink, and there were green forms. The four Airdrie Labour councillors said they had only recently found out that the green forms existed, and were asking what they were for. In a joint statement, they claimed: "People are filling in forms believing they have a fair chance of getting a job, when they don't. Too often the reality is that if you fill in a pink form then forget it."[3] The *Advertiser* began interviewing people who had been turned down after using pink forms to apply for jobs on the council, and relentlessly naming the relatives of councillors and senior officials who joined the council pay roll, usually after filling in green forms. Joseph Brooks, leader of the council since 1982, had two sons in permanent posts, and a daughter in a temporary job; the Provost, Bob Gilson, had a son, daughter and son-in-law on the staff; the brother of ex-Provost Eddie Cairns, who was John Smith's election agent in 1992, was a council foreman. According to the *Advertiser*, eight out of seventeen Monklands Labour councillors had relatives on the council pay roll in one capacity or another. From there, the story expanded to include a claim that all the prestige council development projects of the past decade had been located in Coatbridge, not Airdrie; and that the council's decision to bring out its own municipal newspaper in October 1992 was a simple act of revenge for the investigative journalism of the *Airdrie and Coatbridge Advertiser*. In November, another story emerged about a land deal involving a company run by Councillor Brooks and his brother, which subsequently went into liquidation. By now *The Sunday Times* was taking an interest in the story, and it was raised in the House of Commons by an English Tory MP, David Shaw.

A controversy of this kind is much more likely to blow up in a Labour council than any other, because Labour's heartland is also where unemployment is highest. A Labour local authority is likely to be the biggest employer in town. The children of council leaders in the Tory heartlands perhaps aspire to richer rewards than a post in the local Planning Department. In a town like Coatbridge, a teenager who has learnt about local government from his father may well decide that the best way to a secure future is to obtain the necessary qualifications to be a town planner. Provost Gilson succinctly dismissed the implication that there was nepotism or malpractice involved as "absolute crap". According to the council's figures, released at a special press conference, 81 jobs had been awarded in the previous three months to applicants who filled in pink forms, and 24 to those who used green ones.

There was only one reason for taking the tale south of the border: to drag in John Smith; but in that respect, it resolutely refused to take legs and walk. The recruitment practices of Monklands District Council were not determined by John Smith. His family or friends were not benefiting. If there was discrimination, it was against Smith's constituents in favour of those in neighbouring Monklands West. When the Scottish Secretary, Ian Lang, was questioned about this in the Commons, his answer was that Scotland's Commission for Local Authority Accounts would have to decide whether any council money had been misused, and whether any councillors should be personally surcharged, "but I have no evidence that it would be appropriate".[4] And that was as near as anyone came to digging up a scandal which in some way involved John Smith.

That is why, when the attacks started, they focused on the aspect of his character which marks him out from Neil Kinnock and most other successful politicians. There is an inner calm about Smith. He does not become hyperactive in a crisis, or say things just for the sake of being quoted. He likes to deal with problems as they arise, one at a time, systematically, step by step – like Sunny Jim Callaghan, who stubbornly refused to panic as the Labour government fell apart, and was accused in a headline of asking "Crisis, What Crisis?". In a Shadow Chancellor, this seems like admirable self-restraint; in a leader of the opposition, at a time of crisis, it can look like sloth.

There was some surprise when, after securing the party leadership and appointing his new front bench, Smith's next move was to take a long summer holiday in France with his family. It was a sensible thing to take a break, with four gruelling years to go until the general election, but it was not expected that a new party leader would be absent for so long, with sterling in crisis and parts of the world in turmoil. Whilst he was abroad he took a telephone call from John Major, who informed him that British troops were being posted to Bosnia, to provide humanitarian aid, and to southern Iraq, to protect the Shi'ite marsh Arabs from the Iraqi army. John Smith endorsed both actions, without demanding that Parliament be recalled. The following month he was back, and a crisis was gathering pace in Europe after the Danes had rejected the Maastricht Treaty. Smith assembled the Shadow Cabinet, and announced that he was demanding an immediate recall of Parliament. It seemed to take him by surprise when the government turned him down just forty-five minutes later. To make it worse, Downing Street claimed that Major and Smith had discussed over the telephone the very question of recalling Parliament and had agreed that it would be unnecessary. At this awkward moment, Smith's immense powers of non-recollection came into play. Nicholas Jones, a BBC political correspondent who interviewed him at length, said: "Mr Smith surprised me by saying he had no recollection of every having discussed that with Mr Major. On repeating my question, Mr Smith gave me exactly the same reply. I was in two minds what to do. The obvious next question was to suggest that either Mr Major or Mr Smith was lying but the incident seemed too trivial. However, I was disappointed by Mr Smith's response. He lacked conviction and I sensed I was being fobbed off with a legalistic answer."[5] This mix-up probably did not matter much in the world outside parliament; the average pundit perhaps picked up a general impression that Labour was demanding something be done about the recession and was being given the brush-off; inside Parliament, it gave the impression of a kind of amateurishness.

This was like a prelude to the extraordinary events of the autumn, when Labour was pulled almost simultaneously by two separate currents. The government appeared to be on the point of disintegration, and a large number of people convinced themselves that John Smith's opportunity had arrived to show a killer instinct, and finish off the Tories. As that crisis receded, observers saw not only that the government would certainly survive for at least another four years, but also that the Labour Party leadership was not even convinced that it would win when the time eventually came. For whichever reason, the matter was urgent, but Smith was manifestly unruffled and unhurried. A friendly *Guardian* writer, Martin Kettle, characterized it as "the masterly inactivity of John Smith".[6] A less friendly *Sunday Times* cartoonist caricatured him as "Little Johnny head-in-air, doesn't fight & doesn't care."[7]

Smith never fell for the idea that the Tory government could be brought down in less than four or five years, even though its overall majority in the Commons had fallen to twenty-one. He knew better. He was a senior minister in a government with no overall majority at all, which survived for years by placating the minority parties with items like his own marathon devolution Bill. There was nothing Margaret Thatcher could do then as leader of the opposition to hasten the fall of the Labour government; and there was nothing Smith could now do to force a general election. When the autumn's extraordinary political crisis broke, it was a disaster which the government brought upon itself. The pound's parity at 2.95 Deutschmarks had finally proved unsustainable, and after losing an estimated £1.8 billion of taxpayers' money, and pushing interest rates up from 10 per cent to 15 per cent in a single day, "Black Wednesday", in a vain attempt to defeat the currency markets, the Chancellor of the Exchequer had to admit that the centrepiece of the government's economic policy had collapsed.

John Smith was in no position to claim that he could have done better. With hindsight, it might have helped him to make more noise about calling for a general realignment of European currencies, instead of slipping the idea out in his little-noticed speech in Strasbourg. But ultimately, Smith believed in fixed exchange rates before "Black Wednesday", and still does. He had told the *Financial Times* a year before Black Wednesday that the ERM was "an obligation that has been entered into which we will maintain. It is quite clear and it is quite specific. We are not going to change the rate. I do not believe in devaluation."[8] This prejudice is born of hard experience. Historically, Labour governments have suffered more at the hands of international currency dealers than the Conservatives, so they have more to gain from keeping the value of sterling against other currencies fixed. The new Shadow Chancellor, Gordon Brown, was if anything more orthodox and European on this than his leader. Brown told the Parliamentary Labour Party on 10 September, after Bryan Gould, Michael Meacher and David Blunkett had again raised the question of a realignment, "Our policy is not one of devaluation, nor is it one of revaluation or realignment. . . . One of the things the Germans may wish to propose is whether a realignment of the currencies will bring interest rates down. There is no guarantee that that would happen, and it is not our policy."

If this left Labour without an alternative policy, it also left the government without anyone to blame. Had the Labour Party called for devaluation, the Tories would then have held them responsible for talking down the pound at a moment of national crisis. If Smith's overall performance failed to inspire, at least he had made no mistakes. He displayed his capacity to move with the flow and to make shrewd decisions at times of intense pressure during the extraordinary events of October and November, when John Major's political survival was at stake. The political climate was transformed overnight by Michael Heseltine's abrupt and ill-judged announcement that British Coal would be closing thirty-one pits and sacking more than thirty thousand miners. Coming at a time when the public was beginning to ask what had happened to the economic recovery which they had been promised in return for re-electing the Conservatives, it provoked an extraordinary outcry in the face of which the government had no choice but to sound the retreat. This was a relatively simple political issue for the Labour Party. It was true that past Labour governments had run down the coal industry and a Kinnock administration would doubtless have done so too, but nobody believed that a Labour Trade and Industry Secretary would announce so many sackings in one day during a recession. Robin Cook, as Heseltine's shadow, was able to sustain a highly effective attack on the government without specifying precisely what Labour would have done.

In the excitement generated by the coal dispute, the dry, detailed and highly technical question of a "paving motion" in the House of Commons which would open an extended debate on the treaty which the twelve EC heads of government had signed at Maastricht the previous December suddenly blew up into a crisis. This was due in large part to John Major, who was very proud of the settlement he had reached at Maastricht and hinted via his press secretary that he would take a defeat very personally, even on a meaningless formality like a paving motion, and might resign. The politics in this case was much trickier for the Labour Party than in the coal crisis, or in the other knife-edge vote on the Maastricht Treaty's "Social Protocol" in the spring of 1993. The whole of the Labour Party was opposed to the protocol which set certain minimal conditions about working hours and other employees' rights in every EC state except Britain. Even opponents of the treaty, on the Labour side, would agree that if Britain were to sign up at all it should sign the Social Chapter. So when it came to determining Labour's tactics on the day of the paving motion the first step was obvious: to put in an amendment cancelling the protocol. However, since that was sure to be defeated, the Party was in a real dilemma about what to do next. If MPs were instructed to vote in favour of the treaty, which was party policy, several dozen could be expected to break ranks and vote with rebels on the Tory Party right. Conversely, if they were told to vote against, it was likely that a significant number of Europhiles, led by Roy Hattersley and possibly including some shadow ministers like George Robertson, would rebel and vote with the government. At first it appeared that Labour would have to call off the whips, as the Tories did in 1972, and expose their divisions to public view. It was only when John Major threatened to resign that Smith adroitly saw his opening: if Major chose to make it a personal issue, Labour could take him at his word and they could all vote against the paving motion on the grounds that they had no confidence in the Prime Minister. It worked. On the critical day in November, every single Labour MP voted against the government, reducing its majority to three. It is unlikely that any other Labour Party leader could have pulled that off; but Smith could do it because he was a pro-European of twenty years' standing telling other pro-Europeans to vote against the treaty. The price he paid, of course, was that he risked his own valuable reputation for consistency. The pay-off was that the Labour Party appeared to be united while the Conservatives were tearing themselves apart. It was a triumph of tactics over ideology.

However, when the vote was over and the howls of recrimination aimed at the Liberal Democrats who had supported the government had died down, the cold fact was that John Major and his government were still there and an election was a long way into the future. There had been an expectation in the air that John Smith would be able to go in for the quick kill, but he had not done it. Now that Parliament was back in session, and Smith was pitched into his twice-weekly jousts with John Major at Prime Minister's Questions, those who had praised him over the years as one of the great parliamentary performers discovered that his skill at delivering a well-crafted set-piece speech did not make him an expert in battering his opponent with three quick questions. There were no knock-out questions in these first encounters across the dispatch box. On one occasion in November, John Smith even agreed to ask a question planted by Downing Street, to allow the Prime Minister an opportunity to announce that the Queen had decided to pay tax and to take her children off the civil list. On others, John Major used to good effect the fact that he had the last word.

Smith's approach to the big political questions has been to set up committees and working parties, like the Royal Commissions which proliferated under Labour governments. For general purposes, there was the Leader's Committee, which had existed under Neil Kinnock to plan the Party's strategy, but very rarely met except in the approach to general elections. Under Smith, the committee had met twice before the end of 1992, with Margaret Beckett in the chair. Its membership included the leading members of the Shadow Cabinet, the deputy heads of two of the biggest trade unions – Tom Sawyer of NUPE and Tom Burlison of the GMB – together with the party apparatchiks Larry Whitty, Murray Elder and David Hill. There were also two working parties answering to Labour's NEC, examining the links with the trade unions and the Party's financial crisis; two answering jointly to the NEC and Shadow Cabinet, on electoral reform and Europe, and a fifth, which was billed as a latter-day Beveridge Commission, looking at the whole sweep of the welfare state. This one was an innovation. It had no formal status in the Party, and was chaired by a figure who had never been involved in party politics – Sir Gordon Borrie, the former Director General of Fair Trading. There was also the Plant Commission, set up under Neil Kinnock and still deliberating on proportional representation. The commissions on social welfare and electoral reform both included Liberal Democrats. The Borrie Commission was free to tackle its brief however it chose, and come up with any conclusions it wished, but it was made explicitly clear that neither John Smith nor his Shadow Social Security Secretary, Donald Dewar, was promising to accept its recommendations. At the press conference which launched the commission, Smith was asked directly about whether he still wished the two most expensive items from the Party's 1992 election programme, state pensions and child benefit, to be universally available without means-testing. Smith's reply implied that he wanted them both left alone. This would drastically restrict the scope for any redistribution of state benefits.

These various committees were not told in advance what conclusions the leader wished them to reach and most were quietly set in motion without any accompanying publicity. The operation had none of the political drama of the post-1987 policy review. It could not, anyway, be hyped as a fundamental rethinking of all Labour had stood for because there were huge and obvious gaps in the procedure. For example, the Party was claiming that Britain's first priority was to overcome the recession and its attendant mass unemployment, but no committee was created at this stage to deal with economic policy. And, with the exception of the committee reviewing links with the trade unions, none of the groups appeared to be under pressure from unbreakable deadlines. Altogether it was not obvious when, or if, the procedure would produce results.

This was when the lineaments of faction-fighting in the Labour Party were seen again. It was not like the ideological warfare of the early 1980s, which centred on the definition of socialism. The few stragglers who still believed in the old left-wing concoction of state ownership of industry, withdrawal from the EC, unilateral nuclear disarmament and free collective bargaining had no influence in the Labour Party any more. The eruption in the coalfields, coinciding with a sudden and startling collapse in the standing of the Royal Family, brought figures like Arthur Scargill, Tony Benn and Dennis Skinner back into the public eye; they were even heard with respect and a kind of affection by some of those who had been loudest in denouncing them ten years earlier, but that of itself was evidence that they were no longer seen as dangerous figures by the political establishment. The old dramas in which the Labour leader took on the Bennite left in mortal combat are not likely to be repeated, not simply because John Smith's temperament is different from Neil Kinnock's, but also because the Bennite dragon is not threatening enough to be worth slaying.

A more important ideological battle is between those who are for or against the drift towards the creation of a European superstate. The opponents, who organized themselves into a pressure group in February 1993 with Bryan Gould at their head, are the successors of the old anti-Common Market right, of which Peter Shore is the most notable living relic. They are important because of the bashfulness which overtook Labour's economic team after Black Wednesday. In the months which followed that crisis it became almost impossible to say what Labour's policy was on fundamental matters like exchange rates and the size of the public-sector borrowing requirement. The reason was that John Smith, Gordon Brown and their team were awaiting their chance to reposition Labour as the party of Europe again – more European, at any rate, than the Tories; but the turbulence in the ERM had so discredited the European monetary system and the short-term benefits of Britain's withdrawal were so obvious that it was no time to be caught canoodling with the Brussels bureaucracy. That left an opening for the "Euro-sceptics" to deliver an effective critique of the Party's shilly-shallying on economic policy; but there is no doubt that the pro-EC wing of the Party is much stronger than the opposition, and will continue to be so for the foreseeable future.

The most important political struggle inside the Party appears to be that between the "modernizers" and the rest. "The tensions between the modernizers and those who favour the status quo can be felt at all levels of the Party," the vice-chairman of Holborn and St Pancras constituency Labour Party wrote in a letter to the press. "However, the split does not necessarily fall across the old left–right lines." He went on to complain that "depressingly few" Labour politicians were on the side of the modernizers, and that Smith and Beckett were "proving deeply conservative".[9] But this is not an old-fashioned ideological dispute in which everyone is forced to take sides. It is a difficult task even to say what the "sides" are, because both "sides" accept the analysis arrived at after the 1987 defeat, that the Labour Party must improve its support among the prosperous, property-owning children of the old industrial working class. They agree that the Labour Party should not be associated in the public mind with Scargill-style industrial militancy, or wholesale nationalization, or vast block votes cast without consultation by trade-union barons. They are not arguing about where the future of the Party lies, but about how urgently the journey needs to be completed. Alastair Campbell, then the *Daily Mirror's* political editor, said:

> I see the real divide as between "frantics" and "long-gamers". The long-gamers . . . all believe Labour has time on its side. There is no point, they say, in wasting energies and risking the Tory theft of ideas, in a period that will be forgotten by the next election. But what makes the frantics frantic is that the Party does not know what it is for, other than to oppose the Government in Parliament. There is little sense of the party finding itself a wider role.[10]

He went on to name names, putting Gordon Brown, Tony Blair, Jack Straw, "several lesser known shadow Cabinet members" and backbench MPs Frank Field and Kim Howells on the side of the "frantics", and John Smith, Margaret Beckett, Robin Cook, Jack Cunningham, Frank Dobson and John Prescott with the "long gamers". As with any political dispute, questions of personalities and power politics intermingle with genuine clashes of belief. There is no doubt that the infighting was partly fuelled by fears about the succession, with Tony Blair as the modernizers' favoured candidate. But essentially, it was a disagreement about why Labour lost in 1992.

21
The Modernizers

So why did Labour lose in 1992? Like someone who has fallen out with an old friend and wants to know why, the Party was left asking itself whether it had said the wrong thing or whether its face just did not fit. Had it been a tactical blunder to threaten tax increases on people earning as little as £21,000 a year? Or was the problem that no matter what Labour said most voters were not going to trust them to run an economy? If the Party appeared to be incompetent was that because of Neil Kinnock, who did not look like a potential Prime Minister? Or was the 1978–79 Winter of Discontent, and the internal party warfare which followed, still casting its long shadow. In a piece written in May 1992, Gerald Kaufman claimed:

> Labour was swamped in the 1983 election because it was profoundly mistrusted by a large portion of the electorate, and was defeated in 1987 by a further landslide because the mistrust remained. I fear that the party's defeat last month was due to too much of that mistrust lingering on. . . . The mistrust of Labour . . . came only with the events of 1978–83, most especially the deep split in the party caused by arguments about constitutional changes and by the Benn–Healey deputy leadership contest. The party was still paying the price for those events last month.[1]

Similarly, Jack Cunningham attributed defeat to "the damage that Labour did to its reputation and its credibility way back in the early '80s; surprisingly perhaps, it is still a major problem for us".[2] David Hill's official findings included the observation that: "Our major long-term problem appears to be the fact that we carry too much baggage from the late 70s and early 80s to persuade people that they can fully trust us."[3] This was plainly a commonly held view within the old Solidarity group.

Anyone in the Labour Party who really believes that the 1992 election was lost in 1981 will naturally support what is called the "One More Heave" school of thought on how to win next time. It works as follows: treat 1983 as the starting point, and Labour did not "lose" the election at all, but has been gaining support steadily for a decade. In 1987, Labour's share of the national vote increased by 3.2 per cent to 30.8 per cent, and the number of Labour MPs increased from 209 to 229. In 1992 it went up another 3.6 per cent, to 34.4 per cent; the number of Labour MPs went up to 271. Onward and upward. Next time, Labour should get about 37.8 per cent of the popular vote, and enough MPs to form a minority government; and at the election after that – an outright majority, in about the year 2002.

Unless, of course, there are just not enough potential Labour voters any more, awaiting the Party's call like spirits of the departed around an ouija board, because changing social attitudes and the pattern of property ownership have perhaps wiped out a substantial part of Labour's electoral base forever. It is this last explanation which could be said to sort out the "modernizers" from the rest of the Labour Party. It is the fear that it could be true which fuels the calls for a drastic break with the past. Tony Blair suggested:

> The true reason for our defeat is not complex. It is simple. It has been the same since 1979: Labour has not been trusted to fulfil the aspirations of the majority of people in a modern world. . . . The notion that somehow today's electorate is selfish and self-obsessed, whereas in previous decades they were not, is a foolish and rather arrogant delusion. People have always voted to better themselves. The difference for Labour is that . . . in 1945 they believed that by giving power to the community through the state to act – in housing, health, employment industry and so on – they, as individuals, would be given a better chance in life. . . . When the majority were have-nots, and the vested interests that held them back were those of wealth and capital, the idea of people acting together, through the state, to reform social conditions and redistribute power became a strong political force. . . . But the state as it grew itself became a potential vested interest, with tremendous power over people's lives . . . the majority of people, as they prospered, earned more and began to pay the tax to fund the state, became more sceptical of its benefits.[4]

Labour's "lost" voters are mostly the children of the old industrial working class, who are better educated and more skilled than their parents and do not have the same experience of the job market as an alien force which pulls thousands of people under one roof to service machines. They work in smaller groups, performing more specialized and less monotonous tasks. They have mortgages to pay. They live in streets full of strangers who have made a similar climb up the ladder, far from their relatives and schoolfriends. Such people are conscious of having moved up in the world. Voting Conservative is a way of saying to themselves that they have arrived. They associate the Labour Party with everything they left behind, and would echo what John Major said in his moment of triumph after the general election: "Socialism is dead and gone. Finished, past, out of the window. Nobody believes in it any more. Nobody. Not in this country, not abroad. It is now a museum piece, nothing more. Time has passed it by."[5] The modernizers reckoned something decisive had to be done to persuade the prosperous descendants of the working class that the Labour Party is also on the way up, and eager to join them at their new address. "Until the Labour Party can mentally make the leap that says aspiring to be middle class is positive, the public will always have trouble believing that we want to help anyone less fortunate," one of the new members of the Shadow Cabinet, Marjorie Mowlam, wrote. "People want more money, a decent house, a good car – and so do all of us in the Labour Party."[6]

There is no doubt about how the contest between the modernizers and the rest will work out. One side is well-organized, with strong professional back-up. They have not one but two credible leaders in Gordon Brown and Tony Blair, Neil Kinnock in support, and a clear idea of what they want. Their Labour Party would be more European than the Tories, very strong on law and order, with a promise of electoral reform, and social welfare without excessive tax increases. Its internal democracy would be based on one member one vote, minus the union block vote; and it would rely heavily on professional advisers and image-makers to dispose of the Party's traditional association with dying industries and decaying inner cities. It would be a party where the upwardly mobile could feel at home – not unlike the one which David Owen tried to create a decade ago. On the other side there is not a disciplined army, but a jumble of right- and left-wing factions opposed to one part or another of the Kinnockite project. There are, for example, trade-union leaders who resent being eased out of positions of influence; there are those, like Bryan Gould, with an intellectual objection to the European Monetary System; others opposed in principle to proportional representation, as Margaret Beckett is; and yet others who simply say that the whole process has gone far enough, after eight years of policy reviews and internal reorganization without a general election victory to make it worthwhile. John Prescott put himself forward as principal spokesman of the back-to-basics tendency. His line was that the Party should fight on the old issues of jobs, health, housing and education, with more gut conviction and less packaging. But the traditionalists, if they can be so called, are not a cohesive group with a common set of ideas; they have only a shared sense that the Labour Party has been through too much internal upheaval already. Tony Benn described it as a contest between "the so-called revisionists, who want, in effect, to dismantle the party as it now exists and build a new SDP, and others who are happy to leave well alone and wait for victory by default".[7]

Just as it is sure that the modernizers will win eventually, political imperatives dictate also that when Smith has to take sides, he will be with them every time. If he seems like the last person anyone would expect to preside over the "modernization" of the Labour Party, with his bank manager's demeanour and his outlook on life which predates the swinging sixties, that none the less is what he will have to do, because there is no other serious option. The point was quickly grasped by Gerald Kaufman, who knows the party leader very well and could speak with the freedom of a backbencher. Only eight months after blaming the election defeat squarely on the Benn–Healey conflict, Mr Kaufman was on quite another tack:

> Labour could base its election strategy on industrial workers when those workers, as they did in 1966, formed three in five of the employed population. The party could look to tenants to launch it to victory when, as they did in 1966, council tenants and those paying rent to private landlords lived in the majority of households. But today three in five employees work in white-collar jobs. . . . Labour's extra votes must come from the increasing numbers of men and women who live in the suburbs and work with video-display-unit keyboards. They are employed in modern jobs. They want a modern party.[8]

Intellectually, John Smith need not be uncomfortable among those who want a "modern" party. He has been pro-Europe longer than anyone else in the Labour leadership; he has had an object-lesson in the dangers of fighting an election campaign on a promise of higher taxes, he has committed himself publicly to create a "one member one vote" party, and he is far too pragmatic to throw away the services of professional image-makers. Even on electoral reform, there is no reason to think that John Smith's sentiments are with the status quo. At the end of the 1970s, surprisingly, he sided with the left against Jim Callaghan on whether to abolish the House of Lords; though he might now want to deal with the Upper House step by step, the first step being to take away the voting rights of hereditary peers. He has never staked out a position on proportional representation, but there was an occasion when he spoke indiscreetly to Paddy Ashdown in a taxi on the way to a TV studio, about a year before the 1992 general election. Smith's version of the conversation was that "we did not talk specifics",[9] but according to Ashdown's office, the gist of it was that Smith was ready to concede proportional representation for the Commons, the Scottish Parliament and regional assemblies, in return for Liberal Democrat support for a minority Labour government, should there be a hung Parliament. The conversation took place a few days before the Scottish party conference, at which Smith's old friend Gavin Laird led a call for electoral reform which was overwhelmingly supported by the delegates.

For the modernizers, however, it is not just a matter of whether they win, but how quickly. All the reforms need to be completed by the end of 1993 or 1994, so that the electorate knows clearly and early what a modernized Labour Party means. If Kinnock had still been leading the Party, there would certainly have been more urgency and drama about the process of change. Through strategically placed press leaks, he would have declared himself to be at the head of the reformist faction, and would have set about ramming its programme through a reluctant Party, item by item. Every stage would have seen the leader's authority on the line; every step forward would have been a personal victory. Asked during a long TV interview what advice he would give to his successor, Kinnock replied: "In so far as he would seek my advice, my instinct is that the longer you give yourself with an assembled body of policies, the better. . . . The general thrust must be there and people must be confident about it, and the sooner you do it the better."[10] Some hours after journalists had been treated to a private preview of Kinnock's remarks, it was put to John Smith that he needed to make haste. He would have none of it: "I don't believe that you should rush forward and put everything in your shop window for next Wednesday. I think you've got to do the patient and careful work, taking some original thoughts, working them through in practical ways, and when you're ready to do so, presenting them to the public in a way which commands and maximizes not only the support for the policies but for the Party."[11]

And therein lies the germ of a dispute which could put John Smith on a different side from his predecessor and his presumed successor, Tony Blair – not a quarrel between modernizers and non-modernizers, but between modernizers at cruising speed and modernizers in overdrive. Because it is not about anything tangible, it is apt to express itself in trivial form, as in a meaningless argument which broke out in January 1993 over whether the Party wanted to "Clintonize" or not. None of the protagonists had an agreed definition of what "Clintonization" would mean. It could entail getting rid of John Smith in favour of a younger and more glamorous candidate for the highest office, but no one said that; on the other hand, it could boil down to the aphorism "It's the economy, stupid" – in which case, it is closer to the politics of John Prescott than Tony Blair. However, the argument blew up after Margaret Beckett and then Gordon Brown and Tony Blair had crossed the Atlantic to meet members of the incoming administration, and while Philip Gould of the Shadow Communications Agency, who had participated in the Clinton election campaign, was arranging for senior Democrats to visit London. The alarm was raised by

John Prescott and others who feared that Clinton's victory would be used as an excuse to abandon content in favour of image.

Part of what lay behind this controversy was a backlash which had set in against Labour's image-makers and consultants, after seven years in which they had enjoyed unprecedented influence and prestige. In 1987, they were given credit for the professionalism of Labour's election campaign; in 1992, they were blamed for defeat. John Prescott had made it a theme of his deputy leadership campaign that the "beautiful people" – as he called them – should be kept under political control. "The spin-doctors may have triumphed, but they didn't do much good for the Labour Party," he remarked.[12] They were suspected of being Neil Kinnock's instrument, now at the disposal of the modernizers. This was generally true, but the detailed picture was confused. Philip Gould, for example, had been regarded with suspicion in Kinnock's private office, because he presented the Party's private polling data, which implied that Labour would have had a better chance of winning in 1992 under John Smith. Also, the professionals came under attack from some of the modernizers, like Kim Howells, who let fly at "the clique of spin-doctors and party managers who foisted on us the anodyne policy statements and the gut-churning embarrassment of the Sheffield rally and others like it, all of which contributed so much to the decline in Labour's electoral appeal."[13] The picture was confused because it was not a straightforward ideological controversy. It was an argument – enlivened by personal antagonism and manoeuvring for position – about how party business should be conducted. In the end, Smith put a stop to the "Clintonization" controversy by delivering to his Shadow Cabinet their first talking-to on party discipline. Meanwhile, the professional consultants and image-makers generally lost influence under the new leader, who preferred to turn to old party hands like David Hill. One reason so little appeared to be happening under John Smith is that there were so few spin-doctors about to make drama out of the everyday business of politics.

By contrast, the argument over Labour's links with the trade unions is anything but trivial. It is specific, and it goes back to the beginnings of the Labour Party, which has always looked to the trade unions as a source of funds, recruitment and voting power. The union baron wielding his vast block vote is one of the classic images which voters associate with the Labour Party. John Smith has declared that he will be the leader who puts an end to it. He said in his acceptance speech at London's Royal Horticultural Hall, where he was formally elected party leader, "We must base our internal democracy on the principle of one member, one vote, and not on the basis of block votes." Six months later, he reiterated: "One trade-union general secretary casting millions of votes will not happen in the future."[14] In a party funded and ultimately controlled by the unions, there are only two ways to accomplish that aim: one is to follow the example of David Owen, and break away to found a new party; the other is to prevail upon trade-union leaders to vote their own power-base away. Smith ruled out the first possibility twelve years ago, in strong language. Consequently, his mission is to persuade the leaders of at least two out of the three big unions – the TGWU, GMB and NUPE – that the day of the block vote is over.

The union vote operates in three ways which have taken on a symbolic importance: in votes at the annual party conference, in the selection or reselection of prospective MPs, and in the election of the leader. It also operates in the election of the NEC, National Constitutional Committee, Conference Arrangements Committee, and party treasurer, at regional party conferences, and in the make-up of lowly constituency party general committees, but none of these has been a focus of political attention in the way that the first three have. And behind all these separate examples of the block vote in practice lies the problem of the Party's dependency on the unions for money, and for its main link to the mass of the working population.

Voting at annual conference is the most basic of the three questions. Because the unions are in control there, they also control the rules for other elections. In his election manifesto, *New Paths to Victory*, Smith said there should be "changes" to annual conference, adding: "I do not believe that it can be acceptable to ourselves or to the public who observe our deliberations that the mass membership of the Party should wield only a tenth of the votes at the party conference." Well, neither do the unions. They have already agreed that their joint voting strength will be cut from 90 per cent of the total to 70 per cent. The more controversial question is whether it should be reduced further – to 50 per cent, or even to nil. To the latter, Smith's answer is no: "Labour must and will not sever its links with the trade-union movement."

On the election of the party's leader and deputy leader, Smith at heart shares the view held by political allies like Roy Hattersley and Jack Straw: that the best solution would be to go back to the pre-1981 system, under which both office-holders were elected by Labour MPs. But that would be a move away from his stated goal of creating a "one member one vote" party. Consequently, he proposed in *New Paths to Victory* to replace the eleven-year-old electoral college, which allocated 40 per cent of the vote to the unions and 30 per cent each to MPs and to constituency parties, with a new college made up of 50 per cent CLPs and 50 per cent MPs, with the local parties using one member one vote rather than delegating the decision to their general committees. To get this idea accepted Smith has to persuade the trade unions to vote for it – to vote away their own right to be involved in choosing the party leader. It will not solve one of the big problems about the current system: it is slow and expensive, and makes the removal of an incumbent leader almost impossible. And it will threaten to create an entirely new problem: there could be a closely fought campaign in which one candidate wins a majority among Labour MPs while the other has a majority among the mass membership. Then the Party will have had a leader it did not want imposed by MPs, or vice versa. However, Smith's scheme will finally kill the reason David Owen gave for leaving the Labour Party: that the rules would allow a militant trade-union leader to extend an industrial dispute into politics by launching a challenge against the leader of the Labour Party.

The most urgent of the three big union issues was the selection or reselection of candidates for the next general election. Until it was resolved, local parties could not even begin to choose their candidates. This was the issue which threatened to cause trouble between John Smith and Neil Kinnock.

Kinnock had lived with the problem for the whole of his leadership. It was the first issue on which he was defeated by a party conference – back in 1984 when, aided by John Evans, he tried to introduce a system of one member one vote for Labour MPs whose future, at that time, was in the hands of activists on constituency party general committees. He failed then, partly because of the opposition of left-wing activists, backed up even by MPs who had helped Kinnock win the leadership, like Robin Cook; but more importantly, because the reform threatened to take away the power of trade-union power brokers. Unions send delegates to party committees. In some seats, over half the committee members come with mandates from union branches. The trade unions also held 90 per cent of the votes at party conference. The best Neil Kinnock could do, in his sixth year as leader, was inaugurate a complicated system under which parliamentary candidates were chosen by an electoral college in which a maximum of 40 per cent of the vote was held by the unions, and the rest by the local party membership under one member one vote.

This was a mess which satisfied no one, was very complicated, absorbed a great deal of the time of regional party staff, and produced cases in which a majority of party members might vote to reselect their MP, only to find themselves, in effect, overruled by trade-union delegates who wanted him out – as happened in the case of the Birkenhead MP Frank Field, who was finally saved by intervention from the centre; or, conversely, might vote to sack their MP, only to have him foisted on them again by the union vote – which is what saved George Galloway, MP for Glasgow Hillhead, and allowed a full-time trade-union official named Roger Godsiff, rather than a city councillor named Muhammed Afzal, to become Labour MP for Birmingham Small Heath.

Kinnock wanted to clear this matter up as a final act before he vacated the leader's office by pushing through a decision to do away with the trade-union element in the voting structure, so that all general election candidates would be chosen by simple one member one vote. He wanted the issue settled at the party conference in October 1992, so that the process of selecting parliamentary candidates could begin in 1993. That was agreed by the NEC, without serious opposition, in May 1992. Only a month later, the NEC changed its mind, in the full glare of national media interest. Instead of aiming to settle the issue at the autumn conference, the NEC voted 13:6 to subsume it in a general review of the Party's links with trade unions, whose report would be dealt with by the 1993 conference. That meant that no candidates for the next general election – not even sitting MPs like John Smith himself – are likely to have been selected before 1994. Imposing a year's delay was a very public way of rubbing it in that Neil Kinnock was not giving the orders any more.

What happened in the intervening month was that a number of important trade-union officials had been irritated by what sounded to them like loose talk about breaking the links between Party and unions altogether. In particular, John Edmonds, John Smith's principal union backer, had made his displeasure known; and Smith – who was not directly involved, since he was neither the party leader nor a member of the NEC – indicated that he thought there was no need to rush, and a review covering all aspects of the relationship would be more prudent. It was his campaign manager, Robin Cook, who prevailed upon the NEC to amend its previous decision. The opponents of delay, who either voted against or abstained, made up an unusual mix: Bryan Gould and his two supporters, David Blunkett and Clare Short, plus Tony Benn and Dennis Skinner, plus representatives of the three most right-wing trade unions.

When the trade-union review group began its work, a sharp division of opinion quickly emerged between reformers like Tony Blair, who wanted the trade-union element removed from the selection of candidates, and some of the union leaders and their allies. John Edmonds and Tom Burlison were backing a scheme drawn up by Tony Manwaring, chief aide to the party's General Secretary, Larry Whitty, under which individuals who paid a political levy to their trade union could be given a sort of associate membership status which would allow them to vote in selection contests in their local constituencies. In that way, the block vote would disappear but the union vote would stay.

To its opponents, this plan was simply blocking the way to one member one vote. During November, a series of leaks to quality newspapers revealed that most of the review group thought the idea was at least worth considering. Deliberations were extended for a month, and it was agreed that the group would present options and leave it to the NEC to choose between them. John Smith's opinion of the plan was roughly this: if it could be made to work, it could be an effective way to attract trade-union members into the Party; but it was not going to work in time to select parliamentary candidates for the 1996 or 1997 general election. Some unions, like NUPE or the AEEU, have computerized central membership lists, and could supply the names and addresses of their members in every constituency without much difficulty. In other cases, like the giant TGWU, setting up a proper list could be a nightmare. If the idea is to be introduced at all, it will have to be delayed until the second half of the 1990s. Meanwhile, the only workable alternative was one member one vote. But John Smith chose not to impose his view early on, but to let the review group go about reviewing until all the possibilities had been exhausted. This was a long way from the quick, decisive dash to one member one vote which Neil Kinnock wanted, and fuelled the complaints that there was a dilatory, don't-care air about John Smith's leadership.

No other Labour Party member attacked John Smith during the rest of 1992 as directly and bluntly as Colin Byrne did. However, there were carefully worded expressions of impatience at the pace of reform, all coming from people who could broadly be classed as London professionals. To that class belongs the Greenwich MP Nick Raynsford, who warned: "The party appears to be substituting a state of anaesthetized torpor for the previous mood of hyperactive aggression. If we go on like this, are we not at risk of sleepwalking into electoral oblivion?"[15] That was not an attack on Smith. As a former parliamentary secretary to Roy Hattersley, Raynsford was in the "Smith" rather than the "Kinnock" camp. Hence his tribute to Smith as a leader "free of embarrassing policy baggage from the past". His complaint was that the Party had become so obsessed with freeing itself from any association with ultra-left radicalism that it was all "safety first", with nothing positive to say.

Later, the ex-editor of *Marxism Today*, Martin Jacques – the man who introduced designer socialism to the decaying British Communist Party – let loose in the *Daily Mail* about John Smith's "breathtaking inactivity and complacency", accusing him of being "tied by culture and background to the old Labour universe", and urging him to talk to "entrepreneurs and industrialists, to programmers and advertising consultants, to Essex man and the Femail reader. . . . "[16]

There were complaints similar to Raynsford's in the annual report of the Labour Co-ordinating Committee, which had once been the largest and most influential of the "soft left" pressure groups, and was always a home for ambitious, upwardly mobile professionals. The LCC's criticisms – unsurprisingly – were endorsed by Bryan Gould, who warned of a "lack of direction, perhaps even a lack of vision"[17] infecting the Party. John Prescott was deeply unimpressed, even though he had enjoyed the LCC's backing in the past in his bid for the deputy leadership in 1988. There was no doubt in his mind that the source of the trouble was within the Labour Party, among the network of upwardly mobile professionals who had prospered under the old leader, and that their aim was to undermine Smith:

> "Of course it's personal about John Smith. It's about people wanting to pre-empt discussion and bushwhack people into making decisions that they think are different from what is going to come out. They are the higher strategists, aren't they? They told us everything before the last election and, I might say, the election before that. These are what I used to call the beautiful people who used to tell us all that should be done about the media, how we must dominate the media and get the message right."[18]

There is no denying that six months into his leadership, Smith was going through a bad patch. Ordinary members of the voting public could be heard expressing disappointment in him, complaining that he seemed to be doing nothing and they did not know what he stood for. One couple from Gloucester sent a letter to party headquarters saying, simply: "Dear Mr Smith, Is anybody awake in there? Yours sincerely . . . "[19]

The popular mood was graphically set out in a report by David Hill, shown to the leader's committee in November and leaked to *The Guardian* early in 1993. It disabused the committee of any hopes they may have had that Labour's startling lead in the so-called "quantitative" opinion polls – the ones published in newspapers which give voting intention figures – would automatically convert into a general election victory. Labour's own "qualitative" polling – in which a small sample are questioned in depth about their political attitudes – indicated that nothing had changed since the general election. People were telling pollsters they would vote Labour, because they wanted to vent their dissatisfaction with the Tories; but they had not genuinely and permanently changed their allegiance. Labour had "no clear identity"; it had not made any significant progress since 1987; it was still "the party of the past, untrustworthy, inexperienced, and in favour of minorities rather than the ordinary man and woman".[20] Hill warned that there must be a clear set of new messages to transmit to voters by the 1993 party conference, at the latest.

But if the problems which John Smith had inherited were enormous, so were the possibilities. No government this century has become so unpopular so quickly after being re-elected as John Major's. It was an administration with no excuses left. After so many years in power, it could not convincingly blame anyone else when recession and high unemployment persisted, and crime figures climbed relentlessly. Unlike Gaitskell in 1959 or Kinnock in 1983, Smith faces no organized resistance in his own party. There are no Bevanites or Bennites to speak of, to hold the line against the Labour Party's long march away from the socialism of its intellectual founder towards a mildly reformist social democracy with its face turned to Europe. Where there was organized resistance – as, for instance, when a dozen MPs[21] established the New Agenda group in February 1993 – their objection was that the transformation was coming about too slowly. Yet all that the party leader appeared to have done to make it all happen was to set up committees.

At the time of writing, it is not possible to say whether Smith's strategy of proceeding slowly, by consensus, will work. The final verdict will be delivered by the electorate in 1996 or 1997. It is still possible that all Labour's worst fears will then have been realized. One of those fears is that they picked the right leader in 1992 for the election just gone, but the wrong one for next time round. There was still a real reluctance in the Party to attack Smith openly, by name, though Bryan Gould frequently came close to it. So did some of those who thought the Party was better off under a leader who moved faster, like Neil Kinnock. Early in the year, the TGWU leader Bill Morris felt it necessary to warn that "there is nothing sillier than the sniping campaign that appears to have started in a few unrepresentative quarters against our new leader, John Smith".[22] The case against Smith, in summary, was that for years he had benefited from a remorseless campaign to denigrate Neil Kinnock by any means available. As Shadow Chancellor, he had been able to hold himself in reserve for the occasional Commons speech or television interview, in which he could exude gravitas and an intelligent command of his subject, allowing anyone who wanted to make mischief to say how much better a party leader he would be than Neil Kinnock. But now he was actually in the job, at a time of growing political discontent, he was too slothful and set in his ways to seize the moment and give voice to the public's mood. He was accused – behind his back, of course – of believing what he had read about himself during the Kinnock years, and of not knowing on a Tuesday what he intended to do on Wednesday.

The only certainty is that John Smith, unlike Neil Kinnock, will not be given a second chance. By the end of 1997, he will either be Prime Minister of Great Britain or an ex-leader on the opposition back benches. If he is resident at 10 Downing Street, then he will be remembered, like Clement Attlee, as a man easy to underestimate who none the less moved the Labour Party forwards in the direction it needed to go with a brilliantly controlled display of leadership. If he fails, posterity will probably be more unkind to him than to Neil Kinnock, who at least proved that he was trying hard under difficult circumstances.

Apparently, none of this causes John Smith to lose any sleep at nights. One of his extraordinary strengths in his ability not to let the pressure of life at the top or the fear of failure disturb his equanimity. For one thing, he does not share Neil Kinnock's or John Major's sensitivity over what the newspapers say about him. Just before Christmas 1992 he hosted a reception for political journalists in the Shadow Cabinet room. During a long evening, when drink flowed freely, he gave no indication that he resented the way that most of the national newspapers were then rubbishing him. There are two ways of looking at his stolid refusal to leap into action when he is accused of inactivity: he could be hopelessly self-satisfied and out of touch, or he could be tough enough, and inwardly secure enough, to stick to his chosen course of action regardless of unhelpful criticism. Smith's old friend Jimmy Gordon – who is, incidentally, a successful entrepreneur, and more of a Thatcherite than a socialist – says: "No matter what the pressure, he will get up the next morning and say 'Let's get on with it' – and that will save him. John has got the temperament for it."

He also looks like a political heavyweight. A psychologist specializing in body language could have an interesting time comparing John Smith's demeanour at Prime Minister's Question Time with Neil Kinnock's or John Major's. Kinnock, who had to endure years up against Margaret Thatcher, with her hundred-plus majorities, looked tight, grim and determined to get through with it, like a man walking head down into a storm; but the bulky figure of John Smith takes command of the few square feet of floor allocated to him, and he turns this way and that, with a finger raised to emphasize his point and a slightly pleased-with-himself look, just like someone who has waited a long time to be able to do what he is now doing. In an era when voters ingest much of their political knowledge in sixty-second morsels from prime-time television news, these things matter.

In addition, there is his superb ability to dominate the Commons when he delivers a set-piece speech on the big occasion. His first foray as opposition leader, when the House was hastily recalled to debate Britain's sudden exit from the European Exchange Rate Mechanism, did not disappoint. The political editor of the *Daily Telegraph* judged: "He dented Major's authority and lived up to his reputation as one of the best debaters of his generation."[23]

And behind a solid image lies solid fact. John Smith was a senior government minister when John Major was a candidate looking for a seat; and if he had not been in politics, he would probably have been a judge, or a top-flight advocate earning a six-figure salary. Ming Campbell – who, of course, represents a rival political party – says: "If you look at the things John has done in his life, he has never done an unsuccessful thing. University, the Bar, marriage, politics, recreation – you cannot point to an area in John Smith's life in which he failed to set high standards or to achieve them."[24] Jimmy Gordon claims: "It's not that he could never fail at anything, it's just that whatever it is, he hasn't found it yet."

However, John Smith's personality is not going to be the single factor which decides the next general election. His virtues may give the Labour Party a marginal advantage it did not have under Neil Kinnock, but it should not be forgotten that Labour's gains in 1987 and 1992 were mostly at the expense of the former Liberal/SDP Alliance. The Conservative vote scarcely changed from one election to the next. The Tory Party's strategy centred on a calculation that the recession would end, and unemployment would begin to fall, a clear two years before they needed to go to the country again, and that those who had worked their way into home ownership and the trappings of middle-class comfort in the 1980s would then continue to reward the party under which they had prospered. Under Britain's electoral system, if a little over two-fifths of the electorate have become so prosperous and so committed to the Tory idea that they are willing to live the rest of their lives in a Japanese-style one-party democracy, the majority have to be bound by their decision. John Smith said: "I am a doer and I want to do things, but there exists the terrible possibility in politics that you might never win."[25]

But some of the gloom which descended on Labour Party members as they faced the prospect of being in opposition for life was lifted by the public reaction to the announcement that thirty-one pits were to close. Middle England, apparently, was not prepared to tolerate another bout of mass sackings, even in an old and heavily unionized industry. It was a glimmer of a possibility that something fundamental may have happened. Perhaps the Conservatives have permanently lost a substantial number of their supporters in the recession of 1990–93, as Labour did in the 1970s. If the recently prosperous have decided they want some of the benefits which only an interventionist state can offer – such as free health-care and education, and freedom from the nagging fear of redundancy – then there is an opportunity for John Smith. All his life he has played a long game, often seeming to disappear from sight for long periods without ever being so far out of the game that he misses his opportunity when it arises. He has been in the game longer than almost anyone else in political life, but has never made a serious mistake. He might yet spring another surprise.

Notes

1 The Boy from Argyll

1. Interview, Donald Dewar; speech by Tony Banks to the Tribune rally, Blackpool, 29 September 1992.
2. Information on the Leitch and Smith families comes primarily from an article by John Smith of Tarbert, published in 1987 in *Kist*, the newsletter of the Mid-Argyll Historical Society. This piece was spotted by Neal Ascherson of the *Independent on Sunday*, and passed on to John Smith MP, who provided me with a copy. Some details not included in the article come from a long conversation with John Smith of Tarbert, and from a study of the headstones in Tarbert cemetery.
3. Hansard 18 June 1973, col. 53.
4. Quoted in a profile of John Smith by Isobel Hilton, *The Independent*, 16 July 1992. Unless another source is cited, all the other quotations in this section come from conversations with residents of Ardrishaig.
5. *The Scotsman*, 20 July 1992.

2 Student Days on Clydeside

1. Hansard 11 November 1970, col. 502.
2. Interview, John Smith.
3. *Daily Express*, 14 July 1992.
4. Interview, Tom Clarke MP.
5. Interview, Janey Buchan.
6. Interview, John Smith.
7. *Daily Express*, 14 July 1992.

3 The Lawyer

1. *The Times*, 25 July 1992.
2. Hansard 22 November 1977, col. 1381.
3. Quoted in *The Independent*, 16 July 1992.
4. Quoted in *The Mail on Sunday*, 19 July 1992.
5. Interview, Roy Hattersley.
6. *The Backbench Diaries of Richard Crossman* (Hamish Hamilton & Jonathan Cape 1981), pp. 502, 431.

Notes

4 The Backbench MP

1. Interview, John Smith.
2. Interview, Neil Kinnock.
3. Hansard 20 April 1971, cols. 1097–8.
4. Hansard 13 July 1971, col. 377.
5. Hansard 3 November 1971, cols. 291–2.
6. Hansard 10 December 1973, col. 166.
7. Hansard 22 January 1971, col. 146.
8. Hansard 26 July 1972, col. 1993.
9. *Daily Record*, 9 April 1976.
10. Hansard 18 October 1972, cols. 370, 346.
11. Hansard 30 November 1972, cols. 617–18.
12. *The Sunday Telegraph*, 19 November 1978.
13. Hansard 26 July 1971, cols. 128–30.
14. George Lawson, MP for Motherwell 1954–74, and a government whip.
15. Interview, Roy Hattersley.
16. Interview, John Smith.

5 The Oil Minister

1. Hansard 21 January 1974, cols. 1267–71.
2. *The Observer*, 19 July 1992.
3. Hansard 2 July 1974, col. 326.
4. *The Independent on Sunday*, 26 May 1991.
5. Interview, Bernard Ingham.
6. *The Times*, 13 November 1974.
7. *The Times*, 18 March 1975.
8. *The Daily Telegraph* Magazine, 3 March 1990.
9. Hansard 14 January 1975, col. 317.
10. Hansard 25 February 1975, cols. 421–2.
11. Hansard 17 April 1975, cols. 831–2.
12. *Daily Mirror*, 30 April 1975.
13. *Daily Record*, 28 June 1974.
14. Tony Benn, *Against the Tide: Diaries 1973–76* (Arrow 1990), p. 481.
15. Interview, John Smith. Benn was not able to confirm this story from memory, and it is not confirmed by his diaries, but he says it is "consistent" with his high opinion of John Smith, and low opinion of Labour peers, at the time.
16. Interview, Tony Benn.
17. Hansard 16 February 1976, cols. 921–2.
18. *The Daily Telegraph*, 3 March 1990.
19. Hansard 28 July 1975, col. 1369.
20. Hansard 7 July 1975, col. 121.
21. Hansard 7 July 1975, col. 163.
22. Interview, Bernard Ingham.
23. Bernard Ingham, *Kill the Messenger* (Harper Collins 1991), p. 144.
24. Michael Foot, *Aneurin Bevan. Volume 2, 1945–60* (Davis Poynter 1973), p. 625.
25. Anthony Crosland, *The Future of Socialism* (Cape 1956), p. 518.
26. Hansard 29 July 1975, col. 1575.

27. Tony Benn, *Fighting Back: Speaking Out for Socialism in the Eighties* (Hutchinson 1988), p. 298.
28. *Daily Mirror*, 22 October 1975.
29. Essay by John Smith on energy policy in *Renewal: Labour's Britain in the 1980s*, written by members of the Shadow Cabinet and edited by Gerald Kaufman (Penguin 1983), pp. 55–6.

6 The Devolution Minister

1. James Callaghan, *Time and Chance* (Collins 1987), p. 509.
2. Andrew Marr, *The Battle for Scotland* (Penguin 1992), p. 120.
3. *Daily Record*, 19 April 1974.
4. Interview, John Smith.
5. Interview, John Smith.
6. *Daily Record*, 31 May 1974.
7. *The Scotsman*, 19 August 1974.
8. *The Scotsman*, 7 November 1973.
9. Tom Nairn, *The Break-up of Britain* (Verso 1981), p. 152. The passage quoted comes from an essay originally published in *New Left Review* in 1975.
10. *Daily Record*, 12 October 1974.
11. Hansard 31 January 1978, cols. 403–4.
12. Hansard 10 May 1976, col. 24.
13. *The Financial Times*, 17 June 1978.
14. Callaghan, *Time and Chance*, p. 506.
15. Hansard 13 January 1977, col. 1786.
16. Hansard 19 January 1977, col. 506.
17. *The Financial Times*, 17 June 1978.
18. Hansard 22 February 1977, col. 1360.
19. Ibid., col. 1353.
20. Hansard 1 February 1977, cols. 317–18.
21. Hansard 24 February 1977, col. 1714.
22. Interview, Geoff Bish.
23. Hansard 1 February 1977, col. 262.
24. *Daily Telegraph*, 28 February 1979.
25. Hansard 29 November 1977, col. 309.
26. Hansard 6 December 1977, col. 1214.
27. Hansard 31 January 1978, col. 406.
28. Tam Dalyell, *Dick Crossman: A Portrait* (Weidenfeld & Nicolson 1989), p. 224.
29. Hansard 19 January 1977, col. 504.
30. Hansard 16 December 1976, col. 1744.
31. Hansard 19 January 1977, col. 509; 25 January 1977, col. 1586; 31 January 1978, cols. 403–4.
32. Hansard 19 January 1977, cols. 503–4.
33. Interview, John Smith.
34. Hansard 16 December 1976, cols. 1744–5.
35. Hansard 15 February 1977, col. 540.
36. Callaghan, *Time and Chance*, p. 507.
37. Interview, John Smith.

Notes

7 Inside Trade

1. Tony Benn, *Conflicts of Interest: Diaries 1977–80* (Hutchinson 1990), p. 391.
2. *Sunday Mirror*, 12 November 1978.
3. "Crossbencher", *Sunday Express*, 19 November 1978.
4. *Evening Standard*, 13 November 1978.
5. Hansard 21 January 1974, cols. 1270–71.
6. Interview, John Smith.
7. Hansard 23 July 1980, col. 552.
8. Hansard 30 June 1980, cols. 1089–90.
9. Hansard 19 November 1979, col. 60.
10. Hansard 23 July 1979, col. 123.
11. Hansard 22 January 1980, col. 242.
12. *The Times*, 18 March 1981.
13. *Sunday Mail*, 21 December 1980.
14. Interview, John Smith.

8 Troubled Times

1. *The Independent on Sunday*, 26 May 1991.
2. Interview, John Smith.
3. Labour Party press release, 19 September 1981.
4. Interview, John Smith.
5. The evidence for this was in two surveys by *Labour Weekly*, published 28 September 1979 and 26 February 1982, which gave estimates of 284,000 and 300,250 respectively. Official membership figures published annually in the NEC report to conference are meaningless. See Patrick Seyd, *The Rise and Fall of the Labour Left* (Macmillan 1987), p. 40.
6. *Radical Scotland*, No.1, February/March 1983. My thanks to Alan Lawson for supplying a copy of this interview.
7. Michael Cocks, *Labour and the Benn Factor* (Macdonald 1989).
8. Hansard 14 December 1982, col. 236.
9. Hansard 8 March 1983, cols. 797–8.
10. Interview, Roy Hattersley.
11. Interview, Neil Kinnock.
12. Interview, Roy Hattersley.
13. Hansard 25 October 1983, col. 245.

9 Union Matters

1. Ian McAllister and Richard Rose, *The Nationwide Competition for Votes: The 1983 British Election* (Frances Pinter 1984), p. 15.
2. The ten were Roy Hattersley, Michael Cocks (Chief Whip), Peter Archer, John Cunningham, Jack Dormand (PLP Chairman), Denis Healey, Barry Jones, Gerald Kaufman, Giles Radice and John Smith. There were three others – Gwyneth Dunwoody, Eric Heffer and Peter Shore – who voted for neither Hattersley nor Kinnock. Robin Cook, Michael Meacher, Stan Orme, John Prescott and John Silkin voted for Kinnock.
3. Interview, Roy Hattersley.

4. Hansard 29 November 1983, col. 764.
5. Letter to Nigel Lawson, cited in the *Daily Mirror*, 3 March 1983.
6. *Report of the Annual Conference of the Labour Party, 1985*, p. 155.
7. Ibid., p. 154.
8. *Daily Telegraph*, 30 August 1984.
9. Interview, Graham Allen.
10. Hansard 8 November 1983, col. 164.
11. Hansard 26 March 1984, col. 33.
12. Hansard 27 February 1984, col. 102.
13. *Sunday Mail*, 23 October 1983.
14. *Daily Mirror*, 1 October 1984.

10 Jobs and Helicopters

1. *The Observer*, 24 July 1983.
2. Speech to the Tribune rally, Blackpool, 4 October 1988.
3. *New Statesman*, 28 December 1984.
4. "Social Ownership", *Statements by the National Executive Committee to the Eighty-fifth Annual Conference of the Labour Party, 1986*, p. 2.
5. Lewis Minkin, *The Contentious Alliance: Trade Unions and the Labour Party* (Edinburgh University Press 1991), pp. 431–4.
6. Interview, Roy Hattersley.
7. *Report of the Annual Conference of the Labour Party, 1985*, p. 178.
8. *New Statesman*, 28 December 1984.
9. Bryan Appleyard, *Sunday Times*, 19 May 1991.
10. *The Guardian*, 19 May 1986.
11. *Daily Record*, 27 June 1985.
12. Hansard 16 December 1985, col. 36.
13. Alan Rusbridger, *The Guardian*, 14 February 1986.
14. Hansard, 15 January 1986, col. 1158.
15. Ibid., col. 1153.
16. Hansard 27 January 1986, col. 683.
17. Hansard 25 March 1986, col. 787.
18. *The Financial Times*, 20 November 1986.
19. Hansard 27 January 1986, col. 662.

11 Shadow Chancellor

1. Hansard 23 March 1987, col. 106.
2. *Daily Mirror*, 10 July 1987.
3. *Daily Mirror*, 12 October 1989.
4. *Report of the Eighty-sixth Annual Conference of the Labour Party 1987*, p. 47.
5. Hansard 15 February 1984, col. 276.
6. Hansard 24 March 1986, col. 643.
7. "A Fairer Community": report of the Policy Review Group on Economic Equality, in *Meet the Challenge, Make the Change: A New Agenda for Britain* (Labour Party 1989), p. 31.
8. *Sunday Mirror*, 9 August 1987.

9. *Meet the Challenge, Make the Change*, p. 35.
10. Ibid., p. 36.
11. Hansard 28 March 1983, col. 4.
12. Hansard 3 November 1987, col. 786.
13. Hansard 5 November 1987, cols. 1088–9.
14. Hansard 29 October 1987, cols. 541–2.
15. Hansard 16 March 1988, col. 1116.
16. Hansard 3 May 1988, cols. 814–17.
17. *Daily Mail*, 6 October 1988.
18. Interviews with Alastair Campbell, *Sunday Mirror*, 22 January 1989; and Nicholas Wapshott, *The Observer*, 19 July 1992.
19. Interviews in *The Sunday Times*, 22 January 1989; and the *Daily Mail*, 26 January 1989.
20. *Daily Mail*, 26 January 1989.
21. *The Observer*, 19 July 1992.
22. *The Sunday Times*, 22 January 1989.
23. *Sun*, 17 July 1992.
24. *Sun*, 16 December 1988.
25. *Evening Standard*, 15 February 1989.
26. *Sunday Express*, 15 January 1989.

12 Mr Kinnock and Mr Smith

1. *Sun*, 22 March 1988.
2. Hansard, 15 March 1988, col. 1017.
3. Private information.
4. Hansard, 17 May 1988, col. 799.
5. "This Week, Next Week", BBC1, 5 June 1988.
6. *The Guardian*, 13 June 1988.
7. *The Independent*, 21 June 1988.
8. Andrew Roth, *Parliamentary Profiles, 1987–91*, vol. IV, S–Z (Parliamentary Profiles Services Ltd 1991), p. 1363.
9. *Working for Common Security*, Fabian Tract 533 (Fabian Society 1989), p. 13.
10. For example, Hansard 18 November 1986, cols. 453–4.
11. *Daily Mail*, 28 May 1987.
12. Interview with David Dimbleby, in "Neil Kinnock: The Lost Leader", BBC2, 5 December 1992.
13. *The Scotsman*, 3 October 1988.
14. *Daily Mail*, 26 January 1989.
15. *Daily Mirror*, 2 July 1988.
16. Interview, Jenny Jeger.
17. Interview, John Smith.
18. Interview, Dick Douglas.
19. *The Sunday Times*, 22 January 1989.
20. BBC2, 5 December 1992.
21. Quoted in Colin Hughes and Patrick Wintour, *Labour Rebuilt: The New Model Party* (Fourth Estate 1990), pp. 121–2.

Notes

13 Lambasting Lawson

1. "The World This Weekend", BBC Radio 4, 26 July 1992.
2. John MacIntosh Memorial Lecture, Labour Party press release, 1987.
3. Giles Radice, *Labour's Path to Power: The New Revisionism* (Macmillan 1989).
4. Hansard 16 March 1988, col. 1124.
5. Hansard 7 June 1989, col. 255.
6. Labour Party press release, 12 June 1989.
7. Hansard 24 October 1989, col. 689.
8. Michael Cassell, *Financial Times*, 28 October 1989.
9. "Competing for Prosperity", report of the Policy Review Group on A Productive and Competitive Economy, in *Meet the Challenge, Make the Change: A New Agenda for Britain*, (Labour Party 1989), p. 14.
10. *The Independent*, 19 October 1989.
11. *Meet the Challenge, Make the Change*, p. 14.
12. Hansard 24 October 1989, col. 690.
13. Ibid., col. 691.
14. *Sunday Correspondent*, 5 November 1989.
15. *The Financial Times*, 30 October 1989.

14 Lunching for Labour

1. *The Independent*, 13 November 1989.
2. For example, I wrote a piece for the *Daily Mirror* on 14 July 1990 forecasting that Labour would announce a policy of an immediate return to the rates, and describing this as a personal victory for John Smith and a defeat for Bryan Gould.
3. *The Financial Times*, 30 March 1989.
4. *The Independent*, 17 November 1989.
5. *The Daily Telegraph*, 9 January 1990.
6. *The Independent*, 23 February 1990.
7. *The Times*, 3 April 1990.
8. *Leading Speeches* (City Publications Ltd May 1990), pp. 381–2.
9. "On the Record", BBC1, 1 October 1989.
10. *Daily Mirror*, 8 March 1990.
11. *Looking to the Future* (Labour Party 1990), p. 7.
12. *The Independent on Sunday*, 6 May 1990.
13. Labour Party press release, 14 June 1990.
14. *The Independent*, 2 October 1990.
15. *The Times*, 14 June 1990.
16. "Panorama", BBC1 18 June 1990.
17. *The Independent*, 20 June 1990.
18. BBC1, 21 June 1990.
19. *Daily Express*, 17 April 1990.

15 The £35 Billion Price Tag

1. Hansard 7 February 1975.
2. Hansard 9 February 1976.

3. Hansard 25 February 1977.
4. Hansard 13 July 1979.
5. Hansard 15 February 1985.
6. Hansard 2 May 1985.
7. Hansard 22 January 1988.
8. Hansard 24 April 1990.
9. Press release, Labour Women's Action Committee, 13 May 1992.
10. *The Independent*, 14 May 1992.
11. *The Guardian*, 18 May 1992.
12. Interview, John Smith.
13. Hansard 21 March 1990, col. 1128.
14. Hansard 24 July 1990, col. 315.
15. *Daily Mirror*, 6 October 1990.
16. Hansard 15 October 1990, col. 930.
17. Hansard 23 October 1990, col. 271.
18. *The Sunday Times*, 6 September 1992.
19. "Economic and Monetary Union", statement endorsed by Labour's National Executive Committee, November 1990.
20. Hansard 24 January 1991, col. 486.
21. Hansard 21 November 1991, cols. 508–9.
22. Walden interview, LWT, 2 December 1990.
23. *Daily Mirror*, 3 December 1990.
24. ITN, 16 September 1991.
25. Hansard 20 November 1991, col. 283.
26. *Sunday Times*, 12 April 1992.
27. *Daily Record*, 14 January 1991.
28. Hansard, 13 February 1991, col. 876.
29. "The World This Weekend", BBC Radio 4, 3 March 1991.
30. TV-am, 5 May 1991.
31. *Daily Mirror*, 9 May 1991.
32. Hansard 24 July 1991, col. 1187.

16 A Night at Luigi's

1. *The Independent*, 7 January 1992.
2. "Newsnight", BBC2, 21 January 1992.
3. ITN lunch-time news, 6 January 1992.
4. *The Independent*, 7 January 1992.
5. *Sun*, 9 January 1992.
6. *The Spectator*, 11 April 1992. (This piece was written several days before polling day, evidently in the belief that Labour was about to win.)
7. MORI, *The Sunday Times*, 29 December 1991.
8. *The Independent*, 13 January 1992.
9. The six journalists were Jon Sopel of the BBC, Mark Webster of ITN, Andy McSmith of the *Daily Mirror*, Alison Smith of the *Financial Times*, Alan Travis of the *Guardian*, Jill Sherman of *The Times*. This account of what happened over dinner is first-hand.
10. Hansard 16 January 1992.
11. *Daily Mail*, 27 January 1992.

12. Interview, Roy Hattersley.
13. "World at One", BBC Radio 4, 14 January 1992.
14. Hansard 22 January 1992, cols. 409–10.
15. The Right Honourable Michael Portillo MP, *The Economics of John Smith* (Conservative Political Centre July 1992), p. 14.
16. Quoted from a verbatim transcript of the seminar held by *Roof* magazine.
17. *The Times*, 6 February 1992.
18. Hansard 19 February 1992, col. 364.
19. *The Guardian*, 19 February 1992.
20. Hansard 19 February 1992, col. 363.
21. *Independent on Sunday*, 23 February 1992.

17 The 1992 Election

1. Hansard 11 March 1992, col. 859.
2. *Daily Mail*, 14 March 1992.
3. *Daily Express*, 25 March 1992, *Daily Mail* 25 March 1992.
4. *The Sunday Times*, 22 March 1992.
5. To be precise, the increase in earnings for the whole economy was 7.5 per cent in the year to February 1992, and 8.5 per cent in the year to March 1992: *The Independent*, 1 June 1992.
6. *Sun*, 23 March 1992.
7. TV-am, 22 March 1992.
8. "On the Record", BBC1, 22 March 1992.
9. *The Financial Times*, 26 March 1992.
10. *The Financial Times*, 1 April 1992.
11. *The Independent*, 30 April 1992.
12. Interview with David Dimbleby, in "Neil Kinnock: The Lost Leader", BBC2, 5 December 1992.
13. *The Financial Times*, 4 April 1992.

18 The Leadership Election

1. *Tribune*, 24 April 1992.
2. *The Guardian*, 14 April 1992. Two months later Howells voted for John Smith.
3. *The Sunday Times*, 19 April 1992.
4. Interview with Martin Kettle, *The Guardian*, 16 April 1992.
5. *The Daily Telegraph*, 21 May 1992.
6. *The Independent*, 12 June 1992.
7. *The Financial Times*, 16 July 1992.
8. *The Sunday Times*, 19 April 1992.
9. Press notice issued by John Smith's office, House of Commons, June 1992.
10. Hansard 2 July 1992, col. 1050.
11. *Evening Standard*, 28 July 1992.
12. "David Frost on Sunday", TV-am, 31 May 1992.
13. Tom Sawyer, "Roots and Resources", *Fabian Review*, vol. 104, no. 4, July 1992.

14. From my own note taken at the MSF annual conference, Bournemouth, 19 May 1992.
15. "On the Record", BBC1, 5 July 1992.

19 The Party Boss

1. Patrick Seyd and Paul Whiteley, *Labour's Grass Roots: The Politics of Party Membership* (Clarendon Press 1992), pp. 49–50, 153.
2. *The Guardian*, 12 December 1992.
3. Personal interview.
4. *The Guardian*, 13 April 1992.
5. The Minority Report submitted by Margaret Beckett and Audrey Wise of the investigation into Liverpool District Labour Party – not carried by the National Executive Committee, 26 February 1986.

20 Masterly Inactivity

1. *Scotland on Sunday*, 11 July 1992.
2. *Fabian Review*, vol. 104, no. 6, November 1992.
3. Information on Monklands Council is taken from a sequence of reports written by Eileen McAuley, of the *Airdrie and Coatbridge Advertiser*, over the summer of 1992. There was also a long report in *The Guardian*, 25 January 1993.
4. Hansard, 16 December 1992, col. 417.
5. Nicholas Jones, "Mr Smith Comes to Town", *British Journalism Review*, vol. 3, no. 4, 1992.
6. *The Guardian*, 26 September 1992.
7. *The Sunday Times*, 22 November 1992.
8. *Financial Times*, 27 September 1991.
9. *The Times*, 6 January 1993.
10. *The Sunday Telegraph*, 7 February 1993.

21 The Modernizers

1. *The Guardian*, 8 May 1992.
2. "David Frost on Sunday", TV-am, 31 May 1992.
3. *The Independent*, 13 June 1992.
4. *The Guardian*, 30 June 1992.
5. For a Thatcherite prediction that Labour is in terminal decline, see Patrick Cosgrave's study of the 1992 election, *The Strange Death of Socialist Britain* (Constable 1992).
6. Marjorie Mowlam, "What's Wrong with Being Middle Class?" *Fabian Review*, vol. 105, no. 1, January/February 1992.
7. *The Guardian*, 7 January 1993.
8. *Daily Mirror*, 18 January 1993.
9. *Scotland on Sunday*, 10 March 1991.
10. "Neil Kinnock: The Lost Leader", presented by David Dimbleby, BBC2, 5 December 1992.

11. Interview with ITN political editor Michael Brunson, "News at Ten", 4 December 1992.
12. Walden interview, ITN, 25 May 1992.
13. *The Guardian*, 14 April 1992.
14. Interview on "Breakfast with Frost", BBC1, 9 January 1993.
15. Nick Raynsford, "Sleepwalking into Oblivion?", *Fabian Review*, vol. 104, no. 6, November 1992.
16. *Daily Mail*, 6 January 1993.
17. "World at One", BBC Radio 4, 8 December 1992.
18. Ibid.
19. *The Guardian*, 7 January 1993.
20. *The Guardian*, 5 January 1993.
21. Nine of the twelve MPs at the first meeting of New Agenda had been in the Commons only nine months, including Tony Wright, Malcolm Wicks and Tessa Jowell. A tenth, Nick Raynsford, had just returned after losing his seat in the 1987 election. Two other longer-serving MPs, Calum MacDonald and Terry Davis, also took part.
22. Bill Morris, "Crossroads for Labour", *Fabian Review*, vol. 105, no. 1, January/February 1993.
23. *Daily Telegraph*, 9 December 1992.
24. Interview, Menzies Campbell.
25. *You* magazine, 22 March 1992.

Index

Index

Index

Index

Index

Index

Index

Index

Index

Index